What this individual's life brings forth for others is their knowledge of their own inner attunement. Indeed, it is the human instrument that is played upon. Joel Andrews creates a tapestry of light and sound by using the harp to bring forth that which intimates the divine within us all.
Kevin Ryerson, from spiritual sources

Incredibly beautiful music! As close as I've ever come to the essence of the Universe. Thea Alexander, co-author of "2150 A.D."

I listen to your tape at least once a day and get lots of creative energy from it — actual physical rushes like electricity for hours afterwards.
L.N.

Yours is a very special gift. The vibrations, not of this world, bring peace, harmony, and healing. I am immeasurably helped. U.W.

I've cried listening to my tape because it is so full of Love — something that has eluded me my whole life. The music reminded me that Love IS my being, and helped me reclaim it. J.B.

It was as if I had taken a spiritual vitamin that gave me a certainty, strengthfulness, and innocent wholeness. H.Z.

Having one's soul-purpose put into music and words is indescribable — a great encouragement to say the least. D.B.

It is uncanny. Your tapes have thrown me into a deep trance, and I have realized perfect relaxation and attunement. I feel levitated off the floor and the pain of scar tissue from many cancer surgeries is greatly alleviated. M.M.

I've been getting very positive feedback from my mentally-ill patients. I'm thrilled with the results. Bless you. K.M.

A HARP FULL OF STARS

The Journey of a Music Healer

Joel Andrews

GOLDEN HARP PRESS

Ben Lomond, California

A HARP FULL OF STARS

The Journey of a Music Healer

For information or ordering additional copies, write publisher:
Golden Harp Press
P.O. Box 335
Ben Lomond, CA 95005

Printed in the United States of America

Author photo by Kathleen Thormod Carr.

Library of Congress Catalogue Card Number 89-80782
ISBN 0-9623165-4-7

With deepest gratitude and everlasting love,

To the One Source of all Consciousness;

To all the patient, living Emissaries of Light
with whom I've co-created over the years,
and especially those who have overseen the work reported herein;

To my own shining guardians,
and indwelling Gift of Spirit;

To my beloved wife, friend, and creative partner, Serafina,
for support of the completion and publication of this research.

To all those who helped, some of whom are listed on the next page.

To the thousands of clients who came for help on The Path;

and finally to the musicians, healers, channels,
and students of the Spiritual Renaissance
who have waited for this book.

The Divine in me salutes the Divine in you.

ACKNOWLEDGEMENTS

My heartfelt thanks to Evelyn Keller and Jonathan Forrester, for their vision to invite me into the work; Jean Keyes, for the first suggestion to improvize on a person; Gustave Neumeyer, for his detailed analysis of his reading, corroborating its inherent truth value; Kay Ortmans (real name), for encouragement and suggestions along the way; Nel for her channeling of the symbolism of the alphabet; Bonita Brookshire and Dale Mathis, for their work with the Basic Selves; Marietta Khounal, for suggesting I play the music of the angels; and finally Dr. C. Norman Shealy for his support through the years, his work in expanding holistic medicine and the Foreword for this book.I am most grateful also to Marty Immerman, for editing of concepts and reader response; Erik Tiemens, for cover ideas; Sari Mitchell, for her "tightening up" editing; Desiree and Jim Hurtak, for the use of their IBM PC Computer storage; Desiree, for computer editing and professional advice; Karen Tenney, for excellent typing and appreciation of this material; Arnold Clapman, for logo design; Brenda Plowman, for cover design and production support; Kathleen Thormod Carr for her photograph; Deborah Karaszewski, for typesetting; Mitchel-Shear, Ann Arbor, Michigan, for printing; and finally to those admirable visionaries who contributed financial support for this book's full manifestation.

Disclaimer: No process in this book is to be construed as guaranteeing healing. All of these techniques *can be conducive to* healing and many have brought about significant improvement in conditions or complete remission. If you have a condition which could be serious we recommend you consult a trained health practitioner. If you do, healing music can certainly then provide therapeutic support. The attitude the author takes here is that true holistic medicine means all the health practitioners working together toward the optimum health of us all.

TABLE OF CONTENTS

FOREWORD

"Music is a thing of the soul — a rose-lipped shell that murmurs of the eternal sea — a strange bird singing the songs of another shore."

Josiah Gilbert Holland

"Music: to feel its wondrous harmonies searching the subtlest windings of your soul, the delicate fibres of life where no memory can penetrate, and binding together your whole being, past and present, in one unspeakable vibration; melting you in one moment with all the tenderness, all the love, that has been scattered through the toilsome years, concentrating in one emotion of heroic courage or resignation all the hard-learned lessons of self-renouncing sympathy, blending your present joy with past sorrow, and your present sorrow with all your past joy."

George Eliot

FOREWORD

I had the great fortune of meeting Joel Andrews during "The Week of Attunement" at Virginia Beach in September 1972. There were two highlights of that meeting for me; one was an evening of music by Joel in which he improvised. It was the first time in my life I had ever been in a trance and I was in it spontaneously from listening to his soaring and very marvelous music. Another interesting event was that I sat in on a past-life reverie of his guided by Lindsay Jacob and I also experienced a session with Lindsay. That week changed my life forever. I subsequently invited Joel to come to La Crosse on two occasions; one when he played during a medical conference and another time when he came for a week and did channeled music for me, my family, and my patients, as well as for our clinic. Only when you experience Joel's music can you understand the word "inspired" or "inspiration".

It is difficult to study esoteric healing through any one of the many scientific techniques available. This is certainly no less true with music therapy, but let us recognize that at least 80% of all illnesses are primarily psychosomatic or the result of stress. These illnesses unfortunately are all to often treated excessively with drugs or even surgery when the patient and/or the physician fail to recognize that the primary problem is stress and not a specific illness requiring vigorous intervention. In fact, such illnesses primarily require detachment. In a situation such as this, if the patient is willing to put the effort into it and has any significant belief in it, then music surely offers a safe and remarkably effective method for reducing stress. The old adage, "music soothes the savage beast", is a remarkable truism.

This work, of course, is not and is not intended to be a true scientific report. The fact that there have been only two complaints in 2,000 healing tapes is not meant to imply that the other 1,998 persons were "healed" nor do the many favorable reports prove healing in a scientific sense. Indeed, this is the great problem in all rigorous research. We have to do double-blind studies to rule out the placebo effect. On the other hand, the placebo effect accounts for a minimum of 35 - 50% of everything that is accomplished in all treatments. With many drugs, the actual efficacy is only 38 to 40% and yet they are considered great drugs. Amitriptyline, one of the great antidepressants, is a typical example. Only about 38% of depressed patients given amitryptiline will respond effectively to that drug.

The message in Joel's work is not that his music is better than a drug or surgery. The message is that a majority of individuals have illnesses that are result of stress and they need to choose stress reduction therapy which appeals to them and in which they have great faith. For individuals who are listening to the sounds of the soul, music, there is no more effective technique than inspired music. As you read this unique and personal journey, may you be open to the sound of your own soul.

C. Norman Shealy, M.D., Ph. D
Founder & Director
Shealy Institute for Comprehensive Health Care;
Founder & First President
American Holistic Medical Association;
Clinical & Research Professor of Psychology
Forest Institute of Professional Psychology

CHAPTER ONE

Prelude

Esteemed One:

Welcome to the world of this book! I hope it will be a treasured experience for you. As you can see by our "itinerary" in the Table of Contents, a rich and exotic journey is planned. This odyssey has brought profound upliftment to me, so I know that if you don't become too enamored with one of the enticing "ports of call" on the way, and sign on for the whole voyage, it could change your life. You might end up knowing a great deal more about who you are and what you're about in this particular life.

At the very least you will hear the story of how I trusted spirit enough to evolve a new method of attunement with music which invited over 2,000 people to synchronize with their soul-paths, to transmute the past, and re-create a more love- and light-filled future. This opened them to the potential of more success in all aspects of life and the joy and ecstasy of living in paradise on Earth. (From God's point of view that's what we have here. How could it be otherwise? But we need to learn how to see it and live it!)

Before our cruise ship pulls away from the dock let us meet each other as friends. How about a handshake? Or even a hug? If we're going to be spending some hours together I'd like to assure you that I have the utmost respect for you. In fact, after bringing through these Individual Attunements and with the concerts and seminars I've experienced, I am completely convinced that everyone on Earth is my brother or sister. I've even come to suspect that everyone is trying their best in life (given their past-life history); even beyond this that people are, in essence, divine and therefore lovable! This, of course, includes you.

This leads me to something very important: my approach in writing this book is not to try to prove anything. I agree with Dr. Norman Shealy that this book does not attempt to be a formal, scientific demonstration, although I hope it will stimulate this kind or research; the results could be most interesting and valuable.

You see, I know that there's only one person who can convince you, and that's *you*. So I want you to know I honor your free will. I also know that even if there are universal truths here, their *interpretation* varies from individual to individual. Also, there is deeper and higher personal *timing* which can ignite realization in your being. And this illumination will be valuable *at that time* in enriching your life. Moreover, since a lot of the material in this book is guided by the higher beings who brought through the Attunements, *I don't even know* all that it contains! A phrase in this book could spark a realization for you, *direct from the Sources*, which I could not have imagined. How wonderful! But anything resembling proof here is probably *cumulative*. My job has been to present as sincerely, honestly, and clearly as possible the most important features of this pioneering work that could be put into words.

Not that I don't respect logic or the scientific method! I consider myself a priest-scientist, and in other cultures these two approaches were often blended in the same person. There is no basic conflict between these two - they simply involve looking at reality through different windows - and God invented all the windows! Why don't we, then, become students of windows? My friend, Alan Watts, used to say, "There are those who say the universe is fundamentally *structure* and then those who maintain that it's primarily *goo*, but, of course it's both." Let's give thanks for that!

So you'll find some interesting *systems* here (from spirit) as well as some of the more flowing elements — hopefully in some kind of balance. Surely the Sources in spirit harmonize these two beautifully and in an actual Attunement they are in a most remarkable balance. If I should ever see (clairvoyantly) a client doing something in a past-life that is not reflected by the symbolism of the notes and other elements of the music that the Sources are using my intuitions would be wrong! But this has never happened, if I was in the light trance (expanded state) in which I always do the work. I am what is called a conscious channel.

Another polarity which has been quite a challenge, but for which I have been prepared in past incarnations as well as this one, is to put into words the deeper realities of music, an art of vibration and basically non-verbal. This definitely requires artistry! I find much writing about music by philosophers and metaphysicians that would embarrass the authors if they really studied the true nature of sound and music. Here my three degrees in music have been a great help. To me, there is only beginning to be a body of written material about music that makes sense. Victor Zucherkandl* is one who has asked the question, "Can we look at

*See Bibliography

what the nature of sound and music might tell us about reality before we superimpose our assumptions on it?". This book suggests some answers along the lines of this inquiry.

I think you'll enjoy it more if you can put temporarily aside all preconceived ideas about music and just experience the exploration and discovery. After I bring you safely back home you can get out your "knowledge" of such subjects as the nature of sound and music, names, reincarnation, spiritual growth, and God, and mull it all over. Then you can *analyze* and *assess* what's going to be of value for you and what you'd like to keep and act on. and this is most important. Wise also, is *not to completely discard anything.* It might be just the first time you heard it and later on you might want to bring it up from memory without a black mark across it!

These then have been my purposes:

1. To tell the story of the opening of a musical channel, the transition from a 25-year career in many aspects of professional harp playing to a new life as a psychic and spiritual healer. As a trailblazer, to include some of the vicissitudes of an apprentice healer as well as some of the miracles of personal transformation.

2. To publish the results of 18 years of research into the potentiality of healing with music; and research into channeling past-lives on the harp from "higher Sources".* To share the development of various levels of universal symbolism for the elements of music, and more specifically, music as it is played on the harp. An Appendix includes the code for translating letters into pitches, which composers have used for 300 years, and the meaning of each letter for the emerging age as revealed by the Sources. Then a chapter is devoted to applying this symbolism of letters to the analysis of names and words. This is possible since the system appears to be universally applicable - not confined to my work alone. This research is based on the over 2,000 Individual Attunement Tapes, 1600 Name Analyses, and 100 General Tapes that have been brought through this channel since 1971.

3. To relate many personal experiences that tend to demonstrate the reality of higher beings (ascended masters, members of "The White Brotherhood", and angels and devas), experiences that reveal many psychic and spiritual laws; and to recount events of a "miraculous" nature that are just fun to tell!

This book was also written for all you musicians who came up after concerts to talk about improvizing or working with celestial musicians to create the new healing music. I'm sorry it took so long to get this to you but I had to write the story for a number of other groups of people as well — which took some doing. You'll find a wealth of encouragement here and information about how to get started, as well as a report on the group I helped to found, The Order of Orpheus, which channeled

*Higher in frequency, not a judgement of spirituality

4

music together for healing and upliftment. In the years to come we are probably going to need all the healers we can get. In any case, we are certainly recruiting a *love corps* of artists to spread the word of the growing Renaissance of Spiritual Light and we need to support each other in this unprecedented endeavor!

For those especially interested in reincarnation you will find some significant additions to present theory. These arose out of putting together some seemingly different areas of research I was conducting over a fifteen-year period: (1) the Past-Life Attunements themselves; (2) the Kahunas'* concepts regarding the Low Self (the "subconscious") and the High Self; (3) working with my own Basic Selves (what I like to call the subconscious) with muscle-testing (kinesiology); and (4) a deep study of certain material in the monumental revelation from higher beings, *The URANTIA Book.* Don't miss putting ashore in this fascinating, eclectic, cross-cultural port!

Equal to the miracles reported here, is the continuous guidance the sources gave as I was writing! I asked for further light on what I had been doing, especially the nature of the material and the techniques involved in its transmission, and I am so happy to say they exceeded my request graciously. Imagine my deep satisfaction as I learned much more about the work that has been my major focus for the past eighteen years!

Why did I choose an autobiographical approach? When I read a book or hear a lecture the part I enjoy most is not the rehash of *other* books or papers, but when the author takes a break from the outline and shares with us a personal experience and what was learned from it. I'm a little weary of someone reading five books or taking ten seminars on a subject and then writing their own. I'd rather read the books and take the seminars! This is why I've organized this book as much as possible as a dialogue with a friend (you) and as a report of *my own journey.* Then I can show the repercussions of what I was learning on the evolution of a life immediately. This is also why I thought it would be of interest to begin in Chapter III with my very real and challenging beginnings — to show the rich "compost" out of which it all grew. These early events, in fact almost all the personal incidents included here, are not meant to be in-depth autobiography but just serve to anchor the concepts of spiritual evolution in the progression of a life. They also begin to illustrate one of the central themes of this book: that we never know for what incredibly wonderful future we're preparing, and so should give *everything we've got* to the present, no matter how bleak or oppressive it might seem.

If it's true, as the source called Seth says, that we are conscious in many parallel realities at once, we can begin to open this comprehension by remembering the past and noticing its part in creating our present. This should not be depressing but enormously hopeful since then we can understand, learn valuable life lessons, and transmute and *re-create* our-

*Priest-healers of Hawaii

selves along higher lines! This is what the Attunements I do are all about: reflecting back to you the soul-path you selected at the beginning of the present series of lives so that your past and present experiences *make sense* — whether they appear "positive" or "negative". According to the wisdom of the higher forces, who have infinitely more love for us and understanding of us than we could imagine, all our experiences are "positive" — there are no "failures".

So with their help I have been developing a *totally positive view of reality* — a view which must be a little closer to how things look to God. Isn't this one of our prime objectives, to see things the way God sees them? The last fifteen years certainly have radically changed my world view. I must say this requires a good deal of practice to maintain, with the world going through the throes of a healing crisis! And yet I have come to know that, to God, *Earth is a particular version of Paradise!* How could it be otherwise? To think that God is *ignoring* us is human projection — anthropomorphic blasphemy! This positive view is for everyone — followers of all religions.

It might be appropriate to share with you some answers to your question, "Well, what has it done for you?". This will unfold through the autobiographical narrative, but briefly:

1. Health: I'm living proof that it's possible to renew yourself *at least* every seven years. But without spirit pointing the way I probably wouldn't be alive now! I've received guidance during many life crises, including warnings of accidents. I've had much karma to work through in this life, and a good deal of it with physical repercussions, and at every juncture spirit has helped me re-organize my life on higher principles. By following these insights I have almost completely avoided going to doctors.I appear 10-15 years younger than my years! And feel and act even younger than that!

2. This work has expanded my relationships with my brothers and sisters; wives and children; the other kingdoms I live with on the planet; my position relative to life on other planets; and my relationship to higher beings on up the line.

3. Through this work I've come to know some 59 past-lives of my own, greatly enhancing my understanding of the deeper purposes of this particular life; who I am and what I'm about. I've gotten a rough idea of what I need and want to do to achieve possible ascension (to my understanding, possible for anyone in this life!).

4. I've been able to do Past-Life Attunements for myself and those close to me, greatly accelerating comprehension of the potential of my own achievements and the value of my growing edges.

ALL THESE GIFTS, AND MORE, AWAIT THE PILGRIM OF FORTITUDE WHO WILL WALK THE GOLDEN PATH OF LIGHT AND LOVE.

6

So, dear friend, I hope you will savor this journey as you might a 15-course dinner and, just as you leave digestion to the age-old wisdom of certain organs which you carry everywhere for this purpose, leave the assimilation of this information for now to your higher mind, your subconscious, and your superconscious. Then you can enjoy with me a grand adventure of exploration!

Joel Andrews

CHAPTER TWO

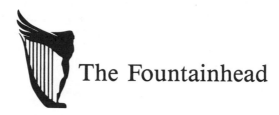 The Fountainhead

First let me share with you two peak experiences which have shaped my work and my life:

1965 (The Santa Cruz Mountains)

I trudge up the path through the redwoods. Overcome with sadness (the illusion of being mistreated), I lean against a redwood tree—tears welling up. How can people be so insensitive? How can I heal this pain in myself? How can I heal it in others? The soft, russet bark of the ancient tree, like the caress of a quiet mother, brings warm peace and strength.

Empty and fresh, I bear left, leaving the path, and after a few steps into the woods I see an arc of stately redwoods on my right. As I descend the gentle slope, the curve of trees continues. The ground cover thins and I am enclosed by a huge circle of redwoods, a spacious amphitheatre, embellished here and there by a few graceful madrones, their coppery skin glowing in the early morning light. I realize that this magic ring, 150 feet across, was too large to have come from one mother tree unless she was of great antiquity. Like a child, I wander in hushed wonder at the power and natural beauty of this ringed and ringing space.

At one point, I think I have crossed over into Pan's world of nature spirits; I see a grand convening of North American delegations in this sylvan theatre-in-the-round, followed by a full-scale, devic, festival ballet! When this image fades, I begin to wonder if I can find the center and I saunter around and down until I stop at what seems the lowest point. Looking down at the leaves, I find no marking of what I feel to be the vortex of energy; then I look up. Directly overhead the branches of three magnificent madrones have come together, leaving a six-foot circle of blue

8

sky. Then I see that their trunks make an almost perfect triangle in the middle of the amphitheatre, and come together as they rise. Just then I feel a surge of energy through me, coming right up out of the ground! My body begins to sway, then rotate, and I raise my arms toward the opening of sky, my entire being dancing with ecstasy! My feet rooted to the ground, I dance with abandon for 2O minutes and I cannot fall — the spirallic fountain of force streams up and holds me in its flow-pattern. Gradually it subsides...and finally I stand for almost two minutes without breathing, just savoring the quality of the vibrations of that sacramental spot...

* * * * * *

Right after this experience, my training as a healer began to accelerate and resulted in the development (in 1971) of the unique healing work with the harp that is reported in this book.

1984

Just a few months ago, I moved to the Santa Cruz Mountains. I thought I understood the reasons for the move. Then, just as I was completing this book, I revisited the amphitheatre and stood once more over the energy vortex. I was moved to ask the nature of it. I had been told that it was a storehouse of akashic* information, and having discovered a few other such "etheric libraries" around the country, I was curious as to what kind of information might be stored here. My vision opened and I saw that on subtler planes this is an archive of information and techniques from past civilizations, especially the Lemurian,* concerning the uses of the arts for healing and the raising of consciousness. Deep in the mountain, I could see akashic records (under the protection of angelic custodians) which can be accessed by those whose motives are pure and who have undergone the necessary training, and whose life-plans include the destiny to utilize these ancient techniques. Here are instructions on how the arts can take people beyond words into higher states such as peace, unity, harmony, joy, spiritual ecstasy, and love. Standing on this access point, I knew that 20 years before, in 20 minutes, I had been healed and programmed with a whole new system of healing with music co-created with Higher Forces and Beings; a system which dramatically changed the course of my life, has brought relief, healing, and upliftment to thousands on various levels of being (mineral, plant, animal, human, and angelic); and has brought me undreamed-of spiritual unfoldment and knowledge. And all this was in answer to my question, "How can I heal this pain in myself and in my brothers and sisters?"
Now the circle closes, the cycle is complete and I will tell you the

*See Glossary
*See Glossary

whole story. But, of course, the end is the beginning and I have returned to The Fountainhead for further inspiration and direction for my never-ending ascension up the spiral of service to The Light. I eagerly await the greater ecstasies to share with you all.

Let us imagine, then, you and I, that for some reason we have become stranded in a secluded house in the woods near the ocean for a long weekend. You hear about the work I've been doing, which just happens to interest you very much. We prepare something deliciously warming to drink and build a fire. You promise to spend a weekend sometime soon telling me about your experiences, and we begin. Are you comfortable?

"In the mother, when the first trace of life begins to stir, music is the nurse of the soul. It murmurs in the ear, and the child sleeps. The tones are companions of his dreams. They are the world in which he lives."

Antoine Bettina

CHAPTER THREE

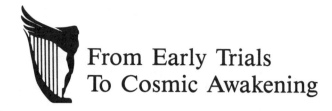

From Early Trials
To Cosmic Awakening

Before I tell you how this work began, it might be a good idea to give you a thumbnail sketch of my early life. Following are some of the things I had to work through from early life, and some of the experiences which were formative, and actually prophetic, of later developments. I will try to "tell it like it was." However, I may not be able to resist some "asides" or comments from where I am now and what I know has taken place!

I entered this physical world May 25, 1928, in Santa Barbara, California. The birth took place in the St. Francis Hospital. (Thirty-two years later I am to begin a nine-year sojourn in San Francisco, patron saint: St. Francis, and 46 years later I am to begin intensive work with an ascended master by the name of Kuthumi, whom many sources believe to have been St. Francis.) As a baby I seem to have been somewhat reluctant to accept embodiment and contracted pneumonia at six weeks and spent a few weeks in the hospital being taken care of by the Franciscan nuns. My mother, Florence, recalls, "for months afterward he responded to anyone dressed in black!"

I was a sensitive child and loved the ideal climate and paradisal beauty of semi-tropical Santa Barbara. I was unusually "awake" from the earliest years, had a very active inner philosophical life, and was more aware of what was going on with and between the adults than with other children. My older brother, Oliver, was not exactly pleased with my arrival (much growth here in later years!). I enjoyed spontaneous playtimes with Gavin, my half-brother (1½ years younger). But usually when Oliver was around, Gavin would respond to his older brother's attention, leaving me alone. This produced first suffering and then development of inner strength, self-reliance and character. I always have been especially aware of "situations" and immediate environments. (Painful at first, this has developed into such abilities as being able to attune to the general vibrations of a town within the first hour after arrival.)

When I was six, my stepfather, Robert Hyde, took the family to live in a cave he had fashioned out of a chalk hillside. This was still the Depression (the Crash of '29 took place when I was one), and Bobby, as he was known, sought the solution to his struggles as a short-story writer on five acres and a huge garden. The family lived in the cave for a year while we built a house. The floor of the cave was smooth as pottery, there was a telephone and, for most of the time, a maid! Of course Anna couldn't sleep with her employers, and there were not servants' quarters in the cave. Until the family moved into the house, which was before the rains came, she would simply appear at the door of the cave each morning and disappear at bedtime. She was of hardy Irish stock and she loved it! She came with a suitcase of service costumes and brought elegance to the cave, sometimes cooking crepes suzettes over the campfire!

There were often wild parties, and we children would be sent to our beds in the far corners of the cave, there to feign sleep and peer at the golden bottles of Muscatel wine passing before the fire. (In the 1970's and 80's, the movement to return to the hills is somewhat different. Part of the motivation is again to secede from the thickening center to the freedom and healing of nature, but we are more likely to find meditation, singing and dancing going on in a cave.)

I learned much from my surrogate father, Bobby, in terms of how to make wine, play chess and build houses, but growth from his authoritarianism was much more difficult. He beat his children for the slightest provocation, believing we should be "seen and not heard," and found it almost impossible to touch us with love. He didn't really want to recognize us as human beings until we demonstrated "adult" behavior. This created some obstacles to growing up which were only surmounted years later.

My grandmother, Florence's mother, was a grand and high-born lady named Lilia Tuckerman. In addition to raising five girls, she was a fine landscape painter. I used to carry her paint box on country outings, and she felt quite responsible for my religious training in the Episcopal Church. However, my earliest spiritual thoughts and experiences were more Eastern than Western. An innate sense of higher truth caused me to react to what man and The Church have made of the teachings of Jesus. Yet I enjoyed going to church with Lilia; her simple faith made an impression on me. She had a strong belief that I would be a great artist one day, and this did much to build self-confidence during these lonely years. (Lonely because, although in my soul I was grateful to be coming into a life which would release a great deal of karma and produce an enormous amount of growth, to my early consciousness this growth would mean learning how to forgive others' transgressions and how to love when not being loved.) Actually, I could only count on the love of my mother, my grandmother, and my Uncle Gavin.

After a few years my grandmother bought me a full-sized, gold harp. I played it for twenty years and, together with her encouragement, it inspired me all through my education.

My father's brother, Gavin, was like another father to me. My paternal grandmother, Myra, recognized in me a deep philospher, even though I was only seven when she passed on, and she extracted from Gavin a promise that he would take care of me. Gavin (actually Chester Alan Arthur III, grandson of President Arthur) built a group of houses in the dunes at Pismo Beach, California, 100 miles north of Santa Barbara. Here, in the '30's and '40's, he headed a spiritual commune which attracted some of the most influential artists, poets, dancers, and spiritual leaders of the day. It was a simple, ascetic life, supported by the natural elements of sand, sun, wind and the sea. Most vital was the famous and tasty Pismo clam, around which the noon chowder was always created. From the age of six, I would visit my uncle at "Moy Mell" (Irish for "Fields of Honey") for two or three weeks at a time, being healed by the elements and expanded much by the enlightened conversation of these precursors of the New Age: Krishnamurti, Isadora Duncan, Frederick Spiegelberg, Alan Watts, and others.

Gavin's specialty was astrology and psychic awareness, so my first brush with such concepts as karma, reincarnation, meditation and yoga, actually took place in the dunes before I was ten. Gavin introduced me to many psychics and their various arts, even though I never dreamed I would use such gifts in my primary work.

My father, Loring, and my mother were divorced when I was six, so I only saw him a few times when he was in Santa Barbara between world travels and sojourns in the South Pacific. Loring was a romantic adventurer who played his way around the world with his guitar and accordion, and then wrote books about it. He contrasted the life of Polynesia, the paradise of being taken care of by Mother Nature, with the American industrial society. He spent five years in India with a master, and practiced his yoga throughout his life. Loring could remember music he heard in his dreams; could play it on his guitar, and had a way of getting people up and dancing when he played the music of the islands. He inspired me with the power of music to move people and raise their spirits.

For as long as I can remember, I've loved music. Before the age of nine, I was already spending long hours listening to the sizable record collection in our house. Included were not only Bach, Beethoven and Brahms, but Mussorgsky, Rimsky-Korsakoff and Wagner, as well as Debussy and Ravel. Such titles as "Die Gotterdamerung," "Aida," "Pelleas et Melisande" and "Scheherazade" had almost magical power to my budding musical curiosity when I pronounced them. Fortunately, there were many cultured people around the house who pronounced them correctly.

One day Bobby decided that all his children should play musical instruments, ("something to fall back on in hard times") and he envisioned a family ensemble. Oliver, who later became a sculptor, said he'd play percussion; Gavin, who became a writer, said he'd play the cello; and I said I'd play the phonograph. But there lived up the road a 16-year-old girl who played the harp, and one day I was sent up to see if she would teach me. What a picture I was! A homely kid of nine with a lot of dark brown hair hanging over my eyes, my trousers rumpled, four years before puberty and yet falling in love with her on sight. (Little did I know that I was destined to be called "the most versatile harpist in America," and to pioneer healing past-lives with music!) Shyly I asked her if she would give me lessons. To make this possible, the young girl's father helped my family purchase a Clark Irish harp, and lessons began after school.

A year past, and I was asked to play for the school P.T.A. It set me back years in the art of performance before a group, but working through the "stage fright" enabled me to learn many techniques with which I have helped students overcome the same phobia. The first calamity: a wire string broke. A replacement couldn't be found, and a welder had to be brought in to patch it—just before going on stage! He lit up his torch, and soon sparks were flying all over the room! I had never seen this before, and it added to my anxiety, seeing my harp laid out for an operation.

Next, the stagehand put the harp on stage wrong way around. Instead of sitting down and playing, I had to turn it around 180 degrees. I had broken my wrist on the playground, and my arm was in a cast from the middle of the hand to the elbow! The doctor had bent my hand downward (the opposite of a good harp playing position) and so moving the harp around and playing was grotesque enough to complete the trauma of the whole experience, which I performed in a state of semi-blackout!

(I can just imagine my High Self chuckling, "Well, I guess we'll see if he REALLY wants to play the harp!" Some part of me REALLY did, and so I persevered with lessons.) For years I struggled with various forms of on-stage fears. At one concert I stopped breathing so long that my fingers simply started to slow down and stop, with the tension. (Although I was far from aware of it, one of my problems then was the ability to tune in and pick up negativity from the audience. In my healing work, this is one of my most valuable sensitivities: the ability to transmute negative energy patterns for entire audiences.)

I was well-educated in private boarding schools, with a smattering of public schools. I had harp lessons from time to time, especially in the summers, and would perform in school concerts. Always there was music in my early life: ushering at concerts, singing in glee clubs, quartets and musicals, acting in plays. I loved sports and excelled at soccer, tennis, ping pong and pole-vaulting.

Once, when I was a senior, I had given a fellow senior a black mark for being 45 minutes late for Study Hall. A group of seniors ambushed me and threw me in a horse trough. Then they went to the headmaster and complained of my behavior. The headmaster upheld them and summoned me. It was a crucifixion. In this instance the headmaster approved (during my formative years) the social philosophy, "you scratch my back and I'll scratch yours"! Not only that, but that it is O.K. to force others, through gang tactics, to conform to this philosophy!

I said that I could not understand it: "Why don't you change the rules, then, to exempt seniors from all rule-enforcement by their peers?"

I made some headway intellectually, but I was agitated and fearful. Of course, psychologically and socially, they had won. How could I really stand up to four of my peers and the highest authority in the school? (This kind of thing happened a number of times in my youth. I am later to become greatly expanded in universal love and service to everyone. I was also to learn that I had actually been crucified in a past-life. I manifest this pattern until I learn to accept it with perfect love, and to love everyone, then it stops.)

Boarding schools led to the University of California in Santa Barbara. Here I received a Bachelor's Degree in Theory and Composition. I was 16 when I entered: prepared for college musically and intellectually, but not socially. During the fourth year (1949), I put all the experience I had gained working on Bobby's houses to good use and built, with a friend, a small concrete-block house.

At this time I enjoyed several religious experiences related to merging with nature, which I recorded in fair, Wordsworthian verse. This began a habit of noting peak experiences in poetry which has lasted through the years. Also, during this period, I began to explore other instruments. For years I had improvised at the piano. Now I bought one and took lessons at the University. Founding a jazz group, playing string bass, and serving as arranger, I took up the trumpet, tuba, cello, marimba, and Japanese bowls filled with water. It was most exciting when friends and I would have a session of free improvization. (This was the beginning of what would become, 27 years later, the Order of Orpheus, the group dedicated to healing with channeled music.) Summers were spent either building houses, planting tomatoes for the family income, playing tennis, or attending the Music Academy of the West. Here I was exposed to the training of professional musicians by some of the top artists of the day.

At the age of twenty, I spent a summer studying with the master harpist, Carlos Salzedo, at his colony in Camden, Maine. There I immersed myself in the harp literature. I also spent time recopying much of the markings on my music, as they had been erased by a bottle of gin in my suitcase on the flight from New York!

I had visited another branch of the Andrews family whose head was the Vice President of National Distillers (Gilbey's Gin). Taken to lunch at an exclusive club, I was told that my branch of the family were "dark sheep" and "going to the dogs." A job was mine if I wanted to turn back to "respectability." This offer was sealed with a gift of a half-gallon of gin. It was quite symbolic, as the Andrews men in general, for two or three generations before my father, hit the bottle pretty hard. And although they were once quite aristocratic and wealthy, they were culturally and spiritually going downhill fast. While my brother, Oliver, and I were still exposed to the cultural heritage of aristocratic lineage, we saw some of the sicknesses of the upper class. In our parents we saw the disenchantment with these values and accepted their calling to rebuild through artistic creativity and spiritual seeking — symbolic, too, that the new birth should begin in the womb of a cave!

When I was 21, I enlisted in the Air Force to avoid the draft for the Korean War. I was placed in a band in San Antonio, Texas, for two years, and then in the Air Force Symphony in Washington for six months. I learned the humility of being a number among thousands. I also made the first real friends I had had among my own kind, musicians. My uniqueness was appreciated and I began to unfold myself a little. I improvized background music for the announcer on the weekly radio show. It was live so the players never heard it. For two years I developed all kinds of ingenious modulations, special effects and thematic metamorphoses. When I finally heard a recording, I discovered that hardly any of it could be heard! Of course, in terms of training, it was invaluable.

Up until this time, I was doubtful whether my technique was ever going to develop sufficiently, but the vicissitudes of being in the service came to my rescue. For band rehearsals I was placed right in front of the brass section! For much of the time, I had to sit there with no part to play. To maintain my sanity I began practicing technical exercises, concentrating on perfect mechanics because I couldn't hear myself. Of course I had to be ready to stop at any moment if the band stopped, or I would have been discovered! I placed complete faith in the system I'd been taught, the Salzedo Method, and my speed and accuracy developed rapidly. I composed for the harp progressive jazz fantasies on ballads that were popular at that time, also some music for two plays produced in Santa Barbara by Iris Tree, a Shakespearean actress, and the Ojai Players.

Now 23, and still in the service, I experienced an illumination: a touch of cosmic consciousness! For over a month I was in absolute bliss, and I have never been quite the same since. I was just standing in the barracks listening to a group of my buddies talking, and I had a vision. It only lasted a minute or two, but it was incredibly intense and vivid. I was existing at the center of an ideal liquid suffused with a pink-violet-beige light. It was ecstatic. Then I moved from the center to view it. There I saw crystallization, as of new growth, forming and as the shapes grew more definite I could feel the growth process. I left the group and sat on the edge of my bunk as the vision slowly faded and the light and ecstasy gradually diminished.

Two nights later I had a night vision (far more intense than a dream) of the same experience, but in a vivid green light, five times more intense than normal color. The following night, the same vision in intense yellow. (Could this vision have been a memory of being in the womb and experiencing soul entry? And perhaps remembering my soul purpose? And could the colors green and yellow have been indicative of the Heart and Solar Plexus chakras?)

Twenty-four hours later, I came down with what is called in Texas a "summer cold." The band flew to Hollywood and I went to the hospital. After a day I began to recover from the cold symptoms, which were quite serious as "colds" go, and rapidly I began to feel more and more uplifted. On the third day, I had twelve visions. The sensation of light was intense. On this day a number of leaps in consciousness took place. I completely accepted my destiny, completely lost the fear of death, knew I was immortal, resolved the problem of duality (two halves of the same thing, depending on each other for meaning), felt unconditional love for everything and everyone, and was no longer afraid to relate to anyone.

Released with a bill of good health, I found the bandsmen were allowed to live off the base. I rented a small room, were I began to keep a journal of the rising tide of revelations. I was remembering all kinds of events in my life, which seemed to be leading up to the experience, such as the time when I was eighteen and walked across my bedroom and wondered what it *felt like* to be Jesus Christ. I remembered books that had been recommended to me years earlier which helped me understand the experience. Chief among these was *Cosmic Consciousness* by Richard Bucke, which describes the illumination experiences of the major mystics of history. It shows that there can take place a sudden leap in expansion of consciousness, more and more humans are experiencing it, and it is characterized by certain aspects of light and love which vary only slightly from case to case. It points out that the experience does not seem to be a respecter of persons in any way, produces profound and permanent changes in appearance and behavior, and that most religions have sprung from such revelations. My whole attitude toward life, my work, and the reality of other planes and dimensions opened up.

In my journal I wrestled with the almost insurmountable predicament of how to express the vibrational realities in words. (It's a similar challenge, of describing music, that we have undertaken in this narrative.) The more paradoxical the concepts became, the better they seemed to express the all-embracing qualities of transcendence into divinity. So I could understand perfectly when I read others' similar struggles! Once you have had an experience of cosmic consciousness, you understand *every other* person's experience of it! The light, the ecstasy, and the understanding lasted a little over a month, then gradually waned. The wisdom gained remained to be tested through the years.

When I was offered a job as script writer for the broadcasts, which would have meant a promotion and no time to play the harp, I declined. And when I was discharged after three years I was only a three-stripe sergeant!

I returned to Santa Barbara at the age of 25, and for six months mostly ate, recovering from one meal just in time for the next! Gayelord Hauser's nutrition books prompted a yogurt diet. One week later, ten pounds lighter, I met my first wife. She was the first person I had met, my own age, who was trying to live by higher principles. She was also beautiful. But it was her higher principles that attracted me most. Soon we were married in a pageant in the family garden in the foothills. I was inspired! Single-handed I built a house of 20-year-old pier timbers. A few friends joined for the house raisings, and the style was called "rustic contemporary." Fearful of damaging my hands with a power saw, I cut the 4 x 16 planks (some 30 feet long) by hand, with an undersized Swedish saw. (This house, which we never actually lived in, has provided a continuous boost to my income, an enormous help during times of preparation and spiritual service.)

The house finished, we moved to Cleveland. I entered the Cleveland Institute of Music; my goal, to study the harp under Alice Chalifoux, the master Carlos Salzedo's star student, an excellent and inspiring teacher. We arrived in the dark city in the middle of winter and deep snow and after California this was a change of life style. (The color of the air actually varied from day to day, depending on what was being manufactured!) The year-and-a-half spent there was a tunnel of hard work and struggle with old world values and conservatism, lit only by our love, the accomplishment of study, and the superb artistry and personality of Miss Chalifoux. (I thought that I was preparing for a career as a concert harpist and composer. In reality, I was undergoing an apprenticeship for much higher work, and Miss Chalifoux's artistic sensitivity was broadening my expressiveness as well as my humanity.)

Actually, my professional career has been somewhat in reverse: At 27, I begin my professional life, as Head of the Harp Department at the University of Texas. I present solo concerts, tour with a quintet, and organize an annual harp festival. This culminates in a national festival drawing fifty harpists including Carlos Salzedo. For these concerts, I direct, compose, arrange, conduct and perform. During these four years (1956-1960) I sometimes play for 5,000 people at a time. (When my art develops into healing, I finally play for one person at a time, sometimes 50, never more than 300.) It is almost as if I am picking up a career that I have left in a previous life. As I will later find, there is much evidence that I was Johannes Brahms — whatever that means (we will discuss reincarnation in Chapter XII). Four years later, I was let go from the University; the ranks were filled and there was no way to recognize my accomplishments without changing my field. I felt rejected and unappreciated. Of course, I had no way of knowing the renaissance of creativity that awaited me in San Francisco (Patron Saint: St. Francis—Kuthumi, who oversaw my birth).

This brief history of my first 32 years, from the human viewpoint, has been hard growth. But it has been full of many rich influences and experiences. Yet from the psychological standpoint, my inner sensitivities have been oppressed by lack of understanding, frequent beatings and other physical hardships, hostility from my stepfather and my older brother, lack of balance between my intellectual and emotional-social aspects, and difficulty in understanding a world filled with so much negativity and lack of empathy between its inhabitants. Later on in life I will realize that, as with the oyster, these are the grains of sand which will produce my pearls. Even though they seem more like boulders at the time, as I surround them with the white opalescent light of love, it will deepen my humility and my understanding of, and compassion for, people and the human condition. Later I will realize that there were karmic debts with these people which I volunteered to ease and release for the soul-growth involved. It isn't until I am 36 that I work things out with my stepfather. Until then, with all my male superiors, conductors and bosses, I don't know whether I want to hit them or hug them!

Finally I undergo a psycho-drama during a 24-hour marathon at the growth center, Esalen. I pick actors out of the group to proxy for my family and then "tell it like it was". I get more and more involved, and they deliver some of the best acting one could imagine. The resentment comes out and just before I'm going to punch out my proxy stepfather the experienced leader, Virginia Satir, puts a thin mattress in front of me. I'm enabled to get my hostility out into the open. Virginia then says, "What happens next?" I and my stepfather sit down for our first man-to-man talk. At the end of the week, I sit in the garden with my stepfather and mother and go over it all. More comes out between us ... tears of realization and healing. I'm able to forgive, aware that they are the products of their own formative influences, they did the best they could, and I can grow from all the ways I was treated.

Realizing that the word "stepfather" does not describe the *function*, which is *fathering*, I accept Bobby as one of my fathers. We all embrace, reconstituting the family. "Poppy" is the name I choose to call Bobby thenceforward because he is a virile figure—a "Pop."

At the end of the 5-hour session, I am called to the house to answer a phone call. As I near the phone, on the very corner of the table is a real estate card. It says in large letters "Poppy Real Estate" and out of the "o" is growing a red, California Poppy! When confronted with the beatings, Bobby described himself as a "fiery, red devil", and so this image becomes transmuted into a beautiful, red flower! (At significant peak junctures of one's life, one can sometimes see unequivocally the operation of the law, AS ABOVE SO BELOW, or AS WITHIN SO WITHOUT.)

Immediately, this catharsis changed how I related to all male superiors. I could now stand on my own two feet, respect their role and positions, while at the same time knowing that in a higher sense they were my equals and brothers. I become grateful that I could do this while Poppy was alive. Later still, I am to learn Gestalt techniques whereby I could have done it without Poppy being there in person. But, of course, my parents might have put the confrontation off much longer. It was my initiative that helped release some of the guilt they were carrying concerning the early years.

Modern psychotherapy is growing by leaps and bounds, and there are literally hundreds of techniques garnered from all over the world, from hundreds of years of history and from our brothers and sisters on higher planes. These techniques of psychological healing are much quicker and more reasonably priced than they used to be, even ten years ago. Anyone can get more affordable help now, instead of carrying around debilitating fears and hostilities everywhere they go!

*　*　*　*　*　*　*

Well, my friend, I've included this short history so that the character of this story will have some human depth with which you can identify. Also so that when I begin to lose my personality, that is, to expand it to include more and more of what is around me and "above" me, you will have a feeling for the compost out of which this grew!

Isn't it amazing how we never really know what we're doing in life until much later? That's why we have to give everything we have to the present moment. The future is made of it and we never know how significant a seemingly small experience may become. *It may contain a vital seed for the future!* I wasn't too conscious of this through the early years, but I certainly did "hang in there." Perhaps it was because I had some baggage from past-lives that I was getting bored with toting around and *really* wanted to set down so that I could move more freely and even help others to free themselves. I am to learn that when we tune in to the creative forces above, around and within us, we can better handle whatever is given us. And whatever our situation, it is potentially optimum for our growth. The more stuff from the past we are working with, the more strength and understanding we have developed to deal with it. Later on, I will take my hat off to those who are manifesting "difficult" karmic patterns, especially those like my own past patterns, and it's like taking my hat off to myself!

Well, friend, you have been most patient. Shall we throw a log on the fire and freshen our drinks before we plunge into the next phase? It might be a good idea as Joel Andrews really starts moving.

"There is music in all things, if men had ears."

Lord Byron

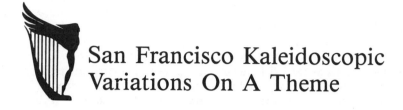

CHAPTER FOUR

San Francisco Kaleidoscopic Variations On A Theme

My life seems to alternate between a period of being stimulated and *created*, and then a period of being sent somewhere to create culture and raise consciousness. After four years of teaching the harp at the University of Texas, organizing annual harp festivals and a nationwide festival, I was glad to arrive in San Francisco for a period of aesthetic recharging. I had finished my formal education with three degrees, been sent out to teach what I had learned, become somewhat disillusioned with the "academic marketplace", and now was ready for some experience! — a logical sequence for the latter part of the 20th century!

For a city, San Francisco is one of the most beautiful, with its clean air, its many hills (which provide a unique perch for each habitation), its two spectacular bridges, and enormous parks. This setting, where the continent meets the Pacific, provides also a meeting-place for East and West, and out of this hybrid vigor have come many creative artists, painters, sculptors, poets and musicians. From this atmosphere have also come new movements in the humanities and religion.

In the summer of 1960 I arrived in North Beach, where the "beatniks" had proclaimed their manifesto a decade earlier. It had become highly commercialized, and the value of store-front property and apartments had skyrocketed. Now the stage was set for the next proclamation from the new youth: the "hip" generation and the "flower children." This centered in the Haight-Ashbury district across town near Golden Gate Park, and the ingestion of consciousness-changing plants brought them much closer to nature. (Later I lived there for a few months and made more active my deep love for the natural world.) I had never lived in a city, and I rented a small basement apartment overlooking the Bay near the Old Ghiradelli Chocolate Factory. Every day, starting out in my car,

I would feel a creative buzz in the air and I would say, "San Francisco — city of promise!"

For nine years I explored the rich versatility of the harp and my own creativity. I also had many experiences that opened me spiritually and planted seeds in my consciousness that flowered years later in the healing ministry of the 1970's (which utterly changed my life). It is these that I should tell you about, not leaving out some of the rich and colorful details of this abundant period.

Some years earlier, through my brother, Oliver Andrews, the sculptor, I had met Jean Varda, a Greek collage-maker and bon vivant. So as soon as I was settled I called him up and he invited me to dinner. I offered to bring my harp, and it was quite an experience, carrying it over the long and somewhat flimsy gangway that led out to the ferryboat on which Varda lived. (Back in those days when they were discontinuing the ferry service, you could buy a whole ferryboat for a song, if you would just not ask to have it delivered! Varda and Gordon Onslow-Ford got permission to dock their's near Sausalito.) After a wonderful dinner which Varda cooked mostly himself, I played for the assembled guests. One guest was so struck by a Corelli Gigue that he came over and asked me to repeat it three times. Then he said he had never experienced such a feeling of "good jazz" in a Baroque piece and asked me if I'd like to do some drumming with him. He produced from his car an array of trapezoidal logdrums, and we sat down in the lotus posture facing each other with the drums between us. He thrust into my hands some mallets, and there followed a "meeting" through rhythmic conversation, punctuated by eruptions of delight from both of us and waves of appreciation from the guests.

In addition to Roger Cummings*, the architect-drummer and gleeful Pan, I inaugurated that night a number of friendships that lasted through the years. A columnist from the San Francisco Chronicle was present and mentioned in his column a harpist in tennis shoes who accompanied dinner with Baroque music and then answered the challenge of the logdrums. At the party, I was so elated that I drank too much wine, and Varda had to lead me to bed. All I remember is ascending an almost vertical companionway. I was awakened in the morning by blazing sunshine and the crying of gulls in a small, completely white room. I had absolutely no idea of where I was! When I emerged from the room I found I was on the roof of the ferryboat. Varda had put me to bed in the wheelhouse!

Ianko (the real name that Varda's friends called him) built a Mediterranean sailing barque. Its sides were decorated with many colors streaming from one great eye, and its sail was of the square, lateen rig. On a Sunday morning it was a privilege to be invited to join other celebrants for a voyage on the bay. Interesting people of all kinds, and speaking various languages, would scramble aboard with wines and cheeses, con-

*All names of people in this book are fictitious unless indicated (real name).

certinas and ukeleles, and plenty of the incomparable San Francisco French bread. Ianko, bald head bronzed in the sun and white hair flowing in the wind, looking like Proteus, God of the Sea, seated himself at the tiller. He bellowed orders to his crew, and we were off. I don't think he ever figured how many experienced sailors there would be. If you weren't sure you'd fall overboard, you "jumped to."

One afternoon a storm came up and without enough experienced hands on board the mast broke. After a harrowing hour we were ignominiously towed to shore by the Coast Guard! Most of these cruises were idyllic however, and as the shore receded, so did civilized cares. There were wonderful times, hilarious stories, and dancing on the deck — all high-lighted by Ianko's incredible fables. These were surrealistic stories, rich with symbolic satire of our times; for, in addition to being one of the leading colorists of the 20th century, Varda was a deeply perceptive, spiritual man. He was also known as one of the best-dressed men in San Francisco. He got all his clothes at the Goodwill and dyed them subtle colors, applying the same alchemy to his dress as to his art.

I soon met Alan Watts (real name), the Zen philosopher, and married his daughter, Ann (real name). Between Alan and Varda and my uncle, Gavin Arthur (real name), the Jungian astrologer, I found myself in an extended society of highly creative people, sensitive to New Age developments; and a number of formative influences began to stimulate my development. (As I look back, these were areas of advancing apprenticeship which would be woven together into a new form of musical healing — a higher octave of music-making.)

My uncle Gavin was like a father to me, but much more. He introduced me to a world of reincarnationists, astrologers, sufis and psychics; homosexuals, bisexuals, omnisexuals; New Age poets and filmmakers and fascinating ex-cons — a sophisticated education. We often attended the Golden Gate Spiritualist Church where Reverend Florence Becker (real name) did some of the most accurate billet reading in the country. You enclosed your question in a sealed envelope on which you wrote a key word or phrase. Seated at a table, heavily blindfolded and with the room well-lit, she would pick up a billet, read off the key word, ask you to speak to her to establish voice contact, and proceed to answer your question. She was obviously helped by her own guides as well as aspects of your deceased kin which would identify themselves by name and items of personal evidential. I was so impressed by these revelations of what was really going on with people that I wondered why the room wasn't filled with the city's top psychiatrists.

I took one skeptical young doctor to a meeting and when I introduced him to Rev. Becker, he said, "If you can see these things, why aren't you working for the government?"

She answered, "Darlin', they're interested in doing what *they* want to do, not in this kind of truth."

When she came to my billets, she would often move her hands as if she were playing the harp, obviously moved by what she heard. She would say, "Do you make music like this?"

Gavin suggested I have some psychic readings of different kinds. I found them most fascinating, especially the process. They were not only instructive but quite helpful — especially in my relationships.

When Alan Watts invited Ann and me to participate in an LSD experience I welcomed the opportunity to explore this facet of our culture, and my own deeper self, under the very best guidance. Over a period of some six years, I took LSD five times, peyote twice, and marijuana occasionally. I came to these experiences with the up-tightness born of 15 years of practicing the harp alone for hours each day, and years of protecting my inner sensitivities from the frequently inconsiderate people around me (or so it seemed).

I could relate to people best when they were in my audiences, but I always had known that one day I would have to open up and reach out to others. I see the drugs as catalysts for psychodramas that were most valuable at that time. They helped me look into the beauty of my own nature (also to shine the light in some dark corners), to reinstate the awe-inspiring beauty of the sensory world, and to feel the growing warmth of intimately sharing these rediscoveries with friends. There were many philosophical illuminations, especially those transcending dualities, but the greatest of these concerned time and the difference between its perception in the altered state and in the normal state. In the transcending state everything was "in the now," and since we could experience all that we were, we were not interested in the step-by-step development of a skill or the working through of a problem.

So I asked myself, "How is the normal state of consciousness different and why is it that way?"

As I came down from an experience, feeling the gradual slowing up of time, I realized what a beautiful opportunity the pedestrian pace of life affords us to grow little by little in areas that are difficult or new. Although at times I did get painfully in touch with some of my fears, they were transcended. These experiences were positive revelations and, in my case, since I really needed to be opened up, highly beneficial.

As so often happens in my life, next came the testing. I became involved in different kinds of encounter groups. These ranged from a leaderless group which unleashed hostility and then seemed devoid of positive methods for dealing with it, to a week at Esalen in Big Sur with a master of the art, Virginia Satir. Her rare combination of technical experience, intuition, and love pulled me through some rather excruciating encounters, and I began to drop the role of "the helpful analyst" which I was using to mask my feelings.

Throughout this period I was exposed to many patterns of Western music (my memory banks becoming well-stocked for the 1970's). I was principal harpist with the Oakland Symphony and San Francisco Ballet (probably reliving karma accrued when I was a composer and a conductor and was hard on the orchestral players). I spent two years editing and learning a harp concerto by a Spaniard, Joaquin Rodrigo, which I performed with the San Francisco Symphony under Arthur Fiedler. I was playing solo concerts, chamber music concerts with "Lyra" groups I founded, including flute, cello and soprano. I transcribed new works for these combinations and composed for them.

For a country wedding of two friends I was asked to arrange Purcell's "Come Ye Sons of Art" and, falling in love with this concept, began to compose some variations. The groom, Alexander Di Tavoli, heard them and commissioned me to complete the set. It is the only music of mine that has been published. I also composed a suite about the sea. I thought that I would be spending much time at the shore for inspiration, but found myself tuning in to the many aspects of the sea very intimately from my studio. (Little did I know that this was training in psychic attunement and developing love for the Earth.)

I played a good measure of very dissonant contemporary chamber music and found much of it unnatural and overly intellectual. I also felt that most of the so-called acid-rock was not truly psychedelic music since it did not take you into the world of nature. Some of it was breaking up the crystallized habit patterns of the past age, preparing us for newer patterns of freedom, but I found the satanic music irresponsible — the product of anemic individuals groping for power. Did they not know they were creating vibrational karma for themselves? — that the patterns and qualifications of energy they sent into the world would return to them, going around the world to hit them in the back of the head? For some, the karma was more rapid and, with chakras blown open by excessive drug use, they absorbed more electricity than they could handle and they died. Others, like John McLaughlin (real name) who is a student of Sri Chinmoy (real name) and founder of The Mahavishnu Electric Orchestra, realized that power in music is not a function of your strength to turn up the knob on the amplifier! Instead it is a quality of music itself, created by the artistry of the players.

I explored new areas of music-making: a program with the dancer, Sheila Xoregos (real name), in which we explored different ways of improvizing with each other; a program with James Broughton (real name), poet, called "The Bard and the Harper," which we presented three times at the Playhouse at the foot of Hyde Street; and I founded the Universal Sound Ensemble to explore the art of completely free improvization. This included a Panamanian (piano), an Englishman (bass), and an East Indian-African-American yogi (conga drum). Then I played for New Age weddings, funerals, lectures, exhibitions and even for the meeting of two minds! (I was *not* allowed to play during a police raid of a commune — where the authorities planted marijuana in the wrong suitcase!)

During this period my solo playing developed nicely and audiences were moved by it, sometimes quite deeply, but I made no connection between their responses and any psychic abilities. There were signs, however, if I had been able to read them. Here is a quote from the liner notes of my first L.P. album, produced in 1966: "What is it that moves the critics to call this artist, 'a most remarkable virtuoso AND musician,' 'a master of his instrument', and 'a musician of the highest stature'? It is not only that when he plays he and the harp seem to become one (one critic said, 'we have rarely heard on any instrument such mastery of technique and complete control'); not only that his training in the Salzedo Method has given him visual style and gesture which bring out the choreographic aspects of the music; not only that he has a warm personality ('an engaging soloist with finesse and glowing charm'); but that his talents as composer, and experience in improvization, give him a breadth of expressiveness unprecedented in a harpist."

"Beyond this the quality that places him with the great bards of the ages, and has moved many of his listeners to tears, is a transcendental quality, which, when the ego is stilled and the artist becomes a channel for the universal forces of light, stimulates in the listener a sense of Cosmic Consciousness. *Joel says, 'We must put ourselves in the service of Art and Light. Then we will fulfill our destiny to be magicians of sound, healers and aligners of the rhythms of the psyche and the body, disintegrators of the crystallization caused by materialism.' "* You will readily see what a prophetic statement this was as this narrative progresses!

After I had lived in the Bay Area for two years, friends told me about a healer by the name of Eleanore Donaven. After a waiting period of three months she gave me an appointment at her "physio-therapist" office in downtown San Francisco. The hour I spent with her was so remarkable that I returned every three to four weeks for seven years. I am still realizing what I learned with her. She had various masters working through her and could call on many psychic abilities. She used colored lights, acupressure, and could apparently see conditions within the body. Every week the masters seemed to be giving her a new ray so she had many to choose from for a particular condition. These I would receive lying on my back. Then I would lie on my stomach and she would place her left hand at the base of my skull and her right hand would move up my spine, chakra by chakra, tuning in to these seven vortices of energy which link our various bodies. With the help of the Higher Forces, she would purify them, balance them, and harmonize them. Eleanore would also see past-life scenes and work with the masters to interpret them. These impressions always helped me with what I was working on at the time, or they helped me to raise the level of my future visions (revelations of my own soul levels). I would get so high in an hour (which seemed like days) that when I descended to the street I seemed to be on another planet! The healing went beyond physical balancing into emotional, mental and karmic causes, and so was deep and lasting. An interesting side-effect was that for three or four days I could tune in to people, especially in terms of their health. I began to experiment with the healing techniques that I was learning from her, and achieved enough success to continue this research.

And research it was, since, as you must remember, I had absolutely no idea that in 1972 I would give up my career as a professional harpist to become a metaphysical healer! From my early days I considered my approach to life scientific, artistic, and musical; I had a strong conscious mind, so psychic experiences needed to make good practical sense to be incorporated into my life. At my concerts, once in a while someone from the audience would come back stage deeply moved, but I never connected it with anything psychic or working with Higher Forces.

One thing I should tell you about before I leave this period is my early involvement with the work of Edgar Cayce (real name). I had been hearing more and more about this remarkable clairvoyant and finally, in 1966, I attended a conference in Monterey on various aspects of his work. I felt drawn to the veracity of this material and began a ten-year study of his readings. I found that their reliability covered a panorama of spiritual growth and, of course, his work imprinted on my consciousness a model pattern for a psychic reading. I began my own personal research (and I really saw it that way) into meditation, dream analysis, reincarnation and the laws of karma. After two conferences, they asked me to give a class in the esoteric nature of music and the basic laws of vibration. This led me to some interesting books and insights, and I developed a six-hour seminar using many aspects of music as windows into the nature of reality. I began to realize what a great teacher of truth art and music can be. Five years later, when I became more seriously involved in the study of metaphysics, I was grateful for so much I had already learned from music — and then I was told by the Higher Forces that the non-verbal arts, and especially music, give us our closest glimpses of the nature of higher dimensions. As for so many others, the Edgar Cayce readings were an introduction and "four year undergraduate degree" leading to my work as a metaphysical healer.

It was during this time that I heard about the music healer, Kay Ortmans (real name). One day I drove down to her center in the Redwoods near Santa Cruz to talk to her about her program and experience some of it. At that time she would improvise at the piano for a client, then provide a permissive atmosphere where they could move and dance to the music, do art work, mold clay, etc. Then she would help them work with whatever symbols came out of this expression that might be keys to helping them understand and release their blocks. The program is powerful in bringing up and "moving out" (her words) the dormant pattern that isn't working. Some of her strongest therapy is alignment through music and massage. Past-life patterns are brought to the surface where the calling forth of higher energies will then harmonize all levels of being. Sometimes these sessions last for three hours! Mine went on for hours, and I experienced four past-life situations!

I was most interested to find this corroboration of Wilhelm Reich's (real name) belief that the past is stored in our "muscular armor." As Kay went deeper into my shoulder it became strangely painful, and I saw myself strapped up on a wall of a cell with metal and leather shoulder straps! It was during the Inquisition and I had been speaking out on religious matters. This is one reason I really appreciate the relative freedom of speech we have in these times, and I intend to make the most of it (doing it a little more carefully!).

It was the next morning that I wandered into the huge ring of redwoods. I found the fountainhead of energy and had the illumination experience related at the beginning of this book. Kay said that I had found the spot where her healing program, "Relax and Rebound," had come to her years before. Once I set up my harp in "The Glade" where she did the movements and art work to music. I was playing some written pieces and she said, "Improvize! Improvize!" She was, and still is, a great inspiration to me.

Years later, when I had started to channel the past-life music, she encouraged me to make the music *healing* instead of just past-life pictures. I had wanted to do this, but didn't have the nerve to take an active part in resolving the disharmonies in the karmic patterns. Of course this was the whole idea behind the new type of channeling, and as soon as I started to resolve dissonance in the music, the Sources came through and helped me. I am grateful for her encouragement.

Before we leave this period, I would like to tell you an experience that I had that was typical of the vicissitudes of an apprentice healer. The brother of a close friend of mine had moved to Sausalito and was opening up psychically a little too fast. He was hearing voices which were telling him to do things which were dangerous for others, under the guise of spiritual help. He had threatened his own son in order to "exorcise the evil spirit in him" and his wife was considering leaving him. I received a desperate phone call from her and was especially concerned because they had very few friends in the Bay Area.

Two or three days later, I arrived home at my studio at dusk, and for some reason didn't turn on the light. As I stood in contemplation, in the growing darkness, I began to wonder what I could do for my friend. I suddenly remembered an experience I had had a month previously where

I had seemed to possess a special sword and was spontaneously cutting away patterns which were attached to me, inhibiting my growth and true purpose. And I remembered how, when I recounted this to my healer-teacher, Eleanore Donaven, she told me I had been given the Blue Sword of Truth (the Archangel Michael and the Lord Krishna are both pictured with this sword). She had said I could use it for others to cut away that which was not for their highest growth.

I knew what I was about to do, but not feeling too confident, I called on my healer-teacher for support and immediately felt her presence in the studio. As I raised my right arm and asked for the power of the Blue Flame, and waited for it to reach sufficient intensity, it seemed that I heard her say, "Well, let's get about it — I have other work this evening." Finally I felt that I was as ready as I was going to be and, visualizing my friend as strongly as I could, formed my hand into a kind of claw and, summoning all the determination I could, raked it down through the image from head to foot to remove any negative influence. The action seemed to be strong and successful, so I thanked my teacher and left the room.

Two days later, my friend's wife called me, and I said, "How's Samuel?"

She said she was much relieved since he had voluntarily entered the psychiatric ward of a hospital. Then she explained that the doctors had administered a new drug which had stopped the voices! I told her I was sorry he had to go into the hospital, but glad the voices had stopped.

As I hung up, I said to myself, "I very much doubt it was the pills."

I had to wait for a week-and-a-half for my appointment with my teacher before I could tell her the story, and ask for some "professional feedback."

She said, with a special curiosity, "On what night did you do this exorcism?"

When I told her she said, "I see. The night after that, I went out with my cat to dump my garbage and was beset by a very powerful dark thought-form (entity). My cat was sick and I immediately returned to the house where I had to do a thorough aura cleansing. What did you do with the entity that you exorcised?" I replied innocently, "What do you mean, do with it?"

She closed her eyes for a moment and then she said, "Now Joel...if you're going to be doing exorcisms, you'd better learn how to do them properly! It won't do to leave these discarnates wandering about looking for a home. I usually bind them and send them to the temples of healing and learning, but I will give you a decree to use. As you finish this type of a healing action, call on the Brothers of Light to seize it, bind it, render it inactive, and conduct it where it's supposed to go."

As I thanked her, I began to realize why I had had to wait for three months to get my first appointment — she was probably thinking over whether she really wanted to take me on as an apprentice healer! — even though it was the furthest thing from *my* mind that I was being trained in the healing arts. I have never forgotten this technique and have been called upon to use it countless times.

These years were, then, a veritable kaleidoscope of creative people and rich consciousness-expanding experiences — many of which were necessary seeds for the unusual developments to come in the next decade. (As I look back it seems to have been carefully planned, either by a deep soul aspect of myself or an extremely wise guardian being — or perhaps both!)

In the Fall of 1968 I received a letter from a friend I had met in the Air Force. His name was Perry Matson and he had been the script writer for the Lackland Air Force Band and Symphonette in San Antonio, Texas, where I played background music for their weekly broadcasts. He was now chairman of the music department at North Carolina State in Raleigh. He invited me to come for a year as Musician-in-Residence, and it seemed attractive.

This period in San Francisco had been almost too active, and what with a number of psychological growth traumas in my personal life, and the strain of supporting a wife and two children, the security looked good for my health, so I accepted. In July, 1969, almost exactly nine years after I arrived in San Francisco, I put a few things in storage, rented the house, piled my wife and two children into the camper and drove East. (Little did I know that it would be another nine years before I moved back!)

*   *   *   *   *   *

Well, my friend, I hope this gives you a rough idea of some of the influences and events that helped to prepare me for the transformations I'm about to describe. Why don't we bring in some wood, throw a few logs on the fire, make some tea, and I'll tell you how my whole life changed and a new form of healing with music was born — or should I say, rediscovered?

CHAPTER FIVE

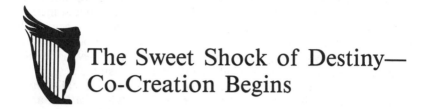

The Sweet Shock of Destiny— Co-Creation Begins

We pulled into Raleigh in early August, 1969, and the weather was like a 24-hour steam bath. I think we could have found lodgings in the psychiatric ward if it hadn't been for the compassionate director of the Student Union who put us up in an air-conditioned room. In four days we were ensconced in a comfortable apartment on the north edge of the city.

My first meeting with Perry Matson afforded humorous reminiscences of the Air Force broadcasts and provided me with an equipped office in the campus theatre building. He then explained that in this primarily agricultural and technical university there were no students majoring in music, and so the function of the music department was to organize a number of musical groups in which students could perform. The Musician-in-Residence Chair was established to fill the lack of performing music faculty. I was to give four or five concerts a year, be a kind of roving musical ambassador on call for important occasions, and talk to various classes about the nature of music.

This was just the type of challenge that has always fired me. It also turned out to be a showcase for all the new things I had been exploring musically in the San Francisco period. The first year I presented five concerts in the Student Union, each featuring a different combination of instruments. Over 450 people attended the first concert. Both Perry Matson and the director of the Student Union were amazed when the audiences continued to be this large throughout the year. I drew more than the chamber music series of internationally-known artists. I can only explain the great popularity of these concerts in two ways. I dressed in a pure-white Nehru suit (instead of the usual black) and set the harp against a rich aquamarine tapestry. Also instead of writing program notes I talked to the audience about each piece. The second factor was that I was beginning to experiment with prayer. Before each concert, I would ask to be used by whatever Higher Forces might be around for the upliftment of the audience. The response to these concerts was most gratifying, and an increasing number of souls came up after the concerts, very deeply moved. Sometimes they would come in tears and sometimes they would be in a state of euphoria. I gradually began to realize that something *supra-musical* was happening. By the time my second year began (the appointment was extended), there were others who also became aware of it, including my colleagues in the music department. They made jokes about my "wings" and some kind of magic I was using.

Again, I was like the apprentice magician who doesn't really *understand* the forces he is trying to invoke — even though he is *talking* about higher dimensions. In an interview at the time I said, "I try to establish a psychic relationship between myself and my listeners. Then if they share psychic energy with me, great things can happen, people can be transported. When I play a concert it brings a vital condition of peace and harmony to the audience." When a musician (or any artist, for that matter) has developed his technique and his interpretive sensitivity to a certain level, he can't go any further until he co-creates with forces outside and beyond him. I was opening up this higher octave and audiences were beginning to feel it.

I developed a close relationship with the flutist there, Jim Hancock. He was involved in most of the chamber music and improvization that I did in North Carolina. We developed a rare rapport, and learned much from each other. He was not too interested in talking metaphysics or psychic phenomena, but he had the most beautiful respect for my interest in these things. Some musicians have developed "perfect pitch" (the ability to identify a note); Alan Watts had what I call "perfect lecture" (he could philosophize engrossingly at the drop of a hat and at any time of the day), and Jim Hancock has "perfect people". He seemed to be able to relate to everyone with a relaxed, humorous compassion without losing his intelligence and integrity. I used to tell him, "You're a Bodhisattva — and don't know it!" It's quite possible that in a recent life he devoted himself to spiritual study and in this incarnation wishes to just manifest the Christ-like virtues without talking about them.

Many friends, and my California agent, advised me to have a New York debut, and it was obvious that while I was in the East was the apropos time. I mention this because it marked the culmination (and the end) of my career as a "professional" harpist. To any aspiring young concert artist, especially one who begins in the West, a debut in New York is a career milestone. The review is necessary to approach the top managers and open up national and international concert touring. An old family friend I had met in San Francisco, Gerry Bodrero, put up the money to engage Hammond Taylor, a manager who specialized in Town Hall debuts. I put together the most challenging program that I could and worked all winter and early spring (1970) for the April 18th date. One of the advantages of my appointment was that it gave me time to finish a few projects of long standing. One of the foremost of these was to complete my transcription of the "Chaconne in D Minor" (J.S. Bach) for the harp. I had always been drawn to the variation form in music, and when I first heard the "Chaconne in D Minor" performed on the Sienna pianoforte, the bell-like tones of which suggest the harp, I fell instantly in love with it and knew that I must transcribe it for the harp. This unique piano, a product of incomparable 18th-century craftsmanship, has only recently been rediscovered. The 32 variations, lasting fourteen minutes, are a minor masterpiece. They were published for unaccompanied violin, although some scholars feel that they must have been originally composed for the lute. They have been transcribed for the piano and the guitar but, as far as I know, never for the harp. The tempo of the changing harmonies fits perfectly the resonance time of the harp, and it was most satisfying to attune myself, with the greatest respect, to the master Bach and to adapt the "Chaconne" as faithfully as possible. I had to draw on the experience of many years of composing to solve the problems of Bach's intricate counterpoint. Then, once it was on paper, I had to learn how to play it and memorize it! This was a challenge since it was the longest contrapuntal piece I'd ever played. Throughout can be found the most subtle interplay between feeling and structure, which appealed to my Geminian nature and helped me resolve dualities. I still call it a masterpiece of reason and passion.

The entire first two-thirds of the Town Hall program (before Intermission) consisted of sets of variations: Beginning in the 1500's with the Spanish lutenists, progressing through Handel and Haydn, including my own set of variations on Purcell's "Come Ye Sons of Art", and culminating with the entire Partita (Suite) in D Minor from which the Chaconne is usually extracted. After Intermission, I played my "Sea Suite" from the San Francisco period, which introduces fifteen new effects on the harp and portions of improvization. Then, to close, I played a piece which I had just completed called "Odyllic Epithalamium". I should tell you about this piece because it represents a bridge or transition between my career as a composer and my career as a psychic musician.

I had promised two close friends in San Francisco that if they ever got married I would write their wedding music. An epithalamium is a piece (usually a poem) in honor of a bridal couple. The word "odyllic" is a word I put together from the word "odic" and the word "idyll". "Odic" force means the energy involved in psychic phenomena, and an idyll is a pastoral love poem. I used the word "odic" because I really felt that I "tuned in" to my two friends during the writing of this piece. The first two sections are portraits of them, and I could almost feel their presence in the room as I was composing. The third section describes their consultation of oracles about the marriage. When I had difficulty representing their horoscopes musically and their correspondence together, I discovered that they had not consulted an astrologer.

When I find myself in a fix, and only then, I consult the oldest oracle in existence, the I Ching. As usual, it illuminated the situation greatly. So there is a section in the music where an ancient Chinese sage interprets the wisdom of the book. The hexagram that I cast describes the conditions when two polar opposites come into union (my friends also lived on Union Street), and I was able to finish that movement of the music. The fourth section is an actual processional to be used at a wedding and is based on the harmony of bells and gongs, a special study that I had made. Bells and gongs, which we find beautiful, are based on two Harmonic (Overtone) Series an Augmented Fourth apart — which should be dissonant. Thus their very nature symbolizes the harmony between polar opposites. Again I was being trained. If some wise lady had entered the room where I was improvising on my two friends as part of the process of composition and told me that in two years I would be improvizing on people for a living, I would have thought she was mad.

My friend, you can easily imagine what kind of a state I was in as the Town Hall concert date approached. My harp playing was cranked up to eight to ten hours a day of practicing. I was filled with expectancy, but it also seemed that every breath I took in through my own aura was filled with destiny. A friend of the family invited me to stay in her apartment the three days prior to the concert and to run through the program for a group of her friends. Then strange things started happening. First my harp was lost at Kennedy airport! Can you imagine something the size and shape of a harp becoming lost? I couldn't risk playing on a different harp since the spacing of strings on each harp varies. I tried mental practice, but was somewhat unnerved with only a few hours to play before the private recital.

Then, Town Hall was so busy that I had only *one half hour* on the stage the day before the concert! The lights were locked up and I couldn't arrange special lighting until just before going on stage. I wore the white Nehru suit and through a miracle was able to find a rich Oriental rug on which to place the harp, but I had very much wanted to do something with lights, especially for the "Sea Suite".

As it turned out, the weekend of the concert was the first fine spring day in New York City and everyone left for the country! I think the audience consisted of 200 people with a special interest in the harp, and I could hardly see anyone as I looked out from the stage! My compassionate hostess sat in the first row, right in front of me, and gave me much moral support. With my natural anxiety over the difficulty of the "Partita" and "Chaconne", heightened by the loss of three days of practice, it was probably the most grueling ordeal of my life! I got through it all right, due to the years of experience in performance, but the "Chaconne" was a bit shaky, with two or three wrong notes. I was in a state bordering on blackout all through that piece, and when I went off the stage I burst into tears under the strain. The second half went well and many people came backstage to congratulate me.

Hammond Taylor said there was no way he could tell whether or not a critic would come, but there was one there and the review was quite good. Of course, it often seems that New York critics can never just come right out and say anything; they seem always to cover themselves by saying something bad and something good in each sentence. The review stated that I was "willing" to extract fresh sonorities from the harp and that my staging was "transparent showmanship — but it worked". If the critic had been interested enough to talk to me, I would have explained that I wore white because white is the mixture of all colors, as is music, and black discourages the exchange of energy. My whole purpose in my stage approach was to co-create with the audience by dissolving the proscenium arch between us. This is why I talked to the audience instead of having printed program notes (I did also have program notes in Town Hall). And this is why I was not hesitant to use such theatrical resources as colorful rugs and colored lights. Used sensitively, I could create the impression that the stage was a room in a home and not some kind of basement or schoolroom, like so many concert halls.

From the standpoint of my "career", I was grateful for the critic's presence and his review, but it precipitated my growing disgust at the pretentiousness of the whole professional concert business. I felt as I left New York that if this experience was an example of a worthwhile goal for a concert artist, I didn't want any part of it. I knew what a truly marvelous program I had prepared and I knew how hard I had worked in the ten years before this concert to try to reach people, to try to involve them in the performance.

In the next days and weeks, I did a lot of thinking. I remembered one informal concert in San Francisco when I was so overcome with love for the audience that I just walked in among them, hugging everybody! And I began to realize that in the traditional framework of concert tours, in the usual halls where organized audience concerts are given, I just wasn't going to be able to establish that kind of rapport. I wondered how many people go to concerts in America for social reasons or as some kind of experiment, and how many of these are really ready for a deeply uplifting spiritual experience. Also how many go for entertainment only? As I look back on it now, I think I had passed some kind of initiation where I had to fully experience the consequences of pursuing a career through the time-worn professional channels. So, as it turned out, my career reached a peak of fulfillment and I retired (or graduated) — all in the same concert!

There is one other experience which I had while in New York that I mention now because of its symbolism. I had a few moments alone in Mr. Taylor's office — which by the way, was stacked two and three feet high on every available surface with old posters, programs, plates, cups, and saucers — and I noticed a poster on the wall. It was a jumble of black and white and I couldn't make out just what it was. Then I noticed some fine print at the bottom which said, "If you will step back fifteen feet you will notice something extraordinary about this picture, which was taken in the snow fields in China."

As I stepped back about ten feet, which was as far as I could go through the "archives of career milestones", I saw the face of Jesus, the Master. It resembled closely the face I had seen in a photograph a child had taken in her garden in San Francisco. She had come in and told her mother that there was a nice man in the garden and she wanted to take his picture. In this photo, unmistakably, is the face of the Master. Between the two, the resemblance was extraordinary. Is it possible that I was guided by some Higher Force to see this poster among the professional debris in those few minutes to plant an idea in my subconscious for consideration after the concert? The idea would have been, "If you will step back to see your career from a distance, the true spiritual purpose of it will appear out of the confusing shapes you now see and the clutter of past programs."

*   *   *   *   *   *

But already in the year before the Town Hall concert, I was having some experiences which were to change the course of my life and align me with my true soul-purpose. As I look back on these purely experimental explorations they certainly seem to have been under some Higher Guidance, but at the time I had no idea of their importance.

If this narrative has an underlying theme, it is that *we never know just what we're doing!* There are inner and Higher Forces guiding us which have access to our optimum Life Plan and often don't reveal the plan until it is safe to do so. The theory of reincarnation was not included in Edgar Cayce's early fundamental religious training. It took him some time to embrace it, even though the healing work accomplished through his readings used past-life material extensively. This is why one must give everything to the present moment. There may be a small but essential lesson or item of information that will turn out to be the piece that completes a larger puzzle later on. This is also why someone who spends his life in a certain discipline and develops a great deal of expertise in it should never put down the novice who passes through it quickly to garner some small thing of later value.

Now that I see my true destiny as a healer and spiritual teacher, when I review my life it appears as if a guide was saying, "Listen to this; no, don't listen to that; remember this idea, discard that one; notice this person, release that one..."

Now that the plan is taking clearer shape I am always finding myself saying, "So that's why I learned that!"

When I arrived in Raleigh, one of the most interesting discoveries was that I was four hours from Virginia Beach, Virginia. This is the headquarters of the Association for Research and Enlightenment, the foundation that guards and disseminates the material that came through Edgar Cayce, the remarkable clairvoyant. His 14,000 readings are on file there for perusal, and a dedicated staff schedules lectures and workshops and encourages study groups all over the world. They also publish many books that mine this rich vein of spiritual wisdom and healing techniques. Like so many workers for the Light, I had my basic education in metaphysics and such subjects as meditation, karma, reincarnation, and healing from this rich and reliable source. In addition to visiting the A.R.E. every few months, I attended a Cayce study group most of the two years I lived in Raleigh.

Virginia Beach itself, and the immediate vicinity, is truly a focus of light energy. It isn't just the salty, clean air blowing in from the Atlantic that gives you that exhilarating buzz. In just a weekend, you feel a special, high vibration whistling down the marrow of your bones! Every time I went there I met the most extraordinary people and had the most mind-bending, and consciousness-expanding experiences.

I had lectured at an A.R.E. conference in California and so was invited to talk about the laws of vibration at a weekend seminar on creativity and music. It was the Spring of 1970. I took my harp and improvized before and after the lectures. After one particular session a lady stood up and asked me if I could improvise on a person.

I replied, "I don't know. Let's try it, but let's make it real; is there someone here who has anyone close to them who really needs some help?"

A lady said her father was dying in a veteran's hospital in California. At that moment, I remembered the code that my harp teacher, Carlos Salzedo (real name), had given me for translating letters into pitches (see Appendix). He had told me that Haydn, Brahms, Ravel and other composers had used it. So I asked this woman for her father's initials and, since it had been some time since I had used the code, I somewhat laboriously translated them into pitches. Then I asked the the whole audience to meditate with me for his highest good, and I inwardly said a short prayer asking for guidance. I played the three musical notes and improvized for about ten minutes.

I had never done anything quite like this before (unless you could include the piece I wrote for my friends' wedding) but the music came out quite definite and beautiful and was much more specific than I expected. I thought it would be *accompaniment music* for a healing meditation. Both the audience and I were deeply moved by the experience, and afterwards one lady came up in high excitement.

She said, "You're a New Age doctor! Could you possibly do one of these for my daughter? I'll be more than happy to pay you!"

I was a little taken aback and said to her, "First of all, you can't pay me; that was the first time I've ever done one and I have no idea how I did it! But I would be glad to experiment again and just see what comes through."

Actually, part of this excitement was probably over the introduction into our time of a new "ancient-future" form of healing and it is probable that many souls in the audience were aware of this subconsciously, on the inner planes of being. Also, they may have been more aware than I was of the guiding seraphim, and possibly even ascended masters, who were in attendance to help inaugurate this new form of healing. These forces knew I was ready, but of course, they can never force anyone. I've always suspected that they gave a slight nudge to the lady that first asked me if I could do it. Fortunately, she was willing! Many years later I was telling this story and a lady in the audience said she was the one who spoke up! I told her she was instrumental in changing the course of my life.

The next day, the mother who was so concerned over her daughter, and I, and another friend I had asked to sit with us (who had some experience in healing groups) met in a small room off the lecture hall. The daughter was in South Carolina. Again I used her initials and said a brief prayer. The music that came through that day was even more detailed. It kept accelerating in rhythm and intensity and I had to bring it under control. This happened a number of times. It was a very moving experience, and I could feel other dimensions opening up. Afterwards, my friend said she could feel a life as an American Indian, and there *was* music that sounded like that. Then I told the mother that I felt this unbridled energy had something to do with uncontrolled sexual expression in a past-life. In the course of the conversation, the mother mentioned that her daughter was an epileptic. It was like a light going on in my head, as I remembered that Edgar Cayce had given a number of readings for epileptics in which he had said that the condition was due to misuse of sexual or creative energy in past-lives. (Subsequently I studied this set of twenty-odd readings, and they almost all say this. Anyone who has observed an epileptic seizure knows that it looks and sounds like an uncontrollable sexual climax. It is interesting that I had witnessed such a seizure a few years before.) I left this session thinking that something mysteriously important was going on, and wondering what it was.

A few months later, I was again giving a lecture at the A.R.E., and decided to close the meeting with one of these improvizations. A friend, Jonathan Forrester and his wife, Evelyn Keller, were in the audience. Jonathan wrote and edited some of the books on the Cayce material and Evelyn is a prominent chiropractor in the East. In improvizing, I chose Jonathan as my subject, and this time the music came through in five different sections, each one with a particular style and feeling. This time I recorded it and gave Jonathan a copy. A few weeks later they called me to say that he had just had a past-life reading from Gay Cormack, an excellent reader, and that they were sure that the sections of the improvized music corresponded to some of the same lives!

On the next trip, in the early Spring of 1971, I had taken my Celtic folk harp along and was asked to take part in an ancient nocturnal ritual on the beach. These spontaneous gatherings often seemed like hand-picked people for the occasion. The ritual was a deep experience for us all, and we gathered afterwards in a room at the Marshall's Motel on the Beach. There was a request for more harp music and I got the idea of tuning into the people of the group. I knew nothing of what was to take place.

The room became highly charged, the music continued for about twenty minutes in a most meaningful and powerful manner, even though the Irish harp is small. When I finished, one of the women was crying and saying, "That's David, that's David!"

I began to explain to her what I felt the music was expressing. She said it was most revealing of what was going on with his condition and was grateful for some ideas as to how she might help him better. It was cerebral palsy, severe enough for him to spend most of his time in a wheelchair over a period of years, requiring a great deal of her time, energy, and concern. As I opened up more and more I said that I thought he had too many uric acid crystals, and that he should be tested for them at Duke University. She reacted with frustration to this suggestion, since she had taken him recently to the Duke University Medical Hospital for tests, but she had been so moved by the music that she agreed to take him again. Two weeks later she phoned me, telling me that they had run tests they hadn't thought of before which indicated that he was loaded with uric acid crystals! This is a condition associated with his malady.

Medication was begun, and he was already feeling better. When her hope had sunk to a low ebb, it was rekindled and she also felt that the music had somehow been beneficial for David as well as for their relationship. Of special significance here is that I didn't know consciously whom I was healing until she passionately burst out his name, and, as far as I know, I didn't know there were such things as uric acid crystals or that they were connected with his disease, or that she had already taken him to Duke University for tests. This was before I did the ten readings for the volunteers at Evelyn Keller's, and so it was quite mysterious and exciting. In this particular case there was not, as there almost always is later, a request for healing. Possibly this took place subconsciously. Also it's possible that the Higher Forces and my High Self wanted to get the healing work started and a formal request was waived.

It was about this time that I remembered being taken, in the '60's, to meet a fine concert pianist in San Francisco who had given up her career to work with disturbed young people with music. I remembered wondering if perhaps the higher octave of music-making was some sort of healing. (Had my destiny guardians planted that experience and that thought in my consciousness for later so that when things began to unfold I wouldn't block my own development with my conscious mind?)

Now we arrive at the zero hour — the initiation that marked the fork in the road of my life. I believe it was August of 1971. Evelyn and Jonathan called me and asked if I would be willing to come and stay with them and do some readings.

I said, "What sort of readings do you have in mind?" (While I had met many psychics in my San Francisco days, I had never fancied myself one, and actually still don't, although I use higher sensitivities in my work.)

They said, "We're quite sure you're channeling past-lives on the harp. We're excited about their healing potential and we have ten people who have volunteered as subjects."

I replied, "Do you really think I can do that? It's an interesting offer, but I'll really have to think it over."

I had been learning something about the laws of karma and was a bit concerned just how they might apply to my reading a person's past. On the other hand, I could see how fulfilling it might be if music that came through me could actually promote healing in a subject. In a few days I called them back. I reminded them that I had no idea what I was doing, but, if it was made very clear to the subjects that I had no responsibility for the effect of the music or the information that might come through, I would come up and see what happened "at their own risk".

The weekend arrived, and I loaded the harp and tape-recorders into my camper, and with considerable expectancy I left for their home. Now, it's a four-hour drive from Raleigh, and for long drives in those days I would place a portable recorder behind my head and play tapes. I was studying the Kahunas, the priest-healers of Hawaii, and took along a lecture by Max Freedom Long on the healing techniques of "Huna". Just before I reached their town a phrase sank deep into my consciousness: "Anything is possible under God." It gave me some much-needed assurance, and I felt I could relax a little. (As I look back, I'm sure my guides put some golden resonance around those words on the tape!)

My friends were in a state of great anticipation about the readings and had scheduled three each day, starting on a Monday morning. They had asked Gay Cormack to sit in on a few to compare notes on my impressions of the "lives" but also to see what her Sources might give her as to how I worked. Part of their excitement was their deep interest in reviving holistic methods of healing, which they felt we had all practiced in the ancient temples — particularly The Temple Beautiful in Egypt. In this temple Ra-Ta (Edgar Cayce) had supervised many such practices to perfect the lower aspects of the people for the reception of the concept of the One God.

Monday morning I arranged the harp and the tape-recorders and retired to my room to prepare myself for "I knew not what". It was not easy for me at that point in my life to talk to God or to pray, but I thought I'd better!

I said, "O.K., God, if it's possible for me to do this kind of work, which I can see could be very high work, without hurting myself or anyone else, let those conditions be established within me such that I can do it."

I felt a heightening of vibrations throughout my body and literally floated into the room where the first subject was waiting. I greeted her, took her initials, translated them into pitches, and then took a few moments of silence to center down. When I was in a meditative state I started the recorders, said a brief affirmation asking for protection around the room, asked to be used by the Highest Forces to which we could attune, played the initials, and then listened.

What I heard first in these readings, and what I played on the harp, was some kind of descending glissando which turned out to be descriptive of the coming into the body of the soul, or whatever you'd like to call the spark of conscious life. Then followed, usually, seven sections of contrasting music. I was sometimes aware of impressions or scenes while playing, but more often would see things after each section. These vignettes lasted between one and three minutes, and the gaps between were 20-30 seconds long, making the average total length around 25 minutes. Each section was a complete statement in itself, and often the key center would change for each one. After I finished playing, I turned off the recorders and gave my impressions, which did come in terms of past-lives. I would see a country or city, get a rough time period, usually a century, and get a feeling for whether the person was male or female. Then I would see them involved in some sort of activity and see how they succeeded at it.

Everyone felt the music had a special beauty. You could feel the increased vibrations in the room and everyone there felt uplifted. Of course these "lives" seemed to be "reproductions," musical portraits, and sometimes dissonant things would come through — so-called negative behavior such as involvement with "black" magic. Then I would help the subject deal with it in a spiritual light. Usually the music resolved the dissonance after a few measures. (Later on this aspect becomes smoothed in the readings, but I assume that the first stage was to bring through accurately what had taken place. Just by being expressed musically, these patterns tended to be harmonized.) After I gave my impressions, there would follow a discussion of what the subject was experiencing in this life and usually what had come through would help to explain this and place it in a larger perspective. After that, Gay would give what she picked up and we found that there was never a contradiction between us — and much agreement. Sometimes she or I would receive different additional material.

Here is her "aura reading" report on how I worked: "When he sits down I see him surrounded by a golden light which is then surrounded by violet. Then I see him ascending through seven planes, and when he reaches the Seventh Plane he is conducting an orchestra. Then I see part of him descend to the Causal Body of the subject where he contacts the personal akasha."

Her conclusion, after three days, was that I was reliably reading the person's past-lives! Her description of the colors and the planes was baffling to me. It sounded pretty esoteric and I really didn't understand what it meant, except that gold symbolizes wisdom and violet, intuition and transmutation. (Later I am to learn what this meant: The gold was indeed the higher octave of conscious mentality, wisdom. The violet was the color associated with the third eye, clairvoyance, but also the ability to represent what was seen in a transmutive light, or "healing by the Law of Grace". The seven levels were the seven bodies of the client and possibly my own as well: 1) Physical-Etheric, 2) Emotional-Astral, 3) Mental, 4) Intuitional, 5) Spiritual, 6) Monadic, and 7) Divine. These could also be related to the chakras. Conducting an orchestra symbolized my getting in touch with a wide variety of vibrations. Then part of me would attune to the Causal Body of the client where I was reading the personal akashic records. At present and for some years there have been other angels who help me access other akashic records. At the time, most of this was a mystery!) After the three days and ten sittings, we all felt that something new, unique and important had taken place. There were some deep discussions late into the night about the possibilities suggested by this "Ancient-New Age" form of healing. I drove back to Raleigh in a warm daze, trying to piece it all together and wondering what my wife and circle of friends would think.

*　　*　　*　　*　　*　　*

Well, my friend, you certainly have been most patient and dawn is stretching and yawning and unfurling rosy-orange arms and fingers across the feather-blue sky. What do you say we take a walk down by the river and watch the trees and the squirrels wake and quiver to the warmth of a new day? We can greet the "sun of God" while I tell you how completely unforeseen experiences lifted me into a higher octave of music-making.

*   *   *   *   *   *

As I went about my duties on campus, I was a man with an inner secret. I felt a growing point of destiny within me which began to change how I felt about many things in my life.

In a very few weeks, I had the first request to travel to another city and do a few readings. At first these requests came in every three or four months, then they became more and more frequent. It was around that time that in meditation I said to God, "If I am going to be doing this work, I would like you to send me those whom I can help, and I won't become involved in suggesting anyone have a reading." I have almost 100% honored this arrangement over the years. Of course, I speak enthusiastically *about* the healing work; but, even though I am sorely tempted at times, when I know a reading would help someone, I wait for a request. (This is most important in healing work. Healers have found that, while it does no harm to pray for someone or to do a healing action on them without a request, they may be wasting valuable time and energy.)

The changes in my consciousness were reflected in dramatic changes in my personal life. In 1971 I met a woman with whom I could really share my spiritual path and with whom I had some important karma to work out. This ended a 10-year marriage. Leaving a wife and two children was traumatic for me and for them, and yet it really seemed destined by some Higher Plan. (In most of my relationships I have been the one to persist, thinking that love would solve all problems. Perhaps enough love will solve anything, but it doesn't necessarily seem to keep people together for a whole life nowadays — perhaps because *growth* is so important in these times of transition between Ages.)

Unfortunately, there is not space here to go into the details of my relationships with women and my three wonderful children, from whom I have learned so much. But I am most grateful to the dear ones who have shared my path and thank them deeply for love, unfoldment, and training. I think it was a case here of what the master Jesus said, "I will separate child from parent, husband from wife", meaning that sometimes the requirements of spiritual growth and service take precedence over family ties — even as important as these are. It depends on the individual life plan.

I began to clean up my body and embraced vegetarianism (continuing to eat fish and eggs, as I had learned that it is not generally wise to make too drastic, sudden changes in diet). I eliminated evening cocktails, Kentucky-style fried chicken and television from my life, as well as cutting down and eventually eliminating smoking (not easy!) I had found occasional marijuana an excellent tranquilizer, but now was afraid it might affect the finer perceptions, so I dropped it. I hadn't had any LSD since the San Francisco days, but closed the door on that possibility as well. I replaced these pastimes with yoga, meditation, nature walks, and more metaphysically-oriented pursuits. I began reading and discussing psychic perception as the extension of our normal senses and explored books on spiritual growth. For the year '71-'72, I accepted a post as Musician-in-Residence at two small colleges in North Carolina with the understanding that I could, between concerts, take trips to do readings.

In the summer of 1972, I moved to Virginia Beach and accepted a position in the Paul Winter Consort (real name). This is a most creative group of musicians dedicated to a synthesis of New Age jazz and Classical music, plus the exploration of free improvization. It was the culmination of a long-held desire to play jazz — a style from which I had learned so much in my earlier years. So I spent the next year touring the colleges half the time (with grey hair and a ponytail!) and the other half developing the readings. The last piece on every concert was "Air on the G String" by J.S. Bach and the Consort always received a standing ovation! It was a clear demonstration that college students appreciate good music if they can get it. I ended up doing a solo improvization based on one's connection with the sun (soon I was to find out that the name of my High Self is "Helios"). I was inspired to write an extended work for the Consort based on the concept of sun energy, and other subjects that tuned into the devic forces of nature, such as "Rain". All of this was excellent training for attuning psychically to these other dimensions and was consciousness-raising for those who worked on these arrangements.

Before concerts I would always say a brief prayer asking to be used as a channel. Some members of the Consort thought me somewhat weird for my constant metaphysical explanations of things, but I had already grown accustomed to this reaction. In past-lives I have been crucified in one way or another for speaking out on religious matters, so I have always been most appreciative of the present era in this country where we have relatively free personal freedom of speech. I wish to make the most of it while I can! Then also I would think, "How can I learn unless I practice; how can I see the deeper laws operating in the outer world of manifestation unless I look for them?" So as I opened my eyes more and more to see what's really going on, I observed the most amazing patterns. (If you persevere in this you will see that most things in this world are not what they seem to be on the surface, but are mostly the reverse. After that comes the realization that they are what they are on this level, but they are the reverse of what they are on the next higher level.) Of course, when you truly wish to see, you get a lot of help.

Not knowing Virginia Beach very well, I took a house right in the flight pattern for the Oceana Naval Air Base where cadets practiced takeoffs and landings. They would fly right over the house, and since their schedule was not predictable I would have to seek guidance as to when to do the readings. It is a fact that the times a plane flew over *during* a life section of music were extremely rare, and the times when a plane flew over *in between* lives, where I could erase it on the tape, were countless. Miracles were beginning to be connected with my healing ministry, many of which I will recount later in this narrative. Since they have steadily increased I won't be able to remember them all!

A significant development in the readings took place at this time, the fall of 1972, and I discussed it with Kay Ortmans (real name), one of my mentors. I began to want the music to be more positive: that is, to begin to harmonize and heal "negative" patterns as soon as they were contacted. She encouraged me that this was possible, so I asked for help and guidance and began to resolve the musical dissonances sooner. Higher Guidance seemed to come immediately, and after a couple of months I didn't even have to think about it — it just happened. I guess in the first stage of clairvoyance you have to learn how to pick up what's there, then you begin to learn higher ways of dealing with what you find. It's also like the primitive form of physical healing where first you take on the condition and then heal it within yourself. Then you learn how to heal it outside of you without ever losing your own integrated balance. Along with this progression of the readings was coming the growing suspicion that all our so-called "negative" behavior patterns were growth in disguise.

The readings increased steadily over these months and in the Fall of 1973 I "took the plunge". I resigned from the Consort and decided to devote full time to the healing work. My income took a dip, then recovered in about four months, and I've been taken care of ever since.

One day I went to my chiropractor for an adjustment and she said, "You know, so many of my patients are out of balance in the Solar Plexus area. Do you think you could channel a general tape for that chakra?"

While I was on tour in Atlanta I was guided to bring it through. She would have patients listen to it while they were waiting for their treatments. It was quite effective and was the first of a long and growing list of tapes for purifying, healing, and balancing the chakras as well as many other tapes for general healing. The Sources had shown that they could give us music which would be safe and effective for everyone. This, I thought, was amazing, and it began to impress me with the enormous potential scope of the new ministry.

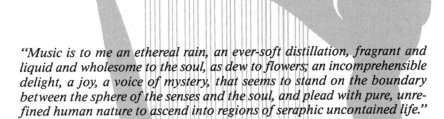

"Music is to me an ethereal rain, an ever-soft distillation, fragrant and liquid and wholesome to the soul, as dew to flowers; an incomprehensible delight, a joy, a voice of mystery, that seems to stand on the boundary between the sphere of the senses and the soul, and plead with pure, unrefined human nature to ascend into regions of seraphic uncontained life."

John S. Dwight

Interlude

At this point, my friend, who had been absorbed in the story, straightened up and said, "This has been absolutely fascinating! These musical healing sessions must have been deeply satisfying and fulfilling to you, to have given up a career that you worked so hard in pursuing. I'm anxious to hear how these readings evolved, and what form they are taking now. By the way, do you have apprentices? And have you considered writing a book to inspire others to expand their musical consciousness into these higher dimensions?"

I answered, "Well, my friend, many musicians who have experienced a spontaneous added dimension in their playing and who feel a new and often strange vibrancy coming into their music have come for support and guidance. When I'm on tour, at almost every concert a musician comes up afterwards, aglow with the joy of having discovered another musician who is actually doing what they have been envisioning or beginning to do themselves. Many of them ask me where they can study the arts of improvization and channeling, and there's very little I can suggest. I mention playing jazz, studying under an Indian master musician, studying with me when I'm not on the road, or just finding other musicians to improvize with. But most of these may be quite difficult for them. I know that if I could take the time to write a book, it could be inspiring to many, as well as publish aspects of my work which are, as far as I can discover, unique on the planet. It could stimulate the evolution of higher music."

My friend said, "That's what I've been thinking! Even as a layman, I'm quite intrigued by the unfoldment of the creative process and what people call inspiration so I'm most interested in how these readings work. What is it like for you as you do them? How does the client experience them? It would be most interesting to explore the patterns of reincarnation that have come through the readings, and especially the systems of symbolism that the Higher Forces working with you have revealed; not to mention the new light that would be shed on the true, essential, meaning of sound and music. I'm sure you've had many experiences doing this work which would be of interest to practically everyone. Since we have two days in this beautiful setting, and nothing pressing for our attention, why don't you tell me about the more important aspects of this work? We can record it as sketches for your book about healing with music in the Spiritual Renaissance."

I said that I really appreciated his interest, and that it would be my pleasure. As the sun arose into the heavens of a glorious day, I began, grateful for the opportunity to distill 18 of the most miraculous years of my life into a narrative. I was somewhat hesitant about whether the words I would use to describe the readings would be universal enough. He reassured me that I should tell my story naturally, the way it happened. He said, "This authenticity is important because of the freshness of much of the material." And he added, "You know, I think it's possible that the terminology you've been given is an integral part of the larger revelation."

Excitedly I said, "Well, this is wonderful! You don't know how long I've waited for this. I think I should start with a detailed description of just how an attunement session progresses."

CHAPTER SIX

The Attunement Experience

To date, I have completed some 2000 individualized healing tapes. While they seem at times somewhat routine, deep down I never really forget that they are, in many respects, miracles. As I tell you about them now, they seem so. When you've gradually developed a skill over a period of time, then you look at it objectively, it can take on an *incredible* quality. Similarly, though I've played the harp for 40 years, if I'm ten feet away watching someone play, it's difficult to see how they can do it! Although a number of variations have spontaneously occurred over the years, let us begin with a standard "life" reading session. I call it an Individual Attunement.

Usually I know next to nothing about the client (we are not supposed to call them patients). I really prefer that they do not tell me about themselves prior to the session so that my mind can be clear. This could be a "long distance" (in absentia) reading where all I have is the complete name, address and birthdate. I have done hundreds of these for clients all over the world, and they come out the same as if they were sitting before me. Roughly one third of the readings have been in absentia. Bear in mind, also, the original pact I made with the Higher Forces: that I would refrain from suggesting anyone get a reading if the ones I could help would be sent to me. Another interesting factor is that, even though music is a universal language and most humans on Earth respond to it, it could be that a large percentage of the people who come for harp readings have a special liking for, and sensitivity to, music. But this certainly hasn't been the case for everyone. They come primarily for healing and the illumination and unfoldment of their deep soul purposes.

Keeping in mind that I'm working under guidance and that there have been a number of surprising variations about which I will tell you later, let us set forth the basic phases through which the average reading progresses:

1. Setting up the room
2. Greeting the client
3. Tuning the harp (ideally done just before)
4. The client writes his/her full name, address and birthdate (not the time) in my book
5. I explain the procedure
6. I check the recording equipment
7. We meditate and center ourselves for 2-3 minutes
8. I say an affirmation to get cleared for the work
9. I start the two recorders and say an affirmation, offering to be used for the highest good of the client
10. I play the notes, under guidance, of the birthdate and the name to call forth the music
11. I improvize, under guidance, the client's music
12. I turn off the machines and go over in my mind the past-life information to be sure I've got it and to receive more
13. I turn over the cassette to do the Interpretation and rewind the listening copy to the beginning of the birthdate music
14. I listen to the birthdate and name, writing in my book the octaves in which the pitches of the initials were played (These are the client's purposes of soul-growth for this incarnation) and the directions, up or down, that the rest of the notes of the letters take
15. Replay the music and record the Interpretation over it
16. Ask the client what they experienced
17. Counseling
18. I often analyze the person's name
19. Label the cassettes, enter the names on the handout sheets, gently ask the client how payment would best be made for the session and if paid, mark it in the book
20. Share an embrace, in universal love, in recognition of the space and time of divinity in which we have met

(In the following amplification of the above steps, I will try to save purely technical data for another place in this book.)

1. SETTING UP THE ROOM

If you wish to do accurate and sensitive work involving expanded states of awareness, you really must have an extremely quiet place in which to do it. While many experienced sensitives seem to be able to work almost anywhere, an apprentice must have a quiet room. A verbal channel working telepathically may be able to tolerate more extraneous sounds in the environment, but if you're using clairaudience, you have to be more careful. A number of times one of my musical sessions has been brought to an abrupt halt by the arrival in the neighborhood of the "Good Humor" man!* I'm listening to far-off music, and sometimes if the radio or television is turned on two rooms away, it can scramble things. With experience has come the ability to concentrate and to screen out these surrounding sounds. But it's best not to use a room where there's a fair chance of loud planes, trains, or trucks, noisy plumbing or fans, playing children, kitchen appliances, or a telephone that can't be turned off. Since body temperature sometimes drops during higher states, you prefer a relatively even temperature and heating or air-conditioning equipment that doesn't make too much noise when it goes on or off. The new silent quartz heaters are a boon. Also, you want to be able to control the light so it's not so bright that it inhibits seeing into other dimensions. In my 18-year ministry, rarely has a neighbor complained about the music, but it has happened, and it's worth checking to see if there is anyone close enough who might object. Then, too, you want a space that hasn't had a lot of stressful situations going on in it, as these patterns are stored in the walls and the objects of the room. As I'm setting up a reading room, I always call on the Violet Flame to flame through, transmuting any patterns that might be negative to the work. (The two affirmations I say repeat this action). I guess it goes without saying that both the channel and the client are going to enter super-states of awareness, so the room should look pleasant and neutral — not too many strong or flashing colors, and it should also smell pleasant and neutral. If you use incense to purify the air, do this sometime ahead so that it's not too strong — some people don't like it.

2. GREETING THE CLIENT

One of the cardinal rules that all healers observe is that we don't give any energy to the problem. I listen compassionately to a limited amount of the client's troubles because I feel it helps the person to get in touch with the desire for healing, but I listen with the inner conviction that whatever is going on is an optimum life plan and is nothing but a learning and growing situation. I resist the temptation to begin to work with these patterns in the sure knowledge that the Higher Beings and Forces that work through this ministry can see these patterns much more clearly, and from a broader perspective, than I can. So my welcome is one of friendship, knowing that the deep soul plan that will be revealed will bring much understanding, as well as healing on many levels. I make the client comfortable, help them to put aside any tensions of the day that they brought with them, and ask them to write their name and birth-

---

*Ice cream truck with amplified music.

54

date in my book. The birthdate is written in numbers. I have previously suggested they dress on the warm side, since body temperatures can drop in altered states.

3. TUNING THE HARP

The reason the music alone is recorded on Side One of the cassette is that this music can be used effectively in many different ways. The most common use is to deeply meditate to the music, allowing it to act fully on you. People also dance or move to it, get a massage to it, do art work to it, take fantasy trips with it, and play it as a background for work and recreation. Since we are creating vibratory patterns which the client is going to use to adjust frequencies in various bodies, and doing this over a period of years, the harp must be tuned as precisely and lovingly as possible. I never rush it, allowing 7-10 minutes. I like to have this done by the time the client arrives. If I do it with them present, it is a meditative experience and attunes us both to the world of sound. Many sensitive people report that just tuning the harp changes the vibrations of the space, and I find this to be true. Since each note has universal symbolism, all of these qualities are being brought from a state of dissonance into one of consonance and harmony. This would then be the second healing action of the session, the first being how I listened to their problems. Here is something that amazed me: having developed pitch discrimination and the art of tuning a harp over 30 years of concerts and readings, I was finally given a better way of tuning it! I now slightly stretch the octaves, as piano tuners do. It takes me about three minutes longer, but I've never heard a harp so in tune. (In tempered tuning, why should the fifth take the full brunt of the compromise? Stretching octaves makes the fifths more in tune — they don't have to be contracted as much!)

4. THE CLIENT WRITES HIS/HER FULL NAME, ADDRESS AND BIRTHDATE IN MY BOOK

This is the granting of permission to consult the client's *akashic* records.* I feel that I haven't the right to consult someone's file without a request, even though the Higher Forces are sending me those whom I can help. I try to be as aware as I can of my own karmic responsibility in this work, and I actually request the Higher Forces to interrupt me if I stray from the straight and narrow path. (This is one area in which, once, they did stop me. See case #11, Ch. VIII.) I ask the client to write the birthdate in numbers, month/day/year, to save one step, since I translate it into the alphabet and then into pitches. I had completed 1000 readings when the Higher Forces asked me to begin using the birthdate, and they instructed me how to translate numbers into the alphabet and then

*"Akasha" is a Hindu word for the basic substance upon which everything is recorded.

into the pitches or notes (see Appendix I). I assumed we were beginning to get people with the same name. So the writing of the names is done primarily for permission and for identification of the personal akashic file. If the client leaves off a name or adds one, it doesn't affect the music. If an analysis of certain past names (such as married names) is desired these can be written down, as well as spiritual names. With the analysis of over 1800 names has developed a whole system, including much new information which is complimentary to numerology. This system will be discussed in chapter XI. The address is just for future use: mailings, a questionnaire, possible follow-up on healing cases.

5. I EXPLAIN (BRIEFLY) THE PROCEDURE

I tell the clients the sequence of events for the session so they will know what to expect, and especially so they won't talk until after I've finished the Interpretation. I tell them that they are the instrument that is being played and that I and the harp are only channels. I suggest that they make their total being, all of their bodies, as sensitive and receptive as possible because the healing energies and patterns are strongest at the time of the session, but the results depend upon how much they can accept. If they seem anxious, I put them at ease by explaining that none of their thoughts or emotions or physical sensations will in any way affect the music, so they might just as well relax. While the music tends to put people into a meditative state, I don't advise them to meditate. The vibrations that come through this music have proven to be truly wholistic, that is, working on all levels, so it is probably best if the client does not willfully withdraw awareness from any aspect of their consciousness. It is possible that a great deal of work might need to be done with the flow and patterns of conscious thinking. I encourage them to assume any position which is comfortable, relaxed and meditative, as long as the spine is reasonably straight and the breathing unimpeded. Most often I have them seated in a comfortable chair about five feet away from me, slightly to the left of center. I have to open my eyes occasionally to look at the strings of the harp, so it might be distracting if they were sitting on that side of the harp and inadvertently moved. Even in concerts, I would rather not be looking at the audience through the strings. Sometimes people assume — or end up in — rather odd positions. A few have insisted on dancing during their music (I ask them to stay out of my line of sight). One was so moved she sang and chanted during most of it. This was somewhat of a challenge for me — and I wondered how she was going to like it on her tape through the months, but she says she loves it. Then one lady insisted on having her reading in the nude! She said she wanted to feel the music on her skin. I replied that I felt there were many positive advantages in shedding all that seems to go with wearing clothes, and that I felt I would be able to do the reading under those conditions. I added that I might join her except for the fact that I'm not in the habit of playing the harp nude! I explained that it's a handicap working the pedals with bare feet, and the picture of me as a nude harpist wearing shoes, doing a past-life reading, was so hilarious I didn't think I'd be able to get into trance!

6. I CHECK THE RECORDING EQUIPMENT

By this time I can be getting quite "high". Ever since the tuning of the harp my consciousness has been expanding in anticipation, so I have to discipline myself to concentrate on the physical-electronic level of the machines and make sure all the necessary buttons are pressed. (This is assuming I've connected everything correctly prior to the session.) I also have to have the microphone ready for the Interpretation, and have clearly in mind how to adjust the recorders for it, since I will be even higher at that time. These readings are a challenge for me to be awake and alert on many different levels at once. I only go into a slight trance — what we call in the profession "conscious channeling" — not in "deep trance".

7. WE MEDITATE AND CENTER OURSELVES FOR 2-3 MINUTES

8. I SAY AN AFFIRMATION TO GET CLEARED FOR THE WORK

With practice has come the ability to release from the body all worldly tensions and emotions. I see my mind as an enclosure of light being gradually cleared of all extraneous thoughts. I feel a strengthening at the core of my being as well as an expansion to include whatever might be for the person's highest good. When I feel at peace and expectant, I say aloud the clearing affirmation (see Appendix II). When I have felt my hearing open up into higher dimensions of vibration and I feel the overshadowing presence, I actually receive a neurological signal that it's time to begin.

9. I START THE RECORDERS AND SAY AN AFFIRMATION, OFFERING TO BE USED FOR THE HIGHEST GOOD OF THE CLIENT

If I pick up that the client might have any qualms about the affirmation being on the tape, I ask about it. It's a beautiful affirmation that has evolved through the years, sets up the conditions for the transmission, and the last word is a signal for me to go into the altered state that is necessary. I highly recommend some kind of affirmation for apprentices in this work, and even after over 2,000 channelings I'm still saying it. I have often felt that I wouldn't HAVE to say it to do a reading, and sometimes in public I don't have much time; yet, I continue to affirm these conditions for two reasons: I want to be as sure as possible that no dark force can contaminate the purity of this music. Then, in the 50 or more past-lives of my own that I know about, I have had slight "brushes" with darker magic, as most of us (if not all) have had. Consequently, I wish to raise as much as possible of my past into The Light, creating as little new karma as possible, working towards my ascension (something I believe to be possible for us all). Of course, it is important that the affirmation be intoned with clarity, expectancy and confidence in its power. (See Appendix II for this affirmation.)

10. I PLAY THE NOTES, UNDER GUIDANCE, OF THE BIRTHDATE AND THE NAME TO CALL FORTH THE MUSIC

As I say the last word of the second affirmation, I feel a gentle shudder go down my being and the settling into me of a Higher Force Field, one of peace, love and truth. However, and I wish to make this clear, THIS IS AN INTELLIGENCE WHICH HONORS MY FREE WILL AT ALL TIMES. I always play the notes of the birthdate in ascending order, and then the pitches of the name. The range of the harp, for this work, is broken up into octaves representing the Physical aspect of the person, the Emotional aspect, and the Mental Aspect, and then on up to the High Self. I play straight through the name under guidance and the initials (which are the Purposes of Growth) fall in one or more of these octaves. The rest of the letters or pitches (archetypal vibrations) are played as a melody moving either up or down to each succeeding note.

The downward direction symbolizes the soul's involution, "getting involved in life for adventure and growth", and the upward direction represents "evolution" or "ascension", learning the universal principles and spiritual laws that build soul qualities with which we evolve toward the realization of the Source and Center of the whole creation. This symbolism also holds true for the music itself with the addition that these movements take the music into the various octaves of being (physical, emotional, mental, superconscious). The sounding of these identifying frequencies is like a clarion call by the individual to the Wisdom and Love of Divinity to reveal the true nature of the Self, to present to parts of the self that feel themselves as separated a model of the Self as a wholism. This is a call which the Higher Forces, of their very nature, cannot refuse. ("Knock and the door shall be opened to you, seek and ye shall find.") On the forehead of the Sphinx in Egypt, which represents our dual nature, animal and god, in its struggle and eventual harmonic unity, is written "Man, know thyself."

It is my understanding that the angels in charge of the akashic record aspect of my ministry have the records stored and filed under a pitch system (which is the language of the angels). When they hear the pitches of the birthdate and name, they take out the file and then under even higher supervision select those lives which 1) will show the person forming a new Soul-Purpose, to be pursued through a series of lives and 2) that will bring the most healing.

That lives can be effectively viewed as a progression along a chosen soul-path is one of the contributions these readings make to reincarnation theory. (Of course the whole subject of reincarnation is something that we're only beginning to understand, and as new, strange cases occur that we can't explain adequately we have to revise our hypotheses. Then, too, the new information coming through excellent clairvoyant channels such as the Seth Material is casting new light on this subject all the time. For further discussion and some of the results of my own research, see Chapter XII.)

11. I IMPROVIZE, UNDER GUIDANCE, THE CLIENT'S MUSIC

As soon as I play the last note of the person's name, I *listen* and hear notes almost immediately, as music on the harp. These tones are the vibratory patterns of the beginning of the first life of the person's current series of lives. Once I begin playing and the music unfolds, everything is in sync: that is, there is no longer a gap between the music I'm hearing clairaudiently and the music that is coming from the harp. Now, on one point we should be clear: this is not like "automatic writing" where the Higher Forces would be moving my fingers. Quite rarely, I will feel this kind of control slightly and I have wondered if a small bit of ego or physical imperfection has gotten in the way (no channel is perfect) and I was about to play a wrong note. Almost always they give the music to my musical mind and I play it on the harp.

How versatile they are! They have at least four methods of transmission: the sounds of the notes (clairaudience), visual images of strings on the harp (clairvoyance), the kinesthetic shapes felt in my hands of the notes to be played (a form of clairsentience), and the verbal names of the notes in my mind and other verbal instructions of what's coming up in the music (telepathy). They seem to use whichever mode, or combination of modes, will be the easiest in each case.

I remember one time at the end of 1975, in Virginia Beach, where I was seeing clairvoyantly a couple designing and producing clothes. My friends in the higher dimensions wanted to get across the idea that the couple also designed jewelry and accessories to go with the clothes. In those days I wore a cross pendant on my chest, and since silver is an excellent electromagnetic conductor, they were able to vibrate it and cause it to *move* slightly. I can tell you it surprised me until I realized what the message was! Fortunately it didn't disturb me enough to hold up the reading. (Perhaps we should realize here that new modes of collaboration between dimensions are always somewhat of an experiment.)

After I finish the first section, which might last between two and three minutes, I ask to see scenes from this first life. (I am so totally attuned to the vibrational aspects of the music that I rarely see anything while I'm playing — although it can happen.) I will see the numbers of the century or an exact year, get a name for the country or city or province, or sometimes see it first before the name comes. Then I get a feeling, if I haven't already during the music, for whether the person is primarily male or female. This last one can be tricky, particularly if the person has been one sex for a number of lives and then takes on the opposite embodiment.

Part of my training has been a deep study of Yang and Yin, the Divine Mother and Father Principles, the two sides of my own nature, and the female and male principles in those around me. With this background, the awareness of these qualities in the music of the readings rarely presents a problem. If the pictures are ever a little slow in coming, I am greatly aided by the system of symbolism for the elements of music which the Forces that work through me are using. *Remember:* I translate letters into pitches to play them on the harp (a system that composers have used for over 300 years) and the symbolisms revealed in the early years of the channeling are another great contribution of this ministry. They have turned out to be a universal system of archetypal meanings for pitches and letters. These objective meanings provide a check on my clairvoyance. If I ever saw something that was not reflected in the notes of the music I could be wrong! But to my knowledge it has never happened! I am very pleased by this joining of the disciplines of science and metaphysics because ever since the illumination I have described I have never seen any basic conflict between these two approaches to life. They are simply two windows through which we can look at the same reality.

For the client this first life of the new series is a formation of a vision, a new path toward God-realization, a setting of higher spiritual goals, and the selection of an ideal principle, the pursuit of which is going to achieve these goals. The model I have been given for this vision is a "Mandala of Purpose", different facets of which the person is going to explore, progressing through the series of lives. So I am shown this symbolic mandala and it evolves out of the music, the events of the first life and higher guidance. The last section of the music is always the present lifetime, but I never know how many lives there are going to be in between. Most often it's two, but sometimes one or three.

These incarnations seem to be chosen mainly for two reasons: to provide a picture of the quality and sweep of the whole series, so the client can get as clear a picture as possible of the significance of this life; and to provide vibratory patterns conducive to healing. These take two forms. Patterns are presented that will bring you your finest moments to stimulate your potentiality, your belief in yourself, your skills and talents, your "good" karma. Then as the so-called negative patterns are touched they're immediately put into perspective so you can see them as patterns of growth, integrated and harmonized with the rest, and thus transmuted and their "negativity" released. (This process of healing is so fundamental and effective I use it also in my counseling work.)

Every note has an archetypal quality, combinations of two or more notes representing aggregate qualities. Meter, which in music is the regular grouping of the beat or pulse into recurring number patterns (groups of notes accented every two or three or four), represents the repetitive rhythmic patterns of life — in shorthand form. This is especially true of the left hand, the lower part, or accompaniment. The right hand is expressing more the actual patterns of the growth of consciousness which are taking place against the background of the routines of life.

What are called "rhythmic patterns" in music, the specific and peculiar arrangements of duration of time and accent, are a shorthand form of the person's actual movements against the recurring patterns of life (pulse of the music) such as minutes, hours, days, weeks, months, years, and important personal cycles of years, such as 7 and 28. All of these elements are combining and recombining, descending or ascending, whether the person is getting involved in life (involution) or pulling out and going back to spirit (evolution). And all of this is playing over the ranges of the harp that represent physicality, emotionality, mentality and the higher octaves of the soulic level.

What we're dealing with here is a rich, highly complex and subtle language of pure vibration which is capable of providing the quintessential patterns of a human life in condensed form. Moreover, it can do this with a power of nostalgia capable of tuning the person into that life and activating important memories on the physical, emotional, mental and karmic levels. And it does it in such a way as to help the client see the higher significance of all these levels. This is art going beyond mere words, which are symbols for something, to the presentation of a much purer vibrational reality. So this music actually comes through in a science of frequency where effects on the client are *calculated*.

The present-life section of the music is always longer (4-5 minutes) and goes into more detail. Due to the special times in which we live, everyone is trying to resolve as much difficult karma as possible, to synthesize the lives of the recent series (a sub-series of a longer series) and to bring it to some kind of satisfactory conclusion. We all hope to reach a fulfillment of the soul-purpose, and fill in and complete the new mandala of vision developed at the beginning of the series. You see, we live in a unique time in the history of life on this planet. There is much evidence that many time cycles, extending thousands and even millions of years into the past, are coming to completion around the year 2000. Most people are responding to the soul urge to fulfill the sub-series and the longer series as well.

Interpretation of the present life is somewhat different. Since the client is pretty much aware of the events of this life, concentration is made upon phases of growth and development, decade by decade, the forces at work behind the events. As the music passes the client's present age (which is fairly easy to get to recognize on the tape), it is reflecting back the highest ideals and purposes for this incarnation. We have gotten these from the client's records, and the music presents optimal life patterns to help realize these highest goals. It actually expresses, in this special language of musical vibrations, the perfect progression from where the client is today to the ideal fulfillment of the mandala of purpose formed in the first life. Of course, this becomes more and more beautiful and spiritual — although it is never clearly defined since it is expressing a potential. Naturally my friends in the higher dimensions have the utmost respect for the free will of the evolutionary creature and therefore I am given no detailed predictions of the future, only music which will keep the client attuned to the highest and help draw on the soul energy. (I have always avoided predictions. The combined free wills of all the people involved so often change what may seem to be an inevitable trend!)

The last chord of the music is almost always the last one, two or three notes in the person's name — unless it goes beyond this to the chord of "Light" (E) or "Service to the Light" (B). Occasionally it will go beyond the short series purpose to the C# Major chord which symbolizes a blessing by the Lords of Sirius, the supervisors of growth in consciousness in this sector of the universe. C# is the Actualizing Principle for artistic patterns, so its higher symbolism would then be the manifestation or actualization of the Higher Creative Pattern or God's Plan on Earth. There is also a definite correspondence between the last one, two or three notes in a person's name and the very beginning of the music, the formation of the guiding soul-purpose for the series. This was one of the great puzzles in the development of this type of reading in the first two years. At first I couldn't understand how the last notes of the name could be the same as the first notes of the first life. It was easier to see how the last chord of the present life could be found at the end of the person's name. The answer finally came when I realized that just about everyone nowadays wants to "get it all together," complete the cycle of lives, and life progression is circular (or, more correctly, spiralic). To complete something you must come back to the place where you started in order to remember your original vision, to find out and accept that you have completed it.

It was things like this that kept happening over and over again that I didn't quite understand, that were tests of faith, but at the same time proof of co-creation with Higher Intelligence. It was fascinating and exciting: the pioneering work of piecing it all together through the years. (By the way, my friend, in order to simplify this chapter, I am purposely not explaining the nature of the Sources that work with me. I am aware of your curiosity and will share with you my experiencing and understanding of them as soon as it seems appropriate.)

Bringing through the music is a supreme high for me — an ecstasy. What more challenging and splendid subject for a musical composition than the evolution of a human soul! I experience all of it as it comes through, and since the dissonances are almost always resolved soon after they're touched, the music is very positive and exquisite. From the standpoint of technical perfection, sensitivity of nuance, and emotional power, I play much better when I'm channeling than I ever did as a professional harpist. It is such a privilege to collaborate with beings capable of such sensitive awareness to all aspects of the client, beings who draw on such vast experience of artistic creativity (some of them belong to the order, "Builders of Form") and who come to us with such deep compassion, respect and love.

12. I TURN OFF THE MACHINES AND GO OVER IN MY MIND THE PAST-LIFE INFORMATION TO BE SURE I'VE GOT IT AND TO RECEIVE MORE

The problem here is one of retrieval — how to bring up to the conscious mind level all that I saw and was given. So I come up and out of the deep state I've been in, about halfway to normal waking consciousness. I go through a quick rerun of what has come through, translating this more into the words I will use during the Interpretation. Seeing it as a whole brings further insights, and the Higher Forces have a chance to amplify sparse information and possibly make a correction. (This is quite rare.) If there should be a change, I always check three times to make sure. And then, once in a long while, I forget to ask when a life was or where it was, and I can ask at this time. Now and then, I actually "dialogue" with the Sources. As I remember, once I couldn't for the life of me remember one of the lives. Fortunately the client was not present, and when I heard the music of that life, I remembered!

13. I TURN OVER THE CASSETTE TO DO THE INTERPRETATION AND REWIND THE LISTENING COPY TO THE BEGINNING OF THE BIRTHDATE MUSIC

14. I LISTEN TO THE BIRTHDATE AND NAME, WRITING IN MY BOOK THE OCTAVES IN WHICH THE PITCHES OF THE INITIALS WERE PLAYED, (THESE ARE THE CLIENT'S PUR-

POSES OF SOUL-GROWTH FOR THIS INCARNATION) AND
THE DIRECTIONS, UP OR DOWN, THAT THE REST OF THE
NOTES OF THE LETTER TOOK

As I do this I confidently place all information on hold. I try to proceed through these operations exactly the same each time so they won't take any creative thought that might bring me further into present time-space reality. Five or six times, things have happened that have brought me out, sometimes right in the middle of a life: someone comes to the door, someone begins pounding with a hammer, a child screams, or a truck goes by where there shouldn't be a truck! In every case, I have been amazed to find that I could get up, deal with the situation, talk to someone at the door or on the roof, come back, sit down and get right back into the other dimensions. It seems to be just a matter of practice and patience in directing one's consciousness.

After I write down the melody of the name I listen to the first portion of the first life. I begin to analyze the meaning of the notes and other elements of the music to correlate with the clairvoyant impressions. Once I am keyed into what these notes are in the beginning, I know the names of the notes for the rest of the music; not through what musicians call "perfect pitch" (the identification of a note "out of the blue"), but through the relative association of one note with the next by the interval between them and the recognition of the notes within a key.

15. REPLAY THE MUSIC AND RECORD THE INTERPRETATION OVER IT

I begin this side of the cassette with a few general comments (the same for everyone). I explain that the music is primarily for healing and attunement, and that it comes in a language of pure vibration, a language which is understood in the deeper levels of being. It is a shorthand for life which nevertheless contains much, much more than I could ever put into words or comment on. I say that it expresses and speaks to many levels of being and play the octaves on the harp that represent the different levels of expression (Physical, Emotional, Mental, etc.). I refer to the sections of the music both as "lives" and "deep aspects of the self." And I say that in general the healing is accomplished by presenting the highest achievements and illuminations of the client, and those so-called negative patterns that are now ready to be understood, transmuted and released. I explain that we will give a few clues as to what the music means and symbolizes, but that it will all come to them on deep levels as the need and receptivity develop.

Then I begin with the first life section and superimpose the Interpretation over it. Even though the information is amplified at this time, there is still opportunity to analyze the symbolism of some of the notes and patterns to show their correlation with the impressions. I am also able to show the progress along the path of the Soul-Purpose and the connections between lives. Occasionally, I report a shift in consciousness that took place *between* lives. On side II I eliminate the pauses between lives which were created by my tuning in to "see" (but which turn out to be rather convenient for the listener on Side I, affording time to allow creative fantasies to play out.) Each one of these life sections is like a window through which you could see and experience various levels of being, Physical, Emotional or Mental, during different listening sessions. These "windows" have even been known to open up vistas of former lives that the person was resonating with in that particular life, sometimes even *before* the current series.

16. ASK THE CLIENT WHAT THEY EXPERIENCED

It usually takes me 20-30 seconds to come out of the trance-like state in which I do the Interpretation. The feeling here is one of great fulfillment and ecstasy. Then I want to give clients a chance to verbalize their experience. When I feel they're ready for this, and sometimes it takes a few minutes, I ask them what it was like for them. Talking about it will help them to remember features which they might otherwise forget as they come back to their normal waking reality. More often than not they have tears in their eyes, they've been deeply moved, and it takes them some time to begin. Most of them appear to be completely transformed, compared to how they looked when they first arrived. If they have a hard time remembering, I ask them how it felt physically and emotionally, if any thoughts passed through their minds, or if they saw anything. But I don't insist on any of these.

As we begin to discuss what came through, they begin to see connections with their everyday lives. As I learn more about them I'm looking for these connections to help them to "own" their reading. It's rather amazing and exciting how fast these connections come, and of course it's only the beginning of many such realizations. What they've been given is a matrix which can explain anything in their lives. If they have received colors, patterns or figures or even new sensations or vibrations in the body, I can help them understand the meaning or symbology of these responses. But I only offer these insights for their consideration — recognizing that they may have their own individual symbology.

17. COUNSELING

This is really mental and psychological healing and is one of the most valuable and fulfilling phases of the reading. It is also one of the contributions that this type of reading has made to the practical application of reincarnation theory to present-day living. The grouping of lives into a series progressing along a chosen path can cast much light on anything that's going on in a person's life. It puts into perspective vexing ideas, disturbing emotional responses, strange-seeming meetings with people, sudden changes of jobs, moves, and so on. It has never failed to be a key that unlocks the mysteries a person feels about life. I'm sure it doesn't provide the final or cosmic answer to the riddles of life, but it can give you large pieces of the puzzle. It can begin to answer fundamental questions such as "Who am I?", "Where am I coming from?", "What is the significance of what's going on now and where am I going?", and "What is my potential?" These counseling sessions may last only 10-30 minutes, but because of what has been revealed in the music I have seen clients resolve four or five of the main questions that have been bothering them for years or for most of their lives! It is this "overall view" aspect of these readings which makes them so valuable as a first reading or at a crossroads in life. They have been described as "master" readings.

18. I OFTEN ANALYZE THE PERSON'S NAME

A great deal of information has come through the readings concerning the symbolism of letters and names. (See chapter XI for a detailed discussion.) From the beginning I have translated the names into pitches (through a code used by composers for some 300 years) and as my friends in spirit revealed the archetypal meanings for the notes I learned what the letters meant. These symbolisms have been corroborated by years of research into how letters are used in the everyday world and by special channelings from my friends in spirit to amplify the system. A name analysis reveals much about who you are in this particular incarnation in the basic areas of OUTER PERSONALITY or INDIVIDUALITY (first name), SUBCONSCIOUS or BASIC SELVES (middle names), and ACTIVITY IN THE WORLD (last name). Your initials are your Purposes of Growth (sub-purposes of the underlying Soul-Purpose) in these three areas. The rest of the letters in each name show what you are drawing on from your rich past-life experience in many times and places (not only the lives that we receive in the reading). It shows the archetypal sequence of qualities through which you progress in all the natural time cycles of life. It shows whether each quality is helping you to "get involved" or "evolve" (ascend), the downward or upward direction of the melody, and through the musical intervals between the letters, it shows how the qualities relate to each other.

19. LABEL THE CASSETTES, ENTER THE NAMES ON THE HAND-OUT SHEETS, GENTLY ASK THE CLIENT HOW PAY-

MENT WOULD BEST BE MADE FOR THE SESSION AND IF
PAID, MARK IT IN THE BOOK

A few years ago I started writing down the names, the direction of
the melody, and the octaves in which the sub-purposes come through
(physical, emotional or mental) so that the client could watch it while
listening to the Name Analysis. It takes some contemplation to apply these
somewhat abstract patterns and symbols to everyday life, and I wanted
to encourage the client to make this rewarding effort. I'm always grateful
to receive the check but often we're both so high we forget about it! This
payment is not compensation for the guidance that has come through,
nor for the healing and deep changes that the client may have received,
but is a remuneration for my time and energy spent, and enables me to
pay the bills and continue the ministry.

20. SHARE AN EMBRACE, IN UNIVERSAL LOVE, IN RECOGNI-
TION OF THE SPACE AND TIME OF DIVINITY IN WHICH
WE HAVE MET

The client and I have shared a very deep experience and usually the
embrace is mutual and spontaneous. We have shared the kinds of things
that build trust, friendship and universal love. I may know more about
the client than many people, or anyone, in their life. I have glimpsed their
divinity. I have a feeling for who they really are, where they're coming
from, and the inner meaning of what they're doing. I see all this through
a lens of love — not to mention the incomparable, unconditional love
that has been showered on us by the Higher Beings. So it is this we
celebrate with the embrace.

I have known for some time that I don't heal anyone, that I simply
officiate at *their* healing. So one of the most important things Joel Andrews is doing is recognizing and linking with his brothers and sisters,
and making friends — and its the same for all healers.

It is one of the deepest satisfactions and fulfillments for me to see
the transformation wrought in clients in just two hours. They arrive in
varying states of disharmony and I see them leaving stronger and more
radiant, more integrated and harmonious, shining with an awareness of
who they are and a new enthusiasm to take on the school of life. They
are taking with them a cassette of their music which can at any time remind them of who they are and put them in touch with their deepest
and highest — the inspiration and motivating energy of their chosen Soul-
Path. I know also that there are vibrational patterns coded into the music for later listenings when they will be ready to respond to them. Many
times clients have written or phoned me years later because they heard
things in their music that they never had heard before and wanted to know

if their music had changed! It is, of course, the "music" of their being which changes, and this enlarges their perception of the music on the tape — and the music of their world.

A reading session leaves the room charged with an ambience of spectrums of light and love, and it leaves me in a state of expanded upliftment — I feel like a godling for an hour or two afterwards. It doesn't actually tire me, but I do need to come down so I can deal with the everyday realities of the life of Joel Andrews, and I do need to get grounded before I do another reading. Some time ago I trained myself to release and forget clients, so my being is cleansed of their vibrations and I can come back into my own scenario, or to the next client with a "clean slate."

The experience of hearing and bringing into manifestation this soul music is an ecstatic one both for me and the client. Surely the music of a human soul in its higher aspects is some of the most beautiful on Earth, and I can say that every Individual Attunement tape that I have co-created is exquisite, the result of at least three divinities: the clients, mine and the Higher Forces. When the readings began it was the heightened vibrations in the room, the direct experiencing of Love and Light, which gave those present personal proof of the value of these sessions. In my own spiritual growth the consistency of this ecstasy has demonstrated to me the fundamental divinity of everyone. I know now that if I did a reading for anyone off the street, their highest Soul-Purpose would be beautiful.

"Music is God's best gift to man, the only art of heaven given to earth, the only art of earth that we take to heaven."

Charles W. Landon

CHAPTER SEVEN

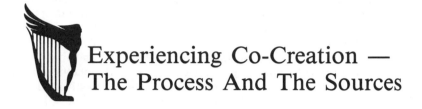 Experiencing Co-Creation —
The Process And The Sources

Perhaps, next, I should describe how I experience an Attunement session. As I am checking settings on the tape recorders, and the client is writing the name and birthdate in my book, I'm feeling a gradual raising of vibrations: a growing energy potential. Then as I tune the harp, which I do as a meditation, without talking, I allow my focus to deepen into the world of sound. As I explain briefly to the client how the reading will go I am already entering the light trance in which I do the channeling.

This is not what is called "deep trance" but rather what is called "conscious channeling." It is definitely not akin to automatic writing where the Sources would be moving my fingers. They impress the musical sounds on my musical mind and I play the music on the harp. While I certainly respect deep trance work, understanding that the putting aside of the conscious mind is the optimum form of dedication and growth for some, I am grateful that I am a conscious channel. I have avoided the physical and psychological problems that often attend deep trance work, and being able to remember what I have brought through has accelerated my own growth tremendously. I have also been able to help others on the path in the role of a guide. I truly believe that what we are after is to expand our consciousness on as many levels, at once, as possible and to be able to shift the focus appropriately.

One advantage of the light trance is that I can do Attunement sessions long distance (that is, in absentia), by myself, without a conductor. Also, I can deal with whatever might come up in the way of distractions during the session. I am so glad that I have not experienced any great physical reactions to going into this altered state over a period of 18 years. Sometimes it can take me a little while to come back to the practical world after a session. Some years ago, when this was a little more of a problem, I included in my affirmation the request that I be returned to the normal functioning state at the close of the session. This did help. I am usually able to deal with the practical world, such as driving a car, at the close of a session where I do spiritual counseling, and have almost always reached the normal balanced state within half an hour after the session. It can be more of a problem after a concert where I go into deeper and more expanded states, but I have learned a technique for closing the chakras which is usually effective. I simply pass my hand slowly over the chakras, decreeing and visualizing that they turn blue and that they be gently closed to the proper degree for dealing with the practical world.

It is my understanding that in these times we are involved in a real struggle between the Forces of Light and the forces of darkness. I choose to see this in a positive light as a healing crisis, an initiation, in which we are going to resolve some important issues once and for all on this planet. Because of this I *always* say my affirmations. I want to be very sure that I am setting up those positive conditions conducive to channeling as much Light and Love as possible.

I actually don't consider myself a psychic: i.e., having the psychic sensitivities on call almost all the time. I use these gifts only under very controlled conditions, only after I have said the two affirmations, and for the spiritual purpose of helping my brothers and sisters to understand who they are. I also never try to read the future. At best, this involves projections of present tendencies which are subject to the aggregates of free will and not very satisfying when they don't come true.

When everything is in readiness, before I turn the recorders on, I say the affirmation to get clear for the work.* As soon as I finish it, I feel a great peace settling over my body and emotions — a centering and balancing — and a movement of awareness inward and upward. When I feel I have come to sufficient peace, I direct my hearing to an area behind and above me, and I contact a group of very high, silvery vibrations. I take this to be what is known as the "sound current."

I was once initiated by a Swami who had been initiated by Charon Singh (real name), the Indian master. A major part of our meditative practice was to listen to the sound current. I was rather quickly successful at this, being able to hear the sound current in my left ear, then my right ear, and finally a third note (the root of the chord) at the back of my head in the region of the medulla, forming a triad. I never do a channeling until I have made contact with the sound current. Then I wait for a few seconds until I know that it's time to begin. It is almost as if I receive a subtle, neurological signal.

I turn on the tape recorders and immediately say the affirmation offering myself to be used as a channel for the highest good of the client. I have set up the last word of this affirmation to act as a signal to go

*See Appendix II for affirmation.

into the light trance. (When I am giving this affirmation to someone, I tell them that I will not say the last word because I do not wish to play lightly with the power of this signal.) Immediately after saying this word a deeper peace quickly passes over my body (and emotions) from head to toe. It is rather like gently but quickly dropping 30 or 40 feet. It also feels like a Higher Force of beauty and truth is overshadowing me and settling into the body. Sometimes it's faster than others and I experience a minor tremor or shudder or a little jerk. The client has never commented on this, so I assume that either their eyes are closed or it's not outwardly visible. Once this incoming force field has reached my feet I am ready to begin.

I play the notes of the birthdate (always upwards) and the notes of the name (under guidance). As soon as I finish the last note of the name, I listen and I am given the opening notes of the music of the first life of the series. In the vast majority of cases, I experience this music aurally and also see the notes on the harp. Once I begin to play, there is no difference between hearing the music clairaudiently and hearing it coming from the harp — these two are in sync. Only when I'm listening just prior to playing am I aware of hearing clairaudiently. But as I have mentioned, the Sources employ various techniques to give me the music depending on which will be the easiest and the clearest. They can give me 1) the clairaudient sensation of pitches, 2) the visual impression of the strings to be played on the harp, 3) concepts or ideas, telepathic words and names of notes or musical patterns that will be coming up soon, such as the idea that we will be modulating soon into another key through a certain chord, or 4) a tactile sensation in my hand of the shape of a chord or pattern about to be played. And, of course, these may be combined. And then, through the years, they have used a number of special techniques to get particular information across to me. Their inventive ingenuity is a constant source of wonder.

In this work I have put at the disposal of the Sources and the client my total experience in this life and in past-lives, and so my physical, emotional, and mental sensibilities are used during the channeling. I fully experience the soul music that comes through. But then this is common to any expression of high musical art: the artist offers all his sensing equipment and capabilities to be used by the composer who has infused such levels of expression into his composition. There is an interesting sidelight here: I am experiencing these past-lives very deeply, (music is not a *symbol for* these lives, as are words, but a purer, shorthand expression of the actual vibratory aspect of them.) So have these experiences not been added to *my own* memory banks? A rough calculation reveals that since 1971 I have probably experienced 7500 past-lives! What a student of history I have become. What a student of what is actually going on with people I have become.

As the music progresses it gets higher and higher in vibration and spirituality, and I am experiencing all of it. Allowing the last pure chord to die away, I turn off the tape recorders. I usually rub my eyes a little and it takes me 15 or 20 seconds to come back to the world enough to speak to the client. I tune into what kind of state they're in and sometimes wait a few minutes for their ecstasy to subside to a point where they would like to talk. Then I ask them what they experienced. This provides an opportunity to verbalize and retrieve important symbolic bits of information which might otherwise be forgotten. For me the experience has been extremely gratifying and uplifting. Not only is it a very high use of my developed artistry as a musician, (since my playing is never better than when I'm co-creating with the Higher Sources), but I feel the great privilege and honor of sharing with a fellow human their highest aspirations and most formative patterns of growth. Experiencing the Love and Wisdom coming through from the Sources is a bonus.

These Attunements have certainly been some of the highest experiences of my life, and the vibrations of the room reflect this for some time afterwards. It is so moving to see a client arrive for a session in a state which I describe as "apparent distortion": they think they're sick; but, of course, illness is nothing but a learning process. Then what a joy it is to see them transformed at the end — shining, much more aware that everything in their life is in Divine Order and according to the plan of their chosen Soul-Purpose, their selected path toward God-realization.

Part of it is knowing that they have a tape that they can take home with them to reconnect with these deeper and higher aspects of self, to help them draw on their own soul energy and keep them "on track." Then there is the knowledge that they are going to be listening to the tape for months and years to come. At the end of a session, I have the feeling that I have been used properly for a high purpose and that I am evolving and growing through being "let in on" the inside story of human spiritual development on Earth.

*　*　*　*　*　*

At this point my friend spoke up, "Well, thanks so much for the detailed description. I can begin to understand why these Attunement sessions are unique. I'm sure this material will be of special interest to anyone studying the versatility of consciousness and the process of healing. And of course it will be a godsend to all apprentice music healers. I feel sure there is not much in print that goes into such detail about the process of healing with sound and music. But could you explain a little further concerning what you refer to as 'The Sources'?"

I shall do my best with this question, but I am always somewhat hesitant when people ask me about The Sources. This is partly because

I do not wish to limit the Higher Forces in any way; also because each developing channel may experience The Sources in a slightly different way, depending on the work to be done. And it is difficult to ascribe words to an experience which is fundamentally vibratory, subjective, and extra-verbal. Over the years, through my own experience, together with reports by sensitives who have observed me at work, I have built up some general concepts about the nature of The Sources working through this ministry. I would be glad to share them with you now. Some day I look forward to being shown precisely how it works.

Immediately over me in this model I see two aspects. One is my High Self and the second is my guardian seraphim (who usually work in pairs). The High Self I understand to be an undiluted fragment of the highest aspect of Deity, which has been assigned to me for this earthly embodiment and for my ascension. I have received the name "Helios" for this aspect, but wish not to limit it in any way. As a portion of Deity, it is like all other High Selves except for the experience it has acquired. I feel that the overshadowing to which I have referred is partly my High Self indwelling at least my mind and perhaps even more of me. I believe its primary function is to provide the purely spiritual concepts and Love, but also to contact and invite the participation of other Higher Beings who might be "on duty" and who have the information we need.

I believe, also, that my High Self helps me to maintain contact with The Spirit of Truth (the spiritual circuit of our local universe representative, the "Son of the Father" aspect) — thus sustaining connections with the Christ Spirit. As I see it, the guardian seraphim — and some years ago I was given the name, Seraptron — act as guardians and stabilizers of energies. They also make connection with other angelic and devic beings, if their services are required for the work at hand, and with the Holy Spirit (the spiritual circuit of the Creative Mother Spirit of the universe). While their energies may be felt within me, I feel that the work of the Seraphim is mostly balancing the forces around me, within the room and the immediate environment. They also coordinate the ministries of the other spirits.

In most of the concerts and general channelings that I do, the opening section of music is in the key of F, which provides a vibration for the angelic forces to awaken the local devas and elementals to harmonize and prepare the room for the coming message. And I imagine Seraptron initiates this preparation. My understanding is that the High Self and the guardian seraphim work side by side, in concert, but on different aspects of the process. (For further information about these two aspects, please consult The URANTIA Book in the Bibliography.)

Then if it is a session involving past-life information, special, what you might call, "karmic" angels are on hand in charge of the Akashic Record Archives. They establish circuits so that when I play the birth date and the name, they know that permission has been granted to consult personal records, the "file number" has been sounded, and the individual's file comes forward. They, together with the High Self, then select the lives that will be the most revealing of the series and the most healing.

Now at every session I invoke what I call the Christ Spirit, by which I mean the highest expression of The Light in the solar system, and I see this at the top of the model protecting everything below it. I picture, then, a gap between the Christ Spirit and my guardian seraphim and High Self. This is a most important feature of my work since any Higher Being who has access to the information we need may be invited to enter this gap of service and align with its purpose. Because of the flexibility of this feature, I have worked with a wide variety of Higher Beings: seraphim, space beings, embodiments of concepts such as Limitless Love and Truth, and what we call Ascended Masters. It is my experience that these beings are less interested in their names, or even the type of being that they are, than the work to be done. Since I have the utmost faith in the power of the Christ Spirit to protect all aspects of the work, I have saved a good deal of time through the years that would have been spent in challenging these beings and checking credentials. When the Presence and Power of the Living Christ is invoked with sincerity, there is no question of the result. I do know other Light-workers who employ various methods of testing beings that come to them on the inner planes, and I understand that many of these methods are effective, but why not go to the top?

At this point, let me give you an excellent challenging decree: "In full faith I invoke the Power, Wisdom and Love of the Living Christ, and I decree that if you come for my highest good, remain and do your work. If you do not come for my highest good I bid you leave at once in the name of the Living Christ."

It has been so interesting and instructive through the years to receive feedback from sensitives in the audience at concerts. In Sarasota, Florida, in 1975, three psychics came up to me with lists of the beings and devas they had seen on stage around, and over me, and over the harp. On this particular occasion, some of the same names appeared on two of the lists, and a few on all three lists! Frequently a large radiant presence will be seen to overshadow and indwell me. Once an extra female arm was seen paralleling mine as I played. Often, huge pillars of colors of the spectrum have been seen behind me on the stage. Another time the whole background of the stage was seen as green (healing) just before I began, and the sensitive saw objects resembling earmuffs on my ears which, as I finished my affirmation, gently swung upwards to open position for clairaudience. Now the significant thing here is that, while I see rather clearly the past-lives, I don't normally see the beings that work with me. I think that if I saw them, it would be so distracting, I wouldn't be able to play! I try to see this as a blessing, but I certainly have developed a curiosity to see them one day. In the meantime I have particularly enjoyed the feedback from clairvoyants in the audience, and the sketches by artists.

For me, my work and my joy is being as totally open as possible to the vibrations themselves, their synthesis and their translation into music which my fellow humans can receive and use. Quite often space beings are seen working through me and I have even channelled verbally from them. This is undoubtedly because I have an aspect within me of space origin and attunement. I have had many adventures in my growing relationship with the Christ and finally have had extremely powerful and vivid "meetings" with "Him." There was evidential that it was indeed The Christ, and these were, of course, peak illuminations of my life.

Co-creating with these Higher Forces has brought me ecstasy, wisdom and the deepest fulfillment. They have never suggested I do anything or say anything which has ended up to my detriment or to anyone else's; they have always honored my free will, and they seem to be unimaginably inventive in promoting the highest growth in consciousness for all life forms. In the week-by-week collaboration over the years, they have earned my respect, admiration and love, and I look forward with the greatest anticipation to meeting them face to face. I would especially enjoy meeting some of the "ascended masters" who have given me their music: Kuthumi, Saint Germain, Serapis Bey, Kwan Yin, Pan, and a number of others. These masters are accessible and will work through the musician who will do the work of preparation, one who offers proven dedication to the work of The Light and whose optimum life plan includes this type of work.

Even apprentices receive vibrations from these masters through their disciples. And they have been known to come through at the oddest times and in the oddest places when a particular piece of work requires their personal attention or if a particularly gifted student needs some encouragement. But if your interest is in what I call "thrills and chills" — far-out phenomena — don't expect to attract a Higher Being. They are more concerned with getting the job done than catering to your ego. Make the experiment of putting the ego aside (expanding it to include as much as possible of life) then you can taste the joys of co-creating with Higher Forces. I use the word "higher" never as a value judgement but to signify a more rarefied and spiritual level of being — and these beings are more replete in intelligence, power, and abilities. But also they are more developed in humility and love, and exhibit the greatest respect for us, or they would not be where they are.

We are going to need increasing numbers of competent healers in the years of transition ahead, and so anyone who will open the door a crack will find the illumination, love and guidance flooding through.

"*Words are wonderful enough; but music is even more wonderful. It speaks not to our thoughts as words do; it speaks straight to our hearts and spirits, to the very core and root of our souls. Music soothes us, stirs us up; it puts noble feelings in us; it melts us to tears, we know not how: — it is a language by itself, just as perfect, in its way, as speech, as words; just as divine, just as blessed. . . Music has been called the speech of angels; I will go further, and call it the speech of God.*"

Charles Kingsley

CHAPTER EIGHT

 How Do Clients Respond?

My friend seemed pleased as he said, "You have presented some most interesting insights and perceptions concerning how you experience bringing through this attunement music. But what about your clients? How does the music affect them? What evidences of healing are there? Also, how do you think sound and music bring about healing?"

Ah, yes, to be sure we have arrived at a paramount place in this narrative. I will give you much information about the results of this fifteen-year ministry; but, alas, I must begin this chapter with an apology and an appeal. We need more scientific research into the effects of sound and music on the body, emotions, and the mind. To my present knowledge, the instruments have not been invented which will measure precisely these responses and transformations. I apologize, but neither myself nor my clients have felt the need for proof of the healing effects of this music for the reasons that I will give you. But I wish now that I had made more of an effort to arrange laboratory testing. One of the chief problems here is that, while there is sometimes immediate release of pain, most of the dramatic healing at deeper levels takes place in the outer, or higher, bodies: the Etheric body, the Emotional (Astral) body, the Mental Body, and the Karmic Patterns. Then it manifests later in the physical body according to the law, "As above so below." Edgar Cayce stated this unequivocally and most experienced healers know it to be true. I will be reporting on some recent tests conducted at Marcel Vogel's laboratory, Psychic Research, Inc. in San Jose. The results were most interesting. (See Appendix II.)

Let us begin with the more obvious effects the client experiences. For most, it is a profound experience: many have tears in their eyes and some actually weep, not out of sadness, but with the ecstasy of coming in contact with their true nature, beauty and destiny. Almost all are moved emotionally. Many feel bodily sensations, some of these quite strong. Others see colors and symbolic images, or receive important mental concepts. Still others see scenes similar to the past-life scenes I have been given for each section of music. They experience all of the effects, to varying degrees, associated with standard music therapy: changes in heartbeat, temperature, perception of the weight of the body, imagery, etc. Many have reported vibrations of varying degrees in different parts of the body. These include steady hums, regular pulsing, isolated internal explosions, nerve impulses like electrical currents traveling from one part of the body to another, sounds in the head, and quite often energy rising up along the spine suggestive of the raising of Kundalini through the chakras.

All so-called "negative karmic patterns" are seen by illuminated beings as nothing but patterns of spiritual growth. So, all such patterns that are contacted in the music are immediately resolved into unity and harmony, and integrated with the rest. It often happens that a client cannot believe they are so beautiful! Then I have to remind them that there were some challenges along the way. Remembering that most of them come with the feeling that they are out of balance and need healing, it is not surprising that immediately after their music they appear to have taken back a good deal of their own power. I have found that so much "disease" results from the giving up of one's own center and power to other people and forces. So my clients usually appear to have been transformed. They look more integrated, showing strength, health, and radiance. and they look expectant — charged up — to pick up their lives with new hope and zest. This is especially because the outlining of the underlying soul-path which they have chosen provides keys to understanding their most difficult present-life challenges, and this can provide one or more major breakthroughs for them during the session.

Through the years I have received some 400 letters from healees. What I would like to do at this point is to invite them to tell you what they experienced. But first, three general appraisals, (these are all exact quotations).

Gustave Neumeyer, psychic and authority on the use of the aurameter to read the vibrations of Tibetan Bronzes and to investigate psychics and mediums, came to these conclusions after a number of tests: "What to me is so fascinating about these harp-testings is that I obtain results with the aurameter during his playing which, later on, Joel confirms without being aware of what I had been getting with my instrument. I found that with many people the readings were centered on the Causal Body (the formless Mental Plane) — the Reincarnating Principle in man. With the more spiritually advanced people, one also finds powerful streams of a very much higher energy (Spiritual, Monadic) flowing in. Occasionally there are filaments of energy running up to the Will aspect of the Divine (7th Plane) and even right up to the highest, the Love-Wisdom aspect. Usually a trance medium works on the 2nd Plane — Astral or Emotional. Good psychics tap the 4th Plane (Intuitional). When Joel explains his music, he vibrates to the 5th (Spiritual Plane), the highest psychic I have ever come across."

Part of a reading by a well-known New York psychic, Venita Mueller: "Many years this man has sought this kind of outlet for his gift...it involves his intuitive attunement with the individual to awaken that tone, that note...indeed the harmony is in the spine and can be reached not only with color, but with sound, and harmonious sound can realign the physical body itself ... this is a means of attuning and awakening the forces that will give the aura of harmony and health to the entire body. Yes, this is valid."

Marlene J. Weiner (real name), Metaphysical Consultant (New York), said, "It is my opinion that Joel Andrews has become one of the clearest channels of healing sound vibration for the benefit of Man. On the physical level, there has been release of muscular and nervous tensions throughout the body under the sounds of my 'own' music."

Here are typical examples of client's comments:

"We've been listening to a wide range of music and, for healing quality and upliftment, yours is still tops! We keep coming back to it again and again." The Clearing, School of the Healing Arts

" 'Locrian Invocation' has stirred me to the very depths." E.P.

"I listen to a tape at least once a day and get lots of creative energy from it — actual physical rushes like electricity for hours afterwards." L.N.

"I had a very strong reaction to my music. Towards the end of it where the bells suggest a breakthrough, I spontaneously wept with a feeling of 'Thank God, at last' - like the end of a tough journey crowned with reward, peace, and goodness, a gorgeous feeling of 'home'. " Ken

"My hands continue to improve. My greatest pleasure is washing my face and feeling the softness of the skin which I have not known for so many years!" Barby

"We play your beautiful tapes at my Hatha Yoga Classes. We're having miracle healings with your Divine help." J.L.

"I've been using my office tape with a gentleman with severe emphysema and asthma. When listening to it and meditating he experiences a great ease in his breathing." S.J.M., M.D.

"I have wondered for a long time how I would find music that is indeed the voice of the soul. I have found it through you." J.D.

"I intended to contact my doctor about a bronchial condition of asthmatic proportions, also a bout of cystitis. The latter condition was cured with the initial playing of 'my music'. The bronchial condition took a little longer — two days!"   A.M.

"I have become addicted to the tapes. I'm afraid I will soon wear them out. I just can't wait to get everyone off to school and work and unplug the phone, and then relax in my easy chair for tape listening and meditation. It makes my whole day."   J.B.

"We are very happy that you sent your records to us in error. We enjoy them immensely."   B.M.

"Your music truly comes from the fount of all healing."   G.S.

"I've been getting very positive feedback from my mentally-ill patients. I'm thrilled with the results. I can't say enough good things about you and your work. Bless you."   K.M.

" 'The Violet Flame' came... floods and waves roll through my four lower bodies! It is beautiful!!! It would delight your heart to see we four sitting night after night listening and absorbing it."   Evangeline von Polen (real name)—The Ruby Focus, an "I AM" group.

"Your work in this field is awe-inspiring."   J.L. (a Yoga Instructor)

"I was lifted from my body by a heavenly force, stroked, loved and nurtured, and then returned to my body, which was, from that moment to this, free of the extreme pain it had known for 20 years as a result of polio."   J.V., (after listening to "Tibetan Gamelan" once on FM Radio!)

"The most celestial music I have ever heard."   S.L.

"He is very pure." Comment made by a Tai Chi master, M.M.D. (after hearing the music channeled for Tai Chi).

"I can't tell you the inspiration and delight your tapes have given us in our Tai Chi club in Ottawa. We'd like you to make us our own tape!"   F.L.

"The most spiritual and beautiful music I've ever experienced. I was told that your music was influenced by the Ascended Masters and I have absolutely no doubt that this is true. The sounds definitely resonate with a very deep part of me which I know to be divine."   G.S.

"Thank you very much for repairing my attunement tape. Now I am back in Divine Order! I couldn't begin to tell you of the complete transformation in my life."   A.P.

"It is uncanny. Your tapes have thrown me into a deep trance and I have realized perfect relaxation and attunement. I feel levitated off the floor and the pain of scar tissue from many cancer surgeries is greatly alleviated." M.M.

"...a glorious afternoon of music — so very inspiring — a once in a lifetime experience and indeed the most joyous two hours I have ever spent." L.K.

"The session to channel this beautiful music for childbirth was one of the highest experiences of my life. The music that your hands and harp brought to earth truly is the sacred energy of birth." P.F. (a champion of home birth).

"How profoundly moved I have been by you and the music flowing through you. I experienced very intense sensations in my Solar Plexus, Heart, Thyroid and Third-Eye chakras, and tears came." A.A.

"You have come into the earth this lifetime with a most unique gift. With it you can and are leading many back to The Father from which we all came." J.J., Minister

"A close friend loaned me your album and I cannot explain with mere words the strength and beauty and calm I have derived from this music. I am intending to use it in my birth experience. It has shown me this beautiful event in a spiritual and joyous light." J.D.

"I've turned to your tapes to pull me (painlessly) out of the distress of long-term fears...Ah! on to solid ground again." S.F.

"The joy I experienced in listening to your music! 'The Music of the Spheres' is exactly what I felt as you and your harp became one with each other and with all of creation. Just recalling it, I experience healing all over again." S.C.

"This important work is surely blessed — forming the foundations of the new Divine Medicine." J.W.

These unsolicited testimonials should give you a rich picture of the wide variety of responses and the great depth and intensity of these effects on the listener. Such results are common with both the general healing tapes I have channeled, and the music channeled at concerts, as well as the individualized attunement music.

Significant in any assessment of the efficacy of this healing music is the fact that out of the over 2000 healing tapes I have produced, *I have only received two complaints*. These turned out to be educational and I will share with you the story of the first. The second account, which is longer, I will save for our discussion on the challenging subject of reincarnation.

Around 1973, after I had been doing the readings for over a year, a man by the name of Art Greenacre came to me for a reading. The reading went very well, and Art returned home with his tape. After listening to it a few times, he wrote me saying that he didn't "agree" with the music and didn't like it. I took his dissatisfaction quite seriously, since as you will remember, I had made a pact with God that if those I could help were sent to me, I wouldn't become involved in suggesting anyone have a reading. I sat in meditation and asked The Sources if this was Art's music.

When it's really important, I actually hear a voice in my head, and the voice said, "Yes."

I then asked "Why was he sent to me?"

After a moment the answer came, "So you wouldn't think you could heal everyone."

What an astonishing answer! When I thought this over, I was grateful for the important insight and *also for Art's submitting to having a reading* just for the purpose of my lesson. Or, on another level: at the point when he became intrigued with the idea of having a reading, was he acting out some karmic pattern of his own about learning how to discriminate what will be helpful for him and what will not? I am sure the laws of magnetism and the guardian seraphim are able to engineer meetings between people where the two karmic patterns complement each other.

In any case, the batting average of this ministry, in terms of positive results, is considerably above most other healing professions, and far above the medical profession. This batting average is one of the main reasons I enjoy a reputation as one of the clearest channels in the profession. I attribute this to a number of factors. First comes my genuine love for my brothers and sisters and a desire to serve humanity. Then comes the desire to avoid building any unnecessary negative karma that would hold up my own ascension at the end of this life. (I believe this to be possible for anyone.) Also, even after 18 years, I still say my affirmation before each channeling.

One reason I have been able to help people so much, especially in the counseling portion of the session, is that I have been shown so much of what's going on with human beings and the true functions of the three major aspects of being: High Self, Conscious Mind, and Subconscious, or Basic Selves. What an education in psychotherapy! Also I have developed a technique that I call SUPER LISTENING. When the client is talking to me about their "problems" (opportunities for spiritual growth), I open up all my perceptive faculties to a high degree of sensitivity. The entire gamut of information is usable: ideas and concepts, key words and phrases, the emotions as revealed in the speech tunes and music of the voice, the body positioning and gestures, and actual subliminal messages from the Subconscious. (You might practice this — you'll be amazed. First: deep centering in peace, then increase the vibratory rate of your perceptive faculties — your receptivity.) As I'm doing this the guides working with me are causing me to notice significant items and impressing on my waiting mind the deep underlying causes of the stressful situations. This SUPER LISTENING is most valuable in work-playshop settings when a subject has just listened to one of the general healing tapes and is sharing their impressions of the experience. It seems to me that from a very early age I have always been asking the question, "What is *really* going on behind the world of appearances?"

Let us now explore further the effects of this healing music. First, however, I should explain why there is such a wide variety of response in different individuals to the same music. We are dealing here with a non-verbal language of pure vibration, patterns of frequencies, with archetypal significance or symbolism, which interact with similar patterns within the subject, and which may be used for a variety of more specific purposes. If twenty different people describe their experience of the same music, as we encourage at many of the concerts, they will use different words and images depending on how they applied the music. But if you know the system of symbolism, you will see a fundamental pattern running through them all. The first and most important division involved here is whether the subject used the pattern in the Physical, the Emotional, or the Mental bodies.

It is now my great privilege to share with you some of the most outstanding Attunements over the past 18 years. Most of these subjects have given their permission to publish their story, but I will still use fictitious names:

#1—(Gustave Neumeyer, age 59): The session at the Keller's, which really marks the beginning of the past-life healing readings, took place in August of 1971. Two months later, I was asked to do some readings at the home of Gay Cormack, the well-known past-life reader who sat in on the inaugural readings. She had invited some close friends down from Washington to check out this new kind of healing. One of them was Gustave Neumeyer, a member of the German Embassy, the leader of a group of twelve psychic researchers, a master in the use of the aurameter, and quite an adept. His past-life Attunement was most powerful, and I felt very high energies coming in.

A month later he wrote a report on his adventure for the group of twelve and in it was information which made currents go up and down my spine. On one page was a chart of three columns. In the first column was my Interpretation, step by step, of his music. In the second column were his internal experiences as the music progressed through these stages. In the third column were the results of his aurameter testings of the music at these same points. The correspondence across these three columns was remarkable and astonished me! When he would do an aurameter testing of something, with the aurameter in his right hand, he would place the thumb of his left hand on a chart of the various bodies — Physical-Etheric, Emotional-Astral. Lower Mental and Upper Mental, Intuitional, Spiritual, Monadic, and Divine. As his developed sensitivities would pick up the level of energy with the device, his left thumb would indicate the level of frequency on the chart. These levels correlated with my interpretation of the symbolism of the notes and musical patterns in relation to his various bodies, and also with the various chakras that he felt activated at the time. For a budding psychic healer developing a new procedure, not really knowing what he was doing, and feeling some anxiety and skepticism concerning the new direction his life was taking, this was just the solid, scientific-type feedback that I needed. It really gave me a lift and impelled me forward, and I am most grateful. I imagine that he was asked by Higher Forces to perform this valuable function.

#2—(The F# on my Harp): Throughout this ministry, rather amazing events have occurred. They usually demonstrate Higher Guidance, and I am including this one as a perfect example. During the week of sessions at Gay Cormack's, I had just begun to channel a client's music when I realized that there was a note, F#, that was noticeably out of tune! This was startling because I had tuned the harp very carefully since I was beginning to realize that these tapes might be played for months or even years. I stopped the recorders, retuned the F#, and then continued.

In those early days the first notes that were heard, after the initials, represented the soul coming into the body at the beginning of the present incarnation. So it occurred to me to ask him during the Interpretation whether there was something that had to be adjusted in him right after birth. At first, he said he didn't think so. But after an hour, he drew me aside and said, "Yes, I now remember my mother telling me that there was an operation right after I was born." These little "miracles" *are* fun. They suggest that Higher Forces *are* operating and they also give us the impetus to carry on.

#3—(Debbie Bremmer, age 31, February, 1973): When I was on tour with the Paul Winter Consort, we would often sleep for a night in the unusual houses of his fans. The Bremmers, Debbie and Tom, had built themselves a beautiful and cozy circular abode, resembling more than anything variations on an igloo. The next morning Debbie complained of a continuing infection in her hands. She thought it might be from the dyes she used in her weaving, but changing dyes hadn't helped. Sometime later in Rochester, we were able to arrange a session in the basement of the campus center in which the Consort was playing. Her music was most beautiful and contained a former life with Tom. The Interpretation and Counseling clearly indicated that the rash in her hands had begun by oversensitivity caused by the dyes, but was continuing as a result of pent-up feelings about the relationship. Also, a unique thing happened: right at the end of the music I actually heard a voice which said, "Slap it out of her hands!"

Now, I'm normally not looking for drama in this line of work, but coming like a command, after that uplifting soul music, I thought I had better do as I was told. I asked her to stand up and put out her hands, adding that I had been told to do something. As I slapped her hands, I said, "Now you're healed if you will accept it." Debbie wrote me many letters over the following weeks and months, reporting on the results of expressing her deep feelings with Tom and listening to her healing music. They communicated some things to each other which they had never touched on before, and they ended up separating eventually. Yet, from the time she started really communicating with him, her hands started feeling better, and a few weeks after they were separated, with continued listenings to her music, her hands were completely healed.

After about a year, a session was arranged with the three of us, and this began my counseling work with couples. Somewhat of a challenge did arise after they were separated. She was so grateful for the help that had come through me, she felt she was in love with me, and planned a visit to pursue the relationship. I was happily married at the time, and wrote her a number of letters in an effort to transmute love into friendship — an art I have had a number of other opportunities to develop over the years. For many people who perhaps have not felt a deep respect and love from another human being, to feel the pure unconditional love and concern coming from the angels and from my higher aspects can be a bit overwhelming.

#4—(The president of a residential water company, age 51): The following channeling illustrates a very different and practical aspect of the work. In 1973, a close relative of mine needed to divide a tract of land prior to sale. The local Water Board, dominated by the president, had been refusing water meters for the lot-split for three years. She had gotten herself up for another presentation, but was anxious and frustrated over the possible outcome. I offered to do a channeling for the situation, even though I hadn't received a request from the man. I explained that we could not exert any influence on his free will and could only appeal to his higher awareness.

I calculated the time difference between Virginia Beach, Va., where I was living at the time, and California, so that I would be playing the music just before he might be waking up on the morning of the hearing. I meditated for a few minutes before the channeling, asking to be able to contact his Holy Christ Self in order to make the appeal at that level of consciousness. The session felt very positive, and in a few days I received a phone call saying that permission for the water meters had been granted! I was tickled, the versatility of the work had been expanded, not to mention the probable healing on deeper levels for everyone involved.

#5—(Priscilla and Rebecca, two girls from the Blue Ridge Mountains, ages 19 and 18): There is a tendency among students of metaphysics, once they realize that everyone is at some level of evolution, to begin to judge the level of others. There is also the temptation to assume that those "less evolved souls" have made mistakes along the path, and are probably being punished, or at least are working off these "negative karmic patterns." For optimum growth this is sometimes true, but it is by no means always the case. These life readings provided a sterling lesson on this principle — one that I have never forgotten.

In 1974 (I think it was May), Virginia Beach was buzzing with concepts and plans for New Age healing centers, and most of these focused around a large structure of futuristic design, often a pyramid. One practical and dedicated Light worker, Jean, decided she wouldn't wait for these grandiose plans to materialize. She met the girl's mother, who told her of her concern and frustration over the girls' apparently retarded behavior and sometimes puzzling antics. Jean offered to arrange appointments with six of the best healers in Virginia Beach and put the girls up in her spare room while she chauffeured them around. By the time their two life readings with me were over, it was quite clear that, given their past-life experience, they were exactly where they were supposed to be, not working off any especially "negative karmic patterns."

Parents of retarded, or extra-gifted, children often forget the valuable opportunity for spiritual growth and evolution these children, these gifts from Heaven, are providing them. Priscilla and Rebecca were certainly intelligent enough to get the message, and it was beneficial for them to receive this positive view, in contrast with the thought forms of many people around them. Of course, the music was uplifting and healing on many levels, and they loved their tapes. This was quite a lesson for all involved. For me, it was the beginning of the awareness that *everyone is, at all times, in the precisely most optimum time and place for the maximum spiritual growth, and that this is a sacred gift.*

There was another enlightening feature in this interesting case. On Saturday afternoon, after all six healers had worked with the girls, Jean arranged a panel discussion. This holistic evaluation of the results was most exciting and valuable since patterns of understanding emerged, by comparing the various healers' diagnostic reports, which never would have been revealed otherwise. Included, besides myself, were a holistic M.D., a chiropractor using the Edgar Cayce readings, an expert hand analyst, and a psychic reader (the masseur did not attend). I was impressed with Jean's forthright plan of action to help the girls. She proved to us that Virginia Beach *already was* a holistic healing temple, and that we did not need to wait for the one-million-dollar pyramid!

#6—(Amandra Larkin, age, late 20's): In August of 1975, I was giving a concert in South Carolina, and at the back of the audience was a girl in a wheelchair. I was told later that the doctors had pretty much given up on her since they could detect very little sensation in her spine. She was beautiful and charming and had been an active girl, then an automobile accident had radically changed her life.

For four years, I had been saying an affirmation before concerts, offering myself for the highest good of everyone in the audience. As Amandra became more and more involved with the music, she began to feel waves of sensation going up and down her spine. She was so moved, she entreated her mother to bring her for a life reading, Attunement. The past-life information explained why she was in the wheelchair, what she wished to learn from her condition, and provided insights into how she could accelerate her healing. In addition to this mental healing, the tape is available to her every day for healing vibrations on the emotional, neurological and physical levels.

In the spring of 1979, a national newspaper interviewed me, and, in preparation for a possible article, checked up on Amandra. She said that her Attunement session had given her a new lease on life, and that she had experienced continuing physical improvement using her music. If I wore a hat, I would take it off to her willingness to open herself to a new form of healing, her readiness to learn some difficult lessons, and her patience and persistence. But the deepest gratitude has to go to the wondrous Deity who acts through the emissaries of light, love and healing.

#7—(Gay Cormack, age, early 40's): A few years after I did the readings at her house, I received a call that Gay was in the hospital, and friends were hoping to take some healing music to her. I channeled the music, and they took the tape with a portable recorder into her hospital room. After she had heard it two or three times, she sat up in bed, wide awake, yanked out all the intravenous feeding and medication tubes that were attached to her, and packed her things. She left the hospital completely well.

My interpretation of this was that while she had learned many New Age techniques for self-healing, and was most of the time in good health, in a weak moment she had gotten out of balance and succumbed to the belief, so prevalent in our society, that only doctors could help her. With all due respect for the medical profession, whose vast knowledge is most valuable if you need their services, I think Gay was affirming her right to claim the health, balance, and harmony that the channeled music was offering her. She probably learned, once again, the lesson about giving up her power to others. Of course if you can't summon this kind of faith, you'd better turn to a health practitioner in whose compassion and techniques you can trust.

#8—(Nan Antanian, Age, early 40's): In the early years of channeling, I believe this was 1975, I would sometimes have difficulty distinguishing between what Joel Andrews was feeling, and what was being impressed on me about the client. Sometimes, momentarily, I would forget that I had made a pact with God to send me those whom I could help and then interpret the feeling I was having as my own inadequacy. Nan was an excellent example. Her Past-Life Attunement seemed positive, but as I finished it, I was overcome with a feeling of sadness and depression. It was a feeling bordering on hopelessness and I didn't see how I could do the Interpretation, but she had requested one. The more I got into it the more I realized I was picking up her anguish at the soul level. She had become so involved in matter that she had almost forgotten her Divine origin and nature.

In our desire to grow spiritually through the advantages that the physical world offers, we can become more and more entangled in its web and forget to look up towards The Light. I explained this to her, and impressed on her the cruciality of her playing down the senses for awhile. Looking to higher things, she should begin viewing the world as an expression of pure Light and Concept in form, and try to think of herself, fundamentally, as a spark of Divinity.

By this time, I was beginning to analyze the clients' names according to the system of symbolism revealed by the Sources: the archetypal significance of letters and pitches. When I looked at Nan's names, I noticed, to my amazement, that they contained nine A's, and that there were very few other letters present. She even had an A as the Purpose of Growth of her last name (her Activity Pattern)! According to the system being used by the Sources, the letter A carries the vibration of the Divine Mother Principle (physical manifestation). I was told that it came from the shape of the pyramid which we now know traps and accumulates cosmic energy and brings it into the physical world, its four sides representing three dimensions plus time. While I have changed her name somewhat, it still shows the A's, N's, and T's that symbolize different aspects of our physical plane. Her initial A is the Divine Mother Principle itself, and shows that she desires to see that everything in her physical world is alive with consciousness and a manifestation of The Light. I pointed out that these realizations could bring about a transformation in her life.

By the time I had finished, I felt fine, quite positive, and enlightened by this lesson from spirit. I was, however, somewhat chagrined by my momentary confusion.

#9—(Erlutah Smith, in her 40's): This one is simple, to the point, and involved the use of the general healing tape I had channeled for the Thyroid or Throat chakra. According to medical tests, Erlutah's Thyroid was so far out of balance it usually required seven grains a day of Thyroid extract to function normally. This extreme medication continued for some years and she had arrived at a state of exasperation. She bought my Thyroid Chakra tape, lay down to fully experience it, and was completely healed. So intense were these 20 minutes for her, and so high was her hope, that she went immediately to the hospital for tests. She was found normal, and there has been no remission. Naturally, the doctors could not believe or explain it.

Out of the 25 general healing tapes that I distribute, this is one of two about which I caution people. It can be "strong medicine" and I recommend not listening to it more than once a day in the beginning. When it was first produced, a chiropractor bought it and set his assistant to work making copies for his patients (unethical). She was attracted to the music, listening to it as she made the copies. After three hours of this she began having very strange sensations in her throat and soon had to quit work and go home with what seemed like laryngitis! The same thing happened to me the next day after I channeled this music. I had ten advance orders and was trying to get these tapes out as fast as possible.

#10—(Spiritual Frontiers Fellowship Concert at Guilford College, North Carolina, August 18, 1978): This was a week-long annual S.F.F. Regional Conference, and I had been asked to play a concert on Friday night. Earlier in the week, they had presented such luminaries of the Spiritual Renaissance as Patricia Sun and David Spangler (real names). As I enjoyed these speakers and the week progressed, I began to wonder why I had been placed last. What acts to follow! Most often my concert is scheduled at the beginning of conferences because the music is so able to relax and open up people to each other, to the immediate environment, and to the purposes of the conference. When I sought guidance about this, what I got was that the music could go beyond words into realms of pure being, and that I was to celebrate the concepts that the others had brought forth. I can tell you I was stimulated by this challenge, and I have rarely been so high.

For some months, I had been retuning the harp to the Overtone Series, the natural Law of Resonance. Half an hour before going on stage, I was still trying to decide whether or not to use it. Concerned that there were 500 people in the audience, I got into such a stit over it that I finally decided to surrender totally to the Higher Force's guidance.

There I was, with my arms stretched heavenward, saying, "Please, just tell me what to do!"

They clearly selected the Overtone Series, and since this takes slightly longer to tune, I finished tuning just in time for the harp to be moved on stage! I walked on feeling the fantastic exhilaration that comes when you know you're being used to your highest potential. I was so turned on, I was on the verge of laughter as I talked to the audience. I shared with them my wonderment at being placed last on the program, and explained that everything had been said so beautifully by the speakers, there was only one thing left to do: *Celebrate It!*

The music was extraordinarily sparkling with beauty and power, and I was aware that the whole stage carried a high charge of Love and Light. After the concert, many people came up to me reporting the signs of healing: intense vibrations and heat in various parts of the body, visions of light, colors and symbols, tears, weightlessness, past-life memories, etc.

Then later, three sensitives reported to me similar visions: that when I entered the stage it was immediately thronged with various Higher Beings. And when I began to play, two columns of monk-like beings came down out of the ceiling in front of the stage, moved single file up the two aisles, and dispersed among the audience, offering healing to all those who would receive it. These psychics told me of many more healings that took place. As I was talking, toward the close of the concert, they filed back down the aisles, back up through the ceiling, and away. The three sensitives said that there must have been between 400 and 500 monks, so there probably was a monk for each person present. I can't tell you how gratified I was to hear these reports. It sounded like one of the miracles out of the Bible, and it called to mind an ancient prophecy that in the "latter days" (toward the end of this century) we would see angels walking the earth and doing their work. I have come to the conclusion that whoever had eyes to see saw them that evening. I suspect that if I had seen them I would not have been able to play! I suppose it's a blessing, and I shall be content with the ecstacy of my love, concern, and harp playing that made it possible. I even entertained the thought (which comes so rarely) that if I didn't do anything else in my life, the revelation of healing that took place that evening was a fitting enough fulfillment.

#11—(Alicia's friend in New York): In the fall of 1976 a friend came to me for a Life Attunement session. Moved by the integrating and harmonizing power of the experience, she thought of a friend who was going through a difficult time, and might profit by one. Her friend, Carla, had recently been admitted to a New York mental institution. Alicia felt that her sensitivities would make it difficult for her to cope with the much more disturbed people around her. She suggested that I do a long distance life reading. She would take it to the hospital with a portable recorder, and it would help maintain Carla's balance. I felt a pang of compassion and thought it would be a wonderful and interesting use for a tape. She gave me her full name and birthdate, and I channeled the music. It came through as usual, but when I listened to the tape to do the Interpretation, IT WAS BLANK! This was a shock because the session took place in my studio where I had been doing readings for weeks, and I knew I had pressed all the buttons correctly. It wasn't until two hours later, after Alicia had left, that I realized we didn't have Carla's permission or request.

For some years, I had believed that I had no right to consult someone's akashic records without their permission. It was as if I had given the Higher Forces permission to keep me on the straight and narrow path. My motive was pure; I was moved by compassion, but they kept me from breaking a basic rule. Of course, there may have been other reasons why Carla should not have had such a tape at that time. I was grateful for the guidance and the lesson. To my knowledge, this was the only time I made this kind of slip. I talk with enthusiasm about the readings, but almost never suggest anyone have one. I wait for this to occur to them. A handful of exceptions to this rule involved suggesting the possibility of an Attunement when I was certain that they would know it was their choice, and take the responsibility.

So there you have it — a rich potpourri of clients' responses, experiences, and reports of healing on a number of levels. There are hundreds more cases in my files, covering an even greater variety; some that would stretch your credulity, or double you up with laughter. I remember one man who wrote me shortly after his Attunement session to say that whatever the long range effects of the music might be, one of his most vexing problems was waking at four every morning to relieve himself. The second morning after he listened to his tape, he slept straight through for the first time in years. He was overjoyed!

Five years after a client's taping, they may write that their cassette has broken, is there any possibility that I still have the master, and could I send them another copy? For nine years, I kept file copies of each Individual Attunement, as well as over 60 general channelings. I had to pack and unpack six or seven heavy cartons of them through eight moves! In 1979, after TWO YEARS of deliberation, I came to the conclusion that I was being everyone's mother and stopped making file copies. (I still have all the old ones.) One of my hesitations was that I wanted to have plenty of readings on hand when some bright, young, New Age music student came to study them for his Master's thesis. I trust that the 1,500 I have saved, plus certain special ones I have retained, will be sufficient for this kind of study. (There are a number of aspects of these tapes which would be fascinating to subject to musicological analysis; especially since, as far as I have been able to find out, they are unique in the world.)

There was some quasi-scientific testing carried out in a pain clinic in Cincinatti in 1979. Three of their patients were asked to volunteer to experience the standard Past-life Attunement. They were hooked up to an electro-encephalograph to monitor their responses during the music. In addition to EEG (brainwave frequency), I believe they were registering also Electromotor Response and Galvanic Skin Response. The doctor had set up the experiment for a friend, but did not show much interest in the project. The equipment operator seemed competent but quite skeptical throughout and, with a cursory examination, the findings were deemed inconclusive by the doctor. For my part, the sessions seemed to go quite well; in spite of the fact that I am always set into motion by *requests* for readings, which we didn't have here. This is important since we have learned over the years that the client heals himself, with God's help, with his desire and willingness to be healed. I had assumed before the tests that these three patients had come forward of their own accord. Another factor that affected these results is that this music, as we have said, usually acts most strongly on a person's *outer* bodies (Etheric, Emotional, and

Mental), and then at some later date sifts down into the Physical body. To make the most of the opportunity, I asked a certified Touch-For-Health practitioner to run a standard Indicator Muscle Diagnosis to check out the strength of all of the major systems of each patient's body immediately before, and immediately after, the Attunement session. The differences between "before" and "after" were dramatic. Many of the weak muscle responses had become strong, and the medium and strong responses even stronger; convincing evidence to the patient, the Touch-For-Health practitioner, and to me. I tried to interest the doctor in some follow-up testing, especially after the patients had listened to their tapes in a receptive state, but he was not interested. He claimed it would be too difficult to isolate the music as a causative factor. This has been a major problem in "proving" the healing effects of music. Even for a client who listens to her music daily and experiences gradual improvement of a serious condition, *how can she be sure it was the music?* We need special methods of testing and more sensitive equipment. Until we have them, we will have to rely on subjective reports of the kinds you find in this chapter.

There is another way in which this lack of scientific proof manifests in my life. If the people who attend my concerts only knew the profound and far-reaching effects of the music they were about to hear, they would be happy to pay $30, $50, $500 or more to attend. Yet they will think nothing of paying $40 for one doctor's visit, $85 for an hour with the psychiatrist, and $900 for two days in the hospital! I suppose this is understandable when you consider the millions of dollars these two respected professions have spent in establishing "scientific" credibility. I wouldn't begrudge them this. But true holistic healing means all of the healing professions *working together* combining their expertise. This is a challenging problem with which holistic practitioners, and every music healer, must deal.

Let me close this chapter with an appeal. I have a strong intuitive conviction that soon laboratory instruments will be developed to measure subtle changes in the outer bodies. My work, together with the work of others, has demonstrated the depth and variety of healing effects possible with channeled music. With sophisticated testing we can begin to learn more about *how* it works and *why* it works. And with publication of the results we can make this truly extraordinary mode of healing more available to the general public.

After all is said and done, still nothing, neither testimonials nor accounts of miracles nor scientific research, can take the place of *your own direct experience.* This is especially true when it comes to something as genuinely *intimate* and as *extra-verbal* as music.

CHAPTER NINE

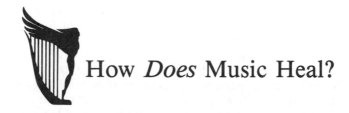 How *Does* Music Heal?

Now you have asked me why and how this music heals. So before we explore symbolic systems, it would be my pleasure to attempt such an explanation. I say "attempt" because, if you will remember, music as a phenomena takes place on a level apart from words. It is *extra-verbal* and so it is always a great challenge to describe it in words. I will try to sum up for you my personal experience of the process of music healing; my observations of how the vibrations of music act on clients, my philosophical knowledge of music, and how these three have interacted over the years.

Everything in creation, in its essential nature, is vibrating to a certain frequency or frequencies arranged in certain patterns. This is an axiomatic truth known to science as well as philosophy. So it is through the Laws of Vibration that we can understand the nature of things and relate one thing to another, though they seem separate. This is because the rates of vibration of an entity are an inherent aspect of it. The question we are addressing is: "How do tones and music produced by an instrument (or the voice), and arranged in space, affect various aspects of a human being?" Let us look deeper into the vibratory nature of both "music" and "human being."

The basic aspects of music are: Pitch, Melody (pitches arranged horizontally in sequence), Chords or Harmony (pitches arranged vertically or simultaneously), Meter (the arrangement and organization of notes into groups along a pulse), Rhythm (the specific attack patterns of pitches, or just *when* the notes occur), and Volume or Loudness (usually measured in decibels, a unit of energy). Researchers for hundreds of years have agreed that underlying these basic aspects of music are vibration, number, and amplitude. It might help for you to picture a vibration as a sine wave: visualize a straight horizontal line, and then a trajectory which starts at a point on the line, curves up above the line in a semi-circle, curves down below the line in a semicircle, and then returns to a point on the line. This is how a vibration is normally represented. Obviously, one vibration might cross the line more frequently in a second than another, and the distance it travels away from the line might also vary. The latter is called *amplitude* and represents volume. The frequency with which it hits the line in one second determines its pitch or its note on the piano. This also would be a convenient way of picturing the vibration of a string on the harp right after I pluck it. The string sways from side to side, crossing through center, gradually diminishing in amplitude until it comes to rest. How often it does this per second remains constant since this is a function of its length and tension. When it comes to the arrangement of frequencies, such as pitches in melodies and in chords, certain relationships are known to exist, expressed by their numbers (vibrations per second) and based on the natural Law of Resonance, the Overtone Series, where the vibrating body produces also higher notes from ever smaller segments of the whole. Where one part or "partial" of the string may vibrate stronger than another, "tone quality" is created.

Then there are Meter and Rhythm. All music has an underlying, regular *beat* or *pulse*: Meter is the organization of pulses into repetitive groupings, usually with some kind of accent being felt on the first beat of each group. Examples might be: 4/4, four quarter notes to a bar or measure, or 6/8, six eighth notes to a bar. This aspect is certainly accessible and understandable through numbers. So is Rhythm, which is the plotting, on the regular pulse, of notes or chords or percussive events. Certain beats are subdivided (according to numbers) and others are only implied or bridged over (long notes and short notes). Anyone who has seen a good quality cassette deck has seen the VU meters which are calibrated with numbers representative of decibels to show the volume or loudness of the music at any point (the amplitude of the sine waves).

Music can truly be said to be the art of vibrations. All of the arts are fundamentally vibratory in nature, but the greatest philosophers and researchers have agreed that music presents the vibrations in a purer more accessible form. It is as if music is a *shorthand* for life, a creation which abstracts for us the vibrational patterns at the very heart of reality, including universal patterns from higher dimensions.

For 35 years I have studied the nature of sound and music to see what it could tell us about the nature of human beings and the worlds that surround them. I have been led to a number of models which have proven to be quite valuable in revealing the essential nature of these realities. (This was part of the preparation for channeling attunement music.)

I hope you have not found these definitions too detailed or technical. I've tried to keep them as simple as possible, but realize that they are necessary to understand the vibratory nature of music, to see how it can be a catalyst for healing for a human being (or an animal, or a plant, or a precious gem, or a piece of furniture, or a town, or anything that has consciousness). I also hope that those lovers of music who have always found the nature of music to be a mystery will find these definitions enlightening and stimulating of further inquiry.

Now let us examine the physical body of a human being from the standpoint of patterns and vibrations. We realize first what a small aspect of the human's total beingness is revealed by this visual picture. On the other hand, with training, we can view the body as a revelation of the deeper and higher aspects of a human being. This is because the body is a manifestation, or expression, of underlying vibrational patterns. Then, note the generic qualities that are common to us all: one head (well, really!), two arms, two legs, ten fingers and toes, one navel and two nipples for both men and women, (but nine orifices for men, ten for women).

We should be immediately aware that one head, two arms and two legs create the basic rhythmic patterns of our walking. Imagine how it would change the basic *sound* of our society if we had three legs, three arms and two heads! We each have one heart, which sends a regular but variable pulse throughout the body, one tongue instead of two, which from a higher point of view keeps our speech rather simple, and two ears instead of three, which means we hear in stereo and can locate sound sources in space. (If we did have a third ear, I wonder if we would be able to hear higher guidance better?)

Every part of the body has a certain vibrational frequency. I once saw a photograph of (and the manual for) a device that could administer a frequency to an organ, with the effect of stimulation and healing. The average common cycles-per-second of the major organs was listed on the machine. A similar device is undergoing some sophistication at this time in England.

If we view the body in motion, performing even a simple act of survival, or playing the organ or the harp, we see many, many complex rhythms all integrated for a certain effect, or result, or task. It begins to resemble the complex, but coordinated, rhythms of a symphony being played by eighty players under the direction of a conductor. We all have one voice (instead of two!) which is produced by vibrating membranes and resonating chambers, a musical instrument *par excellence*. Our voices are capable of producing all the aspects of music we have described as well as the subtle tunes and inflections of speech. Consider, for a moment, how important the rhythms of all parts of the body, and the body as a whole, are to one of the highest human dance expressions: that of lovemaking.

I think we embody chains of frequencies, signals, and rhythms, comparable to melodies, especially when it comes to memories of habitual sequences of physical, emotional and mental events, and projections of these into the future. All important in healing are those sequences of events or melodies which aren't working for us, what we call "negative" thoughts and emotions which eventually manifest as "negative" physical behavior (spiritual growth). And, aren't the chakras, the psychic centers along the spine, just like a chord in music? They each have a fundamental vibratory frequency plus harmonics or higher partials, and are arranged vertically. I am convinced that a study relating the frequencies of the chakras to the Overtone Series would reveal some most interesting and valuable information.

Just how much we love to dance, listen to music, and play instruments is indicative of how musical is our very nature. The great teacher, Gurdjieff, said that there was a definite frequency ratio between the Physical-Etheric body, the Emotional body and the Mental body, indicating that each was going thousands of vibrations per second faster than the next lower body. It is quite possible that this relationship is a geometric one; and this is corroborated by other sources. This fits in with the Great Law, "As Above, So Below", the principle that higher vibrations are gearing down, level by level, into the physical level of manifestation. Probably whenever we do two things at once, at the same instant, this would be comparable to an interval or a chord of notes in music.

We have ears to pick up a wide spectrum of information from the sounds and music of our environment; not only with the eardrum, but with the outer ear itself, which has spread out all over it a map of contact points which transmit information to all the major organs of the body. The marvelous Organ of Corti, within the ear, which transmits sound vibrations to the brain, resembles very much a microscopic piano and contains roughly 24,000 filaments, *each tuned to a different frequency!* Then too, most people are aware of registering sound and music in other parts of the body, particularly the stomach area, and sometimes in the case of very basic rock music, the genital area.

My research leads unequivocally to the conclusion that we "hear" with all parts of the Physical-Etheric body, the Emotional body, and even the Mental body. These three outer bodies are more like force-fields which interpenetrate the physical vehicle but extend out roughly 4, 12, and 24 inches from the body. The etheric is responsible for physical sensations. Healing can be accomplished working directly with all three.

The list could go on and on showing how vital a part in our interaction with our environment our super-sensitivity to vibrations plays: how a baby knows how to pitch its cry precisely to alarm its mother to its needs; how she, in turn, puts it to sleep by patting with a certain intensity, at a certain rate, on certain parts of the body, gradually slowing down; how we can be debilitated by the sounds of machinery at certain frequencies, rhythms, and intensities disharmonious with our own. Then there is the healing upliftment we receive from the vibrations of nature such as the bright song of mountain brooks, the sweet warble of the birds, and the deep hosannas of the sea.

All of this evidence shows clearly that our sound environment is vital to our survival and growth in this plane of existence. Most people take their sound environment for granted, and yet if they were deaf, every hour they would live with a greater sense of insecurity than if they were blind. This is because your eyes, even though they can see farther than your ears can hear, provide you only about one-third of your visual radius, whereas your ears are sensitive to the full 360 degrees. To a student of vibrations, one of the major causes of "dis-ease" in the world today is sound pollution and vibration pollution.

I look forward to the time when my brothers and sisters will awaken to their right to a harmonious sound environment in which to evolve, and will ACT to secure it. I predict that in the next ten years, sound pollution boards will become as important as air pollution boards!

Now, perhaps you can see that a musical view of a human being is not only a sensible one, but a highly revealing and enlightening one. The writings of Victor Zuckerkandl (see Bibliography) report that researchers are applying this view with great success in a number of fields, such as biology, bacteriology and the study of the growth of plants. By now, having seen the basis of music in vibration, and how much all aspects of the human being consist of the same vibratory realities, you can already appreciate that *they are both subject to the same vibratory laws and principles.* Of course, the major difference is that a human is much more complex, consisting probably of hundreds of correlated pulses and rhythms, and possibly thousands of coordinated chords and melodies on a number of levels of being. We are now ready to state the basic theory that I think underlies the interaction between music and a human being (and anything else, for that matter).

The fundamental law of vibration which explains *how* an individual hears music (with all of his being) is the Law of Sympathetic Resonance. This law states that if there are two objects in proximity which are free to vibrate at the same frequency, and one is set into motion, the other will vibrate in sympathy with it. This means that as long as you are open and receptive to the music, and you have within you frequencies, or octaves and harmonics (partials), pulses and rhythms, melodies and chords which are in the music, *these will respond and be set into motion.* To put it the other way around, if a pitch is sounded near you, and it is one you do not have free to vibrate within you, you simply will not hear it. I remember a workshop where I was using a repeated low G for a sound awareness exercise, and one man said he really didn't like that note. I suggested that he must have some past unpleasant association for low G, and that it would be a good idea to work it through. Otherwise, he might eventually find that he couldn't hear it anymore, and the music he heard would be lacking that note. So this is the basic law that explains how we can actually hear. But of course, it's a highly complex and subtle interrelationship.

One interesting question that arises is: as your hearing sensitivity increases, that is, you become freer and freer to vibrate, do you hear more sounds and "musics" around you and more distant sounds? I have certainly found this to be so. While my auditory perception has diminished a little in defense against sound pollution, my body and higher body "hearing" has increased considerably. I know that when I'm on tour and arrive in a town, after the first half-hour, I'm registering the vibrations of that town, not only in the higher bodies, but the thought-forms and emotional patterns. My body is feeling the town. It's as if I'm "hearing it" as a symphony. It also follows that the more you're taking in, the more you would like it all to be in harmony, and so the more compassion and understanding you have to develop if it isn't!

I'm sure human beings have a complex baffling system to prevent certain patterns from being taken in. You certainly would go absolutely mad if you were registering all the radio and television stations in your town at the same time! You'd only last a few weeks longer if you had to hear one station all the time in your head along with your thoughts. I read once that this was one of the most important functions of the brain, to filter out the hundreds of vibratory frequencies that are passing through you at all times, thereby creating a relatively neutral quiet zone in which you might live, grow and have your being.

Now, let us approach the all important question of how music heals. I do not feel that I do anything to the client, that I accomplish any healing. All I do is try to be the best possible *catalyst* I can and bring forth vibrations which the client may use to heal himself. The client who has requested a healing is, in the final analysis, responsible for, and in charge of, his own healing. I think once the conscious mind has made the free will decision and set up an appointment for a healing session, the High Self and guardian seraphim, together with the subconscious or basic selves, who know precisely what is needed, can begin to pattern a selective baffling system to be activated at the session, for what the client is ready to receive, as well as setting up patterns of assimilation — how the vibrations will be used. Ideally, the healer, out of loving compassion for his brothers and sisters, and out of a desire to grow spiritually through service to the wellness and harmony of his world, opens himself to channel the highest and most optimum musical patterns for the client to use. He does this from two ecstasies: the one of his love, and the other of co-creating with the higher musicians. He is not attached to the results, so that he won't get discouraged and discontinue the work.

You see, no healer can heal anyone who is not ready to be healed. It may sometimes take a very special set of circumstances to bring a situation to sufficient intensity for a person to be locked in enough to see it clearly, and to want to learn the spiritual lesson and change internally. Even if it is a serious illness, a person may not be ready to give it up for some time. There may be deep knowledge that those people, places and situations may not be assembled so soon again. *This is why a healer is tampering with a client's karma if he has a desire that healing should take place at any specific time.* This can confuse the learning process. The healer's concern lies in being the best possible channel, not feeding the problem, and to help the client in every possible way to *understand* the situation in its highest light.

The way I picture the healing actually taking place is: the client is suffering from what I would like to call, in musical terms, a negative melodic and chordal pattern — let's say, in the emotional body. He is suffering because the pattern is not working for him. It's not bringing him fulfillment, love, and peace, etc. Really, it's just a pattern of spiritual growth like everything else, but he doesn't know this yet. He comes to the healer in a state of apparent distortion and anxiety — *he thinks he's sick.* But he's opened himself to healing. He doesn't know he can heal himself, with God's help, so he temporarily gives up some of his power to the healer. Inwardly, I don't accept this power, and when I don't, the client's deeper self is reminded of its responsibility and capacity. However, I accept the opportunity to serve a new friend by having faith and calling on the love and the wisdom of God, acting through unseen helpers to provide more perfect and harmonious patterns in the afflicted area. In a state of receptivity, the client takes the new melodic, rhythmic and chordal patterns and *SUPERIMPOSES them over the patterns that aren't working.* Now, if they're too different, they won't fit, but the Sources have provided the perfect patterns for maximum upliftment. The acceptance of this more perfect archetypal pattern, which is charged with Light and Love, even though it may be far simpler than the "negative" pattern he's vibrating to, tends to pull the more detailed vibratory elements into alignment with it.

There is also the strong possibility that the music the healer is producing is a vehicle for higher, more complex vibratory patterns which the client can use to even greater advantage. I think this must be true for the music to act on the higher bodies. Moreover, we know that for my work the range of the harp has been divided into octaves, by the Sources, and designated: the Physical body, the Emotional body, the Mental body, and on up into the Higher Bodies. These are the octaves of the note A, beginning with the first space in the bass clef. So when healing takes place, I really think this is how it works: Along the lines of the client's problem-opportunity, the Higher Forces have created similar but more perfect vibratory patterns which will promote understanding, learning of spiritual principles, fulfillment, and harmony with his world. The client takes on these new patterns, positioning them in the same place occupied by patterns that aren't working. The two become more and more entrained. The things that really don't fit anymore become more and more obvious, and soon will come new ideas about how to do things, the appropriate emotions, and the new behavior patterns, the old patterns being released.

Of course, if the client is physically present at the session he can receive some counseling that can help him understand how the Soul-Path he has chosen is operating in his life, how it can bring everything in his life into a higher perspective. All of this accelerates mental healing.

Here a new pattern is superimposed in the Mental body. As he applies the new spiritual principles to bothersome situations in his life and finds that they work, he adds them to the treasure chest of his soul qualities. Naturally, since every element in the music that I am channeling has a symbolic meaning (pitches, intervals, rhythmic patterns, chords, etc.) there is infinitely more in the language of the music itself than I could ever put into words, and I always make this clear to the client.

If the client has not blocked the taking on of a number of higher vibratory patterns, the healing seems to begin immediately, and transformation ensues. Immediately, the fresh light of hope and expectancy shines in his being, and he takes on new, visible light. He appears more together — more whole — and he begins to take back his own power. This should be a relief to the healer since he should never really have wanted to take on the responsibility for his brother's, or sister's, health. Healer and healee have touched and known each other on very deep and high levels, a privilege for which the healer should feel thankful. I always feel a gratitude that the client's request for healing has enabled me to experience passing the music of a human soul through my being, my fingers and my harp. I don't imagine that there are very many musics more beautiful.

One thing we find corroborated here about the essential nature of music is that it doesn't *represent* anything as do words. Aside from a few exceptions, you cannot understand what a new word means just from hearing it, you have to ask someone what it means or look it up in the dictionary. The response to sound and music is almost universal, and if people are listening and are open to it, they get what it means, or at least what it means to them. It is possible to some extent to use music in a descriptive or "programmatic" way, to imitate life patterns, using universally accepted graphic associations that we have for them.

After hearing a tone poem full of richly-conceived effects, you can say to your friend, "Wasn't that wonderful! Did you hear that section where the flock of swans is migrating south, and they land on the lake to refresh themselves?"

And your friend might say, "Oh, yes, I see what you mean, but for me that was the women of the village going down to the river to do their washing, laughing and playing as they go."

If you asked the composer about that section, he might say, "Well, I'm pleased that my music stimulated such interesting imagery, but when I composed that section, I was thinking of a moving experience I had in Mexico two years ago. In this little village once a year the bells of the three churches ring at four o'clock in the afternoon. All the people stop working and bring offerings to the churches, laughing and singing and playing instruments because they know they'll have the rest of the afternoon off and a feast in the evening." And then if he's enlightened, he might say, "But of course, I was really trying to tune in and express an archetypal pattern: the coming together of beings anticipating joyfully a practical but renewing ritual."

You see, music, fundamentally, is not a *symbol for* aspects of life, it *is* life patterns in a shorthand, abstracted art-form of pure vibrations. This means that *when you experience music you are experiencing life.* Someone conceived a proof of this and wrote out a schemata of the repetition of phrases, with slight variations, in a Beethoven symphony. Then they wrote a poem using the same amount of repetition. Of course it was boring. We enjoy hearing the same thing over and over in music (as long as it's reasonable "good" music) because we're listening to the *real thing.* Another reason we like repetition in music is that our own music is constantly playing and changing so that each repetition we hear sounds different. Have you ever noticed how slowly your thoughts actually change? It may take two or three repetitions for you to take in an idea, but it usually sits there in your mind without changing for some time while you digest it and correlate it with other ideas. The world of thought can certainly sometimes dance, but it normally doesn't dance as freely and as fast as the world of the vibratory arts, and music, and your own music.

For example, a more advanced spiritual teacher, once the student has demonstrated understanding of a new metaphysical principle, will say, "Now celebrate it!" So, again, music is a non-verbal or extra-verbal phenomenon: the direct presentation of archetypal patterns of vibrational reality. And for this reason it is highly *versatile* and transcends the limits of words.

This is just why it is such an incomparable aid in the healing arts. We are all familiar with music's power of nostalgia. Thirty years later you can hear the recording of a song that was popular during your first crush in High School, and your heart can skip a beat, as an emotion of amazing warmth and power surges through you. I mention this because nostalgia is very much a part of the life readings that I do. Not so much in the present century, but back through history the harp was the most common instrument, along with the flute and the drum, so that its dulcet tones are indelibly imprinted in almost everyone's deep memory. And when you hear harp music that is encoded with past-life patterns, *you're there!*

Since the printing of books in our time, we have produced a veritable torrent of words, many of them inspired. Most of the important metaphysical truths have been well stated for those who have the persistence and the response to Higher Guidance to find them. What music can do, and what my ministry has been so involved with, is to bring through higher states that can't be adequately conveyed by words or to celebrate concepts that have already been expressed and received intellectually — to help people *feel* and *dance* the qualities of the spiritual principles in their everyday lives. Concepts such as Peace, Love, Joy, Spiritual Ecstasy, Harmony, Unconditional Brotherhood and Sisterhood, Oneness, can never be communicated solely by words: THEY MUST BE EXPERIENCED. Music can provide the essential vibratory qualities of these concepts, especially if it is co-created with Higher Forces. These are the qualities that are being channeled through the sensitive artists of today, and they are the qualities that fill the music of this ministry: bringing deep healing and expansion of being to individuals, as well as concert audiences and other kingdoms of the Earth. Isn't this how music and musicians can begin to fulfill the highest destiny?

CHAPTER TEN

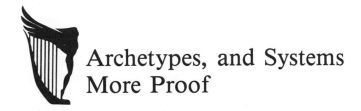 Archetypes, and Systems
More Proof

At this point my friend jumped up, did a little dance, and said, "I didn't realize I was so inherently musical! I think I'll replace a little of my thinking and talking with singing and dancing. And you know, I bet a lot of people have been programmed in early childhood by parents and teachers with the idea that they're not musical. They just need to be shown that they *are* music by their very nature! All they need to do is allow it to express."

After two or three quite impressive turns, he sat back down and said, "What about this system you've been referring to, the one that links symbolic meanings with the elements of the music? I should think apprentice music healers would be most interested in checking this out and integrating it with their work — if they don't find they've been using it already, intuitively. It might even have far-reaching effects, being a kind of restatement of Kabbalistic truth for the New Age. So how did you discover this system?"

I was so pleased and relieved when I began to notice that the Higher Beings working with me were using a system of symbolism for the elements of the music, which correlated with the clairvoyant impressions I was receiving. Relieved, because I knew this new and unusual form of healing would be more convincing if it incorporated an objective, scientific aspect. And I was pleased because my own nature includes a very good balance between the objective and the subjective approaches to life, between reason and spontaneity. (Ever since the illumination I had at the age of twenty-six, cosmic consciousness had resolved most problems of Duality, particularly the conflict between science and religion, metaphysics). Little did I realize the far-reaching implications and consequences of this valuable system — that it would result in a world anthem written in a new language to bring the peoples of the world together in peace and brotherhood.

Here's how the system was revealed. After the first few weeks of past-life readings in 1972, I began to notice that whenever I saw a person involved in a certain type of activity, the music was always in the same key, or at least repeated the same note, or family of notes. If the person was some kind of artist, it would be F#. If they were in a monastery, attuning directly to the Light, it would be in the key of E; and if they were growing primarily through physical experience, the music would be in the key of A. You can imagine my intense curiosity and excitement as I began to look for the system in the music and found it. I began to make rational, common-sense predictions of what was what, and they often turned out to be right. My knowledge of the system grew rapidly over the early months and years, but it was 1975 before the last remaining major gaps were closed.

As background for the following story, keep in mind two things: first, up until then, I had assumed that the system had been devised by the Higher Beings, just for my work. Second, at the beginning of the session I translate the client's birthdate and full name into pitches. I utilize a letter-pitch equivalent code used for over 300 years by many composers. As I was learning the meaning of the notes, I was also learning the meaning of the letters of the alphabet.

In 1975, I received an amazing disclosure which confirmed the universality of this system and I would like to recount how it came to me. I was married to a very fine psychic, Nel. We did a great deal of work together, from which I learned much, and for which I am truly grateful. One day the two of us were lingering over lunch, and Nel, closing her eyes, said she felt a shining presence and heard the name of an angel being sung in pitches.

Now, I didn't usually call it "my" system, but that day I said, "If you could sing me the notes, I might be able to translate them into letters with my system, and we would have the angel's name."

Nel was silent for a moment, and then replied, "She's saying, 'You mean *the* system.'"

What a revelation was contained in those four words! I was so excited by the possibility that the system of archetypal significance for each letter of the alphabet might be a *universal* system that I began to check out words around me at once. This became an interesting pastime while on tour. What I discovered quite simply was that the letters people chose for words pretty much showed an intuitive knowledge of the system. The words that didn't, I suppose, were created by extremely mental people who were not tuning in, or possibly by satanic individuals (or forces) who were trying to confuse the rest of us.

I was discussing this at a workshop in Winston-Salem, N. C., and we were talking about the letter K symbolizing "the spiritual teacher." I chose, as an example, "Krispy-Kreme Donuts." I said that I had learned that this was the first donut company to develop a national chain and that I would expect its founder, even though he was working with the mass appeal for sweets, to be in some way spiritual. A man spoke up, saying that he had just read an article about the founder of Krispy-Kreme Donuts, and that he was known in business circles for the considerate way he treated his employees.

I said, "Well, I'm glad to hear it. Let's take a closer look at what this man is actually doing: he's turning out thousands and thousands of these little round objects, symbols of perfection and wholeness, and he's making them so delicious that he's getting people to eat them! Couldn't we say he's some sort of spiritual teacher?"

Let me share the other significant event that took place that year, which was an even greater disclosure. But first, I should explain that Nel's primary Sources were the Lords of Sirius. It was as if she had a built-in cable connecting her mind to their intelligence, which, when she was in full trance, nothing on earth could influence. One afternoon, she disappeared into the bedroom to take a much-needed nap, and then reappeared twenty minutes later, groggily muttering something about a Mystical English Alphabet — that they wanted her to tell me something about it. She sat down on the couch, going directly into trance. I grabbed a cassette recorder, slapped a fresh cassette into it, and recorded the date as I had been trained.

The Lords of Sirius proceeded to present the origins of language! They said that in the dawn of human history (I got the impression of Lemurian times), the more advanced humans could, on making a sound with the voice, see the form it created in the Etheric field around them. Very soon, they learned that if they wished to communicate a certain tree to a friend, they would make a sound that would create in the Etheric an exact replica of *that tree, which the friend could see! It was explained that this grew into a language. The early languages, then, were based on an exact correlation between a sound, the letter that represents that sound, and that to which it refers.* They were implying not only the essential vibratory oneness of object, sound and letter-symbol, but also that any one of these could stimulate the full experience of the others. (In English, onomatopoeia approaches this: "A *buzzing* bee," "a baby's *ma-ma*," and "*humming* a melody." Sanskrit contains what remains of one of these early languages, and we find this link-up in it to a high degree.)

As the centuries passed, and more and more of the humans using these ancient languages could not see the forms their own speech created, their sense of the living relationship between sound, linguistic structure and actual meaning became less exact, and so they created new words lacking in vibratory integrity and not exemplifying the oneness of all creation. (This was probably the truth behind the Tower of Babel allegory in the Bible. Do we need to blame this, too, on God? We shouldn't "blame" anyone, but we might more sensibly attribute this confusion to the "anti-life" forces personified by "the devil," which is "lived" spelled backwards, and our weakness in responding to them.)

The Lords of Sirius explained that, at the present time, you can express a thought in high-vibration words or low-vibration words. You could write a book using words made of letters that do not support the meaning of the words, or employing letters that do.

They then announced that they would present the "Symbolism of the Mystical English Alphabet for the New Age," which they proceeded to do, letter by letter. It became clear that they were attaching symbolic meaning to each of the *basic strokes* of which *capital* letters are made (they did not use lower case letters) and that they were viewing letters as having chakras (levels of being). *It was so exciting for me to see them corroborating the system I had been developing for two years, and to have them add to this system some higher and lower meanings.*

I had an opportunity to ask questions and was able to clear up some confusion concerning three of the letters. A few months prior to this reading, having learned so much about the significance of the letters, I had begun to analyze clients' names after their Attunements. I discovered that this information went right along with the Interpretations of the channeled music, and amplified it — the name being an expression of who you are and what you're about in this incarnation. The Lords of Sirius gave me additional symbolism for names, and they asked me to start playing the birthdate translated into pitches along with the name. (I suppose we were beginning to get people with the same name and more identification was required.) They also suggested I make available to musicians, and anyone else who was interested, the basic elements of the system.* This has been obtainable from me on three sheets comprising the symbolism of musical intervals, how to translate numbers into pitches through the alphabet, the code composers have used to translate letters into pitches, and the basic symbolism for the letters and pitches revealed through the readings and The Lords of Sirius. Also available, has been a set of two cassettes of the first lecture I gave on the system, in Pittsburgh, in February, 1976. (It lasted four hours! so I edited it down to three.)

Two other highly significant events took place in 1975. Since I was becoming so familiar with the significance of each letter, the Masters invited me to co-create with them an anthem for world unification. We would create a new language for it, one that had not been on Earth before; a language of great power and clarity, so that everyone on Earth could sing it in the same language! No one could say, "Oh, that's in *their* language." I will be telling you the rest of this story in Chapter XV.

The second event had to do with a deep, growing curiosity about

*See Appendix I

just who Jesus was. When I was a child, I had been put off by the constant symbol of Jesus in anguished death on the cross in the various churches I attended. In more recent years, I had become acquainted with a more Esoteric Christianity which often portrays the Living Christ as the "Master of Masters." I began to really want to know why Jesus was called this, and other masters were not.

A young blond friend, Peter, used to drop in and out of Virginia Beach on his travels, looking for wisdom. He was quite a master of sleight-of-hand, and one of his specialties was making cigarettes disappear, which I thought was uplifting since I was trying to stop smoking at the time. He came for an attunement session with me, and then gave me in return a large book called "The URANTIA Book." I had not heard of this book, and didn't think it could have cost quite $35.00, which was what I was charging for sessions then. But he recommended it highly, and said that he really felt I would find it rewarding, and I accepted it. Little did I know that it would become the most important book in my life; that I would discuss it in study groups once a week, (unless I was on tour) for the next eight years, and that it would answer the most important questions about life that I have had. What was important then was that I soon discovered that out of the 2,000 plus pages, 800 are devoted to the most complete and accurate account of the life of Jesus available anywhere, and an explanation of who he really was and is. How about that for an answer to my curiosity!?

At this point, to prepare you for what follows, you might like to look over the Appendix which contains the letter-pitch equivalents and their archetypal symbology.

*   *   *   *   *   *

There is much more I should share with you about various aspects of this system. First, let's begin with translating numbers into pitches through the alphabet, and let's make sure we understand the directions The Lords of Sirius gave us for this procedure. The numbers 1 through 22 are equivalent to the corresponding letters; that is, 1 equals A, 2 equals B, 9 equals I, and 22 equals V. Any number higher than 22 is broken down into its individual digits and then translated into its letters. Thus, 23 would be the second letter and the third letter, or B and C. 257 would be second letter, fifth letter, and seventh letter, or B, E, G. Then we simply translate the letters into notes with the Letter-Pitch Code. I should add that while this method has worked perfectly well for my work over a period of eight years, I have not made a deep study of numbers, and also don't know just how useful this system might be to others. And whether it works in other languages is a matter of research. I did have a friend make a comparison with numerology and there were quite a few correlations even though this system is based on a 7-code (musical scale) and numerology on a 10-code.

Next, let's take a look at the Letter-Pitch Equivalent Code. Be sure to notice that only the letters A through G have the same names as notes. It will perhaps seem obvious and yet I would like to have you remember that the alphabet was chosen for our names of notes. It looks as if when H was reached in the code, the next line starts with B to introduce new notes. German musicians, for 300 years have written the note B as an H—a nice corroboration! (Note that in much of Europe the "Sol-Fa" system is used to name the notes: C—Do, D—Re, E—Mi, F—Fa, G—Sol, A—La, and B—Ti.) Now observe how this code is organized (and this is what you need to know to write it down if you don't have it with you, or memorized): it consists of four natural minor scales erected from four notes, a whole-tone apart, starting with A—one from A, one from B, one from C#, and one from D#. When you first approach it, it seems strange and then begins to make sense and turns out to have some nice features. Some pitches have one letter only (F-F, C-C, A#-Z, and E#-W); some pitches have two letters (G-G and M, D-D and J, F#-L and R, C#-I and O, G#-S and Y, and D#-P and V); and three pitches have three letters (A-A, N and T, E-E, K and Q, and B-B, U and H).

For our purposes, it makes sense to arrange our notes (and letters) around a circle in fifths. The interval of the fifth symbolizes Creation and Manifestation. We might remember, also, that the Cycle of Fifths is well-known in music. The progression of one chord to another chord, a fifth away (like tonic to dominant or C—G), is the most powerful progression in music and dominated final cadences for almost 300 years. Also in the Tempered Scale (began circa 1680), the closest keys to which to modulate were those keys a fifth up and a fifth down because they contained only one new note in their scales. The Cycle of Fifths is especially illustrative for us as each archetypal quality is the Actualizing or Manifesting Principle for the quality before it in the Cycle. The note or quality a fifth *above* any particular note or quality is always it's Actualizing Principle. The note, another fifth higher, is the quality which acts it out, step by step, since that note also turns out to be the interval of the major second above the original note an octave higher, and seconds symbolize patient steps we take up the scale of growth. So this is why I have arranged the symbolism chart according to the Cycle of Fifths. In music, they also call it the *Circle* of Fifths. Written in this fashion, we begin with F at the top, positioning the notes (and letters around the Circle clock-wise. You will notice that they overlap since F# and G♭ are the same pitch written differently.

Another equivalence is F-E# and this seeming oddity turned out to have a great deal of significance in my readings since F-F represents the Angelic Order, and E#-W represents outer space or other planets, and many "space people" have come to me for attunements over the years. I found that they can either try to bring in their special gifts from space directly or enlist the aid of angels to help translate them into more earthly terms.

I learned about this Letter-Pitch Code from my harp teacher, Carlos Salzedo, twenty-three years before I needed it in Virginia Beach, when the lady stood up out of the audience and asked if I could improvize on a person! I have not been able to discover its source but many composers have used it, notably Haydn, Brahms, and Ravel. Another letter-pitch code has not come to my attention.

Let me share with you my views about systems in general. It seems to me, theoretically, that there must be a number of systems covering more or less the same phenomena that will work as long as they're used consistently. A good system strikes a balance between being simple and abstract enough to use, and yet covering a wide gamut of possibilities. I should think this would certainly hold true for a system used in co-creation with Higher Beings.

If you take the range of the flute, for example, you could either break it up into Physical, Emotional and Mental octaves, beginning with the Physical in the lowest octave. Or, you could follow the system given us for the harp, where the lowest notes of the flute begin in the Emotional octave; that is, from the A below middle C to A, an octave higher (second space in the treble cleff), then the next octave would be the Mental, and above A, first line above the staff, would be higher bodies (Intuitive, Spiritual, Monadic and Divine). There is some evidence for this latter system in the work of John Diamond, who found his patients responding to the flute predominantly in the upper part of the body, especially in the area of the throat. You might be interested in his study (through kinesiology — muscle testing) of which instruments were found to be the most therapeutic for different parts of the body, "BEHAVIORAL KINESIOLOGY" (see Bibliography).

When we study this Cycle of Fifths, it seems to make more sense as to why there are three pitches for some letters, two for others, and one for still others. The three in the middle, A, E, and B, certainly are the most active qualities in our world. The E, the Divine Father Principle, provides the pure pattern; the A, the Divine Mother Principle, brings it into form, and the B, the Actualizing Principle for the Light, tells us what it's all for: To manifest The Light in the Earth. And for us humans, the B symbolizes growth in consciousness in the service of this purpose, and this is the most common soul-path to God-realization chosen by human souls over the long series of lives on Earth. When I'm saying these are central, I'm leaving off the A# and the E#, which are outer space vibrations. Then we find E, The Light of Creation, right in the middle. Even if we wanted to delete the F of the Angelic Order, since this Order is not so present in the *perceptions* of humans (in spite of the fact that there are over 500,000 pairs of Angels on the planet at this time); and if you left off the D#, Universal Love, which is only beginning to be common in the hearts of men and women, (F and D# are quite rare in names), E still remains in the center.

There are some other symbolisms which I should mention, and I will try to move from the more generally applicable ones to those which might be more specific to my work with past-lives. Let us begin with the symbolisms of pulse and meter. To be versatile with this, you really should study numbers and what they mean, but I will give you a basic symbology here.

What about the speed (tempo) of the steady pulse or beat of the music? In general, tempos (more correct: "tempi") faster than the heartbeat, or tempi that accelerate, are stimulating, and tempi that are slower than the heartbeat, or slowing up, are relaxing. But tempi are relative in their effect, and a tempo that starts out very fast, and slows down to a tempo still above the heartbeat, could produce the effect of relaxation. Similarly, a very slow tempo that accelerates to a faster tempo, even though it's still under the heart rate, could stimulate. While we're speaking of the beat, let me observe that even though a steady beat is not going fast enough to be heard as a tone or a pitch, it is still a frequency. If you recorded a drum beat of 64 beats per minute, slightly faster than one per second, and speeded it up to 64 beats per second, you would actually hear the pitch two octaves below middle C. If you wanted to take the symbolism of numbers deeper, you could apply it to the numbers of vibrations per second of each note in the music. So here we can see how just two aspects of music are relatable through numbers.

Then in my work, the left hand usually plays what is called in music, "the accompaniment." Its rhythmic patterns are usually fairly regular and are expressing the recurring routine patterns of living: minutes and hours, days, weeks, months, years, and cycles of years. To understand the meaning of the meter groupings that are common to the left hand patterns in this music, we need to talk about the basic symbology of numbers.

One sound, pitch or chord expresses an event. It also might symbolize "unity," "focus," some specific thing, act, emotion, idea, a beginning or an end. The gradual dying away of the tone of this event, quite noticeable on the harp, might symbolize the consequences of the event, suffusing through, and influencing, other levels of being or reality. One pitch, or any musical element which is repeated continuously, has an effect of focusing, collecting, bringing to center, contracting, simplifying, and even producing altered states. If it is sustained long enough some listeners can become bored (and with further listening could become interested again). These effects have been most valuable in inducing meditation and hypnosis.

The meter, or how the beats are accented in recurring groups, is also symbolic. Duple patterns (notes accented every two) express walking, day and night, vibration itself slowed down, an individual's inside and outside world, male and female, Father God and Mother God, and a host of other polarities. (Our world is often called the Plane of Duality).

Three, physically speaking, is a turning pattern and can express spirallic movement. It can suggest the rich associations of the waltz, whatever a triangle might symbolize, any two opposites plus the contemplation of them as a polarity, beginning to free oneself from the limitations of Duality, and a host of trinities reaching all the way up to Deity Triunity such as Father, Mother, and Son.

Four is a compounded form of two since in most four meters there is a slight accent felt on three (halfway through the measure), as well as the stronger accent on one. Four suggests a longer stride, more grounded than three, since four expresses the four basic dimensions of this world (height, breadth, and length, plus time). Four is moving out on a longer journey—an extension and subdivision of two.

Five has been called, "The Number of Man", and could express the fingers of the hand or the toes of the foot, four limbs and a head, breaking away from four since it's an odd-numbered meter (and isn't man's purpose to transcend this four-world to higher dimensions?) or perhaps a protest against limitation. Also, two fives could express the decimal system.

Six is a compounding of three since normally there is a slight accent on four, half-way through the measure. Six, like four, is extending the involvement into more variations of the spirallic dance (expanding from duality). But if six can be accented in two groups of three, does it not tend to integrate the turning dance of three with the two of the world of duality? And the same integration would be expressed by accenting six in three groups of two. And do not three plus two make five, the number of Man? 6/8—3/4 is one of my favorite meters, and I definitely find its effect to be integrative. It is quite prevalent in Spanish and Latin American music, where one also often finds three and two following each other.

Seven would express more prolonged working to expand from the duple patterns of this world, placing them in a larger context. Since it can be accented in groups of four and three, or in groups of three and four, it might tend to integrate these patterns. It could also be accented in groups of five and two, but this is not as common. It could also express the weekly routine of seven days at a time. I have found that humans are more influenced by the four seven-day phases of the moon than they are by the western weekly routine.

I would like to digress at this point to give you the dynamics of the moon phases because I have found that anyone who works with other people should be aware of them. Most people who are not aware of the changes in quality of energy through the moon phases are more influenced by them than those who are. The apprentice healer should take into account various factors influencing the client and if the healer should be called upon to act as a focalizer for group or public events, this knowledge can be used creatively. Phase 1, First Quarter, is the time of the birth of thought-forms and goals that you wish to experience and accomplish during the month. Notice wishes and desires, and if you wish to be creative, focus repeated energy on a few that are truly important. Don't put too much energy into action, unless it's just preliminaries, because Phase 2, Second Quarter, tends to be the correct time for the first major actions. I have found so often that actions undertaken in the First Quarter have to be done over again in the second quarter. The energy of "Manifestation" increases until the Full Moon which begins Phase 3, Third Quarter, during which projects begun in the First Quarter usually manifest and come to fruition. The climaxing energies gradually diminish to Phase 4, Fourth Quarter, when the time of "Evaluation" begins. It is at this time that people are moved to *assess* what came forth in the Third Quarter. They are asking the question, "Is this something of value we want to integrate with our lives or was it perhaps not so well-conceived in the first place (First Quarter)?" The energy gradually runs down and it should be a time for feelings of satisfaction and fulfillment, also for rest, to accumulate energies for the next month and to receive guidance concerning what you would like to initiate in the coming First Quarter.

We all exist in an over-stimulated, caffeine-hyped, panting society, most of whose members think that the dark of the moon, or the portion below the line in their biorhythms, is a "drag", a "downer". The solution is to ingest more drugs or seek out other stimulants in order to "ride out" these "meager" times. The result is that during the waxing of the moon, and the biorhythm cycle, most people don't have the accumulated reserves of energy to carry through to completion and fulfillment the opportunities they have set in motion. It is important that the healer understand this phenomenon because it explains why all the techniques that somehow coax the client into taking a vacation from hyperactivity, coming back to center, and spending some time in deeply relaxing and meditative states, brings about such remarkable healing effects. In a society which was too lax, healing techniques would be predominantly stimulating, leading to outer creative activity, but we in the West are coming to the end of an Age which has emphasized scientific mastery of our outside world. For the past 200 years we have been experiencing a swing toward the Yang principle (contractive, active). Of course, clients may need help with their creativity *once they have reached* a state of contemplation and been able to view the addictions and obsessions of their hyperactivity. They can begin to call forth natural flows of energy.

Now let us return to our discussion of the symbolism of numbers in music, more particularly in the left hand, "routine" patterns. Eight appears to be a compounding and subdividing of four, and so would symbolize a further extension of the earthly journey. In addition, the number eight has some very interesting connotations. The figure eight traces the circulation of energy between two halves of a polarized relationship, and in its higher aspect, lying on its side, infinity. I wonder if this is because it expresses the never-ending circulation of creative energy in the Deity Polarity, Divine Father Principle—Divine Mother Principle, when God, the One, splits into God, the Two, for creative manifestation. Just as there is a basic spirallic flow in a human energy field (symbolized by three meter), most human bodies have also a characteristic figure-eight energy flow between the top half and the lower half. Then there is a good deal of esoteric information emerging linking the number eight with The Lords of Sirius, the Christ, the Holy Grail, and dolphins. (See the book, *Holy Blood, Holy Grail.*)

Nine in numerology symbolizes completion just before the new beginning of the ten and is a rich and versatile metric pattern: three groups of three, but also many combinations of three and two. The master Bach developed a great love for 9/8 meter and its even more extended first cousin, 12/8. The meter 11/8 is quite rare, but perhaps it is only just about to enter our music, under Higher Guidance, to bless us with its special qualities.

This should give you a start with the symbology of numbers in music, and I hope it will stimulate you toward further inquiry. You might like to consult a book on Numerology. Of course, these symbolisms apply equally to the broader aspects of *form* in music: the number of measures in a phrase, the number of phrases in a section, the number of sections in a movement and the number of movements in an entire composition. The relationship between all the numbers involved in a piece of music, including pulse, rhythm, meter, frequencies (pitches), chords, dynamics (variations in loudness) and the broader aspects of form are really *all* involved in what we call *harmony*. Wouldn't it be fascinating to take a piece of highly inspired, channeled music and analyze every number aspect of it?! (The Schillinger System provides means for doing just this. See Bibliography.)

Then my friend broke in saying, "Well Joel, if the left hand, I mean the lower part, is expressing the accompanying patterns of life, what are they accompanying? What is the right hand—I guess you'd call that the melody—expressing? Also, I'm curious about what you have to say concerning how these two relate to each other."

Yes, and here the revelation of this channeled music makes a significant contribution to the general theory of the meaning of music. The right hand, the upper part, usually, but not always, melody, is expressing the *actual growth in consciousness* for which the left hand is providing the scaffolding. The upper part is presenting the less mundane, but more evolving, patterns of human consciousness trying to perceive and prove the higher principles of spirit. It does this by mediating between these spiritual principles and worldly experiences (includes Karma or experiential patterns from the past). Of course, this will effect evolution of the patterns of routine. In this music, the right hand plays mostly in the Mental octave, dipping down occasionally into the upper Emotional octave, or even lower, and sometimes ascending into the octaves above the Mental (Intuitional and Spiritual). I find it interesting to note that here in the West, the majority of people are right-handed — the left side of the body and left hand (right brain) being the *receptive* and the right side of the body and right hand (left brain) being the *active*, creative expression; and, of course, a lot of what the right side is expressing is the *growth in consciousness* of which we are speaking.

Now when the two hands are doing the same thing at the same time, it tells us that these two aspects, "routine pattern scaffolding" and "actual spiritualization of human consciousness," are in congruence, or entrained. There are a number of possibilities here. If they are playing in their respective ranges, they would be expressing the alignment that occurs between different levels of being, or consciousness, according to the great law: "As Above So Below." If the right hand descends to join the left hand in the Physical and Emotional octaves, the Mediator (the mind) might be taking a closer look at these more earthly patterns in order to learn more about their fundamental spirituality (since everything is spirit in some form). Similarly, if the left hand joins the right hand in the Mental and Intuitional octaves, it would suggest that the lower patterns were being taken into the mind, or Higher Mind, as thought-forms and subjected to mediation with Higher Principles. (In this book, the words "higher" and "lower" are never to be construed as value judgements, they are simply convenient words to denote planes of slower and faster vibratory frequency.)

A fascinating question that Victor Zuckerkandl brings up in "Sound and Symbol" is whether "higher" notes in music are, in any real sense, higher. Do they collect up near the ceiling in a room? Do "lower" tones settle to the floor? On the harp, "lower" notes are away from me, and "higher" notes are close to me. On a piano, it's to the left and to the right. For a cellist, it's pretty much down and up. So what's going on? Wouldn't it be more realistic to refer to their frequencies and say "slower" and "faster" notes? Even with the Earth itself, the "higher planes" surround the globe, so where is "up"?

Another one of Zuckerkandl's revelations that I love is: if you play one note, it fills the room. If you play three notes, they fill the room. If the 89 players of an orchestra all play a chord together, it still rather nicely fills the room! What can the nature of music tell us then about the nature of space? We suddenly realize we've been a bit brain-washed by basic science, which gives us the "juxtaposition theory," that a thing can only occupy one position in space at a certain time. One good guess is that the nature of music is exhibiting the *transmission* aspect of space. Another lesson here is that the 89 notes filling the space that one note could fill is showing us something about *co-existence*. (There may be some saturation limit here.)

To get back to how the left hand and right hand relate: sometimes the two execute one pattern together, either working equally or one helping the other. The symbolism here might be a focused concentration of energy into co-creation between your Receptive and your Active Creative sides for the accomplishing of a single task. The way this happens most often in the music I channel is when a blessing of higher energies enters the Upper Mental Plane with a trill or tremolo (circular or revolving pattern played by two hands) and moves on down through the bodies into the Physical. This could be seen as a demonstration that these higher energies of illumination have the ability to enlist the cooperation of the levels below them according to the Great Principle: "As Above, So Below."

Then my friend said, "This is very exciting material even though my technical knowledge of music is somewhat limited. How much of this kind of information is being taught in the music schools?"

I answered, "Very little symbolism for the elements of music is taught in the regular classes in universities and conservatories. You might find some in a composition class or in a book in the music library. But when it comes to symbology, you would probably find it scattered through biographies and reviews, certainly not in a textbook, and the philosophical, metaphysical or esoteric symbolisms are much rarer than that."

My friend responded, "Well, then, I think that the consistent way in which all these symbolisms unfolded, and the intercorrelations between different aspects of the system, should be most valuable to many kinds of musicians, students, professors, composers and reviewers, because it suggests a number of new ways of looking at music of the past, especially the more inspired composers. I should think it would be of tremendous value to any performer studying a composition for the first time! These deep elemental symbolisms should prove essential in understanding and interpreting the life of the music, if, as you say, life is music, and music is life. In fact, I could see a whole new school and generation of interpreters and composers basing their work on this system."

And I said, "...not to mention a new generation of music therapists and healers."

We were both becoming more and more exhilarated over the richness and precision of the information I was putting into the tape recorder. I confessed to him that, as I opened up to the subject, I was asking for guidance for the best possible presentation of the system and that a number of the ideas that were coming through were new to me! I remarked, "I guess, since I've been co-creating with these Higher Intelligences using this system, if I focus my energy and attention on the subject it is impossible for me *not* to be channeling."

He said, "Great! Then you'll be learning and expanding from this book yourself, and this in turn will expand the work. But there's something that I've been wondering about? Don't you have in music, spaces between the notes in a tune, and are they the same kind of spaces between the notes of a chord?"

"You're absolutely right. The pitches outline these spaces and they're called 'intervals'. I've spent a great deal of time trying to figure out their true nature. What I have come to is that if one pitch is played after another, since your consciousness is pretty much continuous and not intermittent, you *journey* from one note to the next across the distance of the interval. Whether it's a long journey or a short journey is not so involved in the meaning of "interval," but is a function of the beat and rhythm in the music. So it's an experience of traversing space apart from how long it takes you, except that a wider interval could symbolize a wider leap. This is a space you can measure by the two frequencies involved, but as an aural, vibratory experience, it is more realistically defined by the psychological dynamics of *expectancy* and *fulfillment*."

You see, within a key or a family of notes, some are more "active," which the listener would like to resolve into those that are more "passive" (or at rest). What makes a note more relatively active or passive is the numerical ratio (a two-number fraction) of its frequency to the frequency of any particular note in the music context, especially the keynote as the fundamental of an Overtone Series of which the note we are considering is a part (even though we are in a tempered scale).

What we have touched into here is a precise definition of consonance and dissonance (apart from an individual's *association* for an interval) based on a note's relationship with its fundamental, expressed as a two-number fraction. The more complex the fraction, the more dissonant the note; the simpler the fraction, the more consonant. By "complex" is meant: "the higher the numbers involved, after the fraction has been reduced as far as possible." By "simple" is meant: "the lower the numbers involved after the fraction has been reduced."

All we need to know for our discussion of the journey we experience from one note to the next, is that the note you have been hearing creates anticipation of the next note according to its "activity" or "passivity," which is either satisfied, or not satisfied, to some degree. The regular beat and the rhythm would also affect this anticipation. So after at least two notes are struck, you are experiencing them, sustained or dying away, and you have embarked on an anticipatory trajectory toward the next note. Of course, the next pitch may be one of a myriad of frequencies, each one of which will provide you with a different experience of relative fulfillment or expectancy (you could also call it *tension* and *release*), and which sends you off on the *next* journey. You usually hope that the next note isn't going to be too outrageously shocking, and that it will be fulfilling, or at least interesting, and stimulating within the context of your own taste. But you could be a listener who is so bored or jaded in life that you crave the excitement of "outrageous" notes!

In any case, the aural adventurer sets forth on the journey from each note innocently and hopefully, putting his psyche into the hands of the composer. So the pitches are like fixed points, steps or plateaus, and the intervals are like momentary flights. Of course, we experience a melody more as flights than steps since we get to know the frequencies fairly quickly.

Since we've delved so deeply into the experience of traversing pitches, perhaps we should notice some other features of experiencing a melody. Just as the progression of tones conditions the experience of each succeeding tone, the frequency of each new tone changes the significance of the preceding tones! Here's an example: If you start with middle C and proceed up the scale with D, E, F, G, A and B, you have established the first note C, as the key center and you have created a strong anticipation to hear the next note, C, as a resolution (like coming home to a home away from home). However, if you were to play after the A a B♭, you suddenly shift the feeling of the key center from C to F, and you might rather hear it resolve downwards to an A, the third of the F chord, and you now hear the original C as a dominant of F. If you play this on the piano it will become immediately clear. So, when you're hearing a melody, you're locked into the present, but you are relating, in an ever-changing way to past "presents" and future "presents." This is a very interesting philosophical model because we are learning something from the nature of the succession of frequencies in music and how we experience this which we can apply to how we live life. Live fully the present moment, relating to past "presents" and future "presents."

Another interesting facet of this model is that it provides an answer to the question, "What is moving in a melody?" You see, the problem is that the pitches (fixed steps) do not move one to the other and, as a matter of fact, if they did slide one into the next, it would *destroy* the melody! And yet when we hear a succession of tones we experience it as a trajectory! Now we can see that what is moving in a melody is our own continuous consciousness taking off on flights of adventure, short hops in a longer, aural odyssey!

But you asked also about the intervals in chords. These are more illusory because a voyage is not involved. They are experienced more as the positioning or placing of the constituent parts of a whole. And this experience is really more than just a function of frequency, because you can take the same four notes and arrange them in a number of different patterns, all having different intervals between the notes even though the arrangement is still simultaneous (vertical in the written music). Here's a good example of the difference in how we experience melody and chords even though the pitches used might be the same. Let's say you visit a new town and your friend offers to take you for a drive to check out four of the surrounding prominent landmarks. It's a journey and you experience going from one to the next and then back home (like a melody). The next morning he announces that he's just gotten his license to fly and he's going to take you up. He flies you up high enough so that you can see all four landmarks at once. That's like a chord and you experience the distance between them and their relative positioning in a different way. The chart in the Appendix on the symbolism of intervals is concerned somewhat with how one experiences traversing an interval but even more with the "position in the chord" aspect. It should be mentioned in passing that the faster the notes are in a melody, the more you are liable to hear them as chords, and that chords can be strung out as melodies.

Let us begin with the first note, or Root, of the chord. The next most closely related note would be the same note an octave higher. We are basing this on the first division (into two) of the string producing the Overtone Series. Whenever you have a note and its repetition an octave higher in this system, it symbolizes the higher significance of whatever archetypal quality the first note represents. This is why the range of the harp is broken up into octaves each representing a higher frequency-level of being.

The next note to consider would be the fifth which, as we have said earlier, is the Actualizing or Manifesting Principle of the Root, the interval of the fifth symbolizing Creation.

The next two intervals are the Major third and the minor third and when we add these intervals between the Root and the fifth, we get the Major and minor Triad, the building blocks of western traditional music. Now the thirds and their inversions, the sixths, are the color intervals in music, providing its richness and beauty. So they symbolize the Sense of Beauty of the Root quality, the Major symbolizing the Yang, right side, Active Principle, the Outer Expression; and the minor symbolizing the Inner Expression of the Sense of Beauty of that quality, Yin, left side and Receptive. These significances are, of course, related to an individual in my work but, by analogy, have wider application.

Next come the Major and minor sevenths expressing the relationship of the individual to the group immediately surrounding. And similarly to the thirds and sixths, the Major seventh has to do with the outer, active, more physical, Yang activities with the group; whereas the minor seventh has to do with the Yin, inner modes of working with the group, using probably more intuition and awareness. The Major interval would be more objective and the minor more subjective.

The next interval that appears in the series is the second, the inversion of the seventh. (An easy way to find the inversion of an interval is to move the lower note up an octave.) Seconds are the intervals of which scales are made, and so they symbolize the steps we take, larger or smaller, progressing toward a goal (the Octave). Major seconds would symbolize steps in the outer world, whereas minor seconds, steps in the inner world. Now this gets even more interesting because, as individuals, we might tend to think of the seconds coming before the sevenths, but in the natural generation of tones from the Fundamental (the Overtone Series) the sevenths come first. We can infer from this that the more consonant and unifying and stabilizing sequence of events is to take care of your relations with the group immediately around you, and then turn to your individual activities. And isn't this true in society? Going off to pursue your life alone is a rarity and growing through family, friends, and profession is far richer and healthier and is supportive of culture, civilization and racial evolution. Just like the thirds and sixths, the seconds and sevenths are inversions of each other, and have to do with growing and progressing—the sevenths being a much more expanded way of growing than the seconds, just as the sixths are a much more expansive Sense of Beauty than the thirds. The Major seventh inverts to the minor second, the minor seventh inverts to the Major second, the Major sixth inverts to the minor third and the minor sixth inverts to the Major third.

I have found that intervals larger than the octave have to do with an individual's relationship with the wider world beyond the immediate group. The Major and minor ninths are the only ones that I seem to comment on with any frequency in the readings and they express outer and inner steps an individual takes in the relationship with city, state, country or world.

There is another interval which becomes symbolically important once in awhile, and that is the Augmented Fourth or Diminished Fifth (C-F# —or C-Gb). This is the next new note that appears in the Overtone Series after the ninth or second degree of the scale, and symbolizes the relationship of polar opposites. It is halfway through the scale C to C. If this interval appears alone in the music without any "tonal friend" for support and harmonization, it would symbolize dissonance in some kind of relationship, but within a dominant seventh chord becomes (as the third and seventh) much more integrated and harmonized. A beautiful example of this is how much we love bells and gongs. These instruments embody the blending of two Overtone Series an augmented fourth apart! It should be noted here that the augmented fourth is not quite so dissonant when it occurs naturally in the Overtone Series. It's lower than on the piano where it's about as much too high as the Major third, but not quite as high as the Minor seventh.

* * * * * *

You can perhaps imagine my intense satisfaction as each piece of this system revealed itself and as the coherence of the system as a whole became evident. As more and more details appeared, the fact that it really came all at once, that is, ready to use with clients, seemed more and more as some kind of miracle. Then there was the exhilaration of being involved in the birth of a new form of healing. I had heard of one or two musicians who would tune-in to a person and play their music and one of these, listening back to the music, would receive impressions of past-lives. In neither case were the lives specifically integrated with the music. There wasn't a section for each life or a system of symbolism for each element of the music. Nor was there the correlation of the letters of the name with the music through the use of a letter-pitch equivalent code.

At this writing, eighteen years and 2,300 attunement sessions later, I still have not heard of another music healer using this system even though I have done these sessions and presented workshops throughout the United States and Canada and five countries in Europe. In the past few years I have heard of five or six musicians who do "music portraits" and some of these receive past-life impressions but don't have the system. I meet many musicians after concerts who would like to open up to this kind of work, who have a smouldering fire in their eyes when they talk about it, and are obviously under guidance to develop it, but are struggling as to how to begin. For most of these, I am the only music healer they have met who is actually doing it. It is especially for these valiant souls that this chapter, so full of scientifically demonstrable systems, is written. I hasten to add that I don't present any of these findings as finally proven facts! This is a system that seems fairly unified and which has worked for me, over a period of years, in over 2,000 cases. Check it out for yourself and see if it works.

Then my friend said, "You know, this might be as good a time as any to give some pointers to musicians who would like to channel healing music for others. How can they get started or at least prepare themselves so the Higher Forces can lead them into it?"

"Oh, thanks. I've been waiting for an opportunity to do that." First of all, most of the music healers I know are doing quite different types of work, so there is a lot of room in the field. Since it is a young profession I guess the Higher Forces have decided that more clients can be served by a variety of music healers. I have felt for many years that in the general field of alternative medicine we are going to need all the good healers we can get.

The first thing you will need to do is develop your improvizing skills to a fine art. Learn many different patterns: scales, chords, meters, rhythms, styles, etc. The more extensive your musical vocabulary, the more the higher musicians can bring through you! Of course the more promise you show, and the more you sincerely *ask* for guidance, the more they will actually *teach* you as you improvize.

Then, when the improvization is going well and you've gained some fluency with patterns, especially those that feel uplifting and meaningful, or symbolic, in the healing process, I strongly recommend saying an affirmation. Develop the habit of saying it before you play to set up the conditions of protection, the purpose of the session, and to open you as a channel to co-create with Higher Forces (see Commentary in Chapter VII, and the two affirmations in Appendix I. After all these years I still say my affirmations!)

You will need to practice putting the ego aside (actually expanding it with universal love) and becoming super-receptive, and in this state you will want to feel protected. Begin to play for groups and then individuals. At first it might be a good idea not to charge for this (if possible) — keep it a pure offering (later on you can charge for your time). In your heart offer your music for whatever and wherever God would like to use it. The requests will start coming to you, providing you've done your homework and it's within your life-plan to grow through channeling music. But also, go ahead and offer your services (non-aggressively) to churches, New Age centers, study groups, weddings, funerals, meditations, rituals, etc. Say your affirmation *every* time you play.

You could also ask that your psychic perceptions be gently opened, and begin to practice clairvoyance and clairaudience, etc. All the time hold the thought that you will stay in balance and harmony, and ask for this guidance. Constantly ask for protection. It might help also to have a practice time at a certain time each day or each week, if possible, to show your dedication and to make it easier for your guides to meet with you (they have other duties, you know!)

Then, when you feel guided, and you see someone in need, offer to play some music for them. Without making any specific claims of healing, you can say general things like: "This music I've been bringing through seems to have an uplifting effect on people" or "Maybe if we ask for it, we can bring through some music that could bring you some peace, some balance, some harmony" or "Maybe the music could be a catalyst for a change in your condition; it has happened, you know." Call forth the words that the person could handle. Or you can mention a past case where your channeled music did help someone (especially if they know them). If it doesn't make either of you nervous, do record the music so that your friend can use it, providing you feel good about how it came out. You will know by how charged you and the room feel afterwards. Keep a copy for yourself so you can study it—there may be new patterns in it. Tell your client how the tape may be used. Then phone them up a few days later to check on the effectiveness of the music and to remind them to use the tape.

Here is something very important to remember: always encourage other channels. We are all one family and you will be encouraging *yourself* —and keeping your channel open. On a basic level: the "potential market" for healing with music is practically everyone in the world since the whole world is so out of balance at this time and music can take a person to such high levels of awareness. Truly, there is no competition; growth through competition is a scaffolding we want to drop as soon as we can. Then we can bless everyone's creativity and be stimulated by it. Co-create with other channels whenever possible— you'll learn a lot this way. Also this "consorted" music can be most healing for the listener, helping with *relationships.*

Then if you need to charge your clients so you can take the time to keep up with requests and your new activities, it's perfectly all right: you're not charging for the healing that gets done—just your time. Your rates can be adjusted to your realistic needs. The Law here is: "If you're serving life, life will serve you."

The Higher Forces are just waiting for artists with which to co-create who are dedicated enough to service. Examine your heart and if you find any ulterior motives there, better process them or go into some other line of work! They would backfire on you! Not that it is required that you be perfect to be a good channel—just that your intentions be pure, and that you can develop the habit of putting aside everything but those intentions when you channel for others. Hence the importance of the affirmation—it creates a habit of intention. It's a signal to which you train yourself to respond.

Another aspect of your training: keep your ears tuned for music with powerful healing qualities and start a collection. Check out its effect on yourself by sitting in a meditative state: body, emotions, and mind, very relaxed but alert. Then ask yourself to be super-sensitive to the sounds and music you are about to hear. Notice just how you respond to the music and its effect on you afterwards. Observe any changes in your physical body, your emotional body, and your mental body, and also how changes in these relate to each other. Did the music tend to harmonize and align them?

In this way you can really begin to find out which music is good for you and which isn't. Often after this realistic appraisal people will throw out two-thirds of their music library! When you have collected a number of tapes or records containing healing patterns you might want to adapt some of these patterns to your instrument and then see if you're guided to use them. There are, of course, many patterns in this book which might be valuable to you. But seek your own guidance: perhaps new material is going to come through you in some of these areas. There is a great richness in what has come through this channel and, having seen what it can accomplish, I feel you could do a lot worse than use this material and see where it leads you, being open to its further evolution. But you and your guides be the judges. It's possible also that you are to be stimulated to co-create something different but somehow related to what has been developed through me. It would be a joy to me if you did and I would support you all the way in this. I welcome you to the Fraternity of Musicians of the Spiritual Renaissance: explorers of the highest destiny of music: to transcend words and bring to a world in need: peace, beauty, transformation, ecstasy and spiritual upliftment, to build the rainbow bridge to higher planes, beings and forces.

If this chapter stimulates experimentation, research and corroboration, as well as extending lines of discovery, it will have served its purpose. There is an interesting study that I have been wanting to make which might be suitable as a master's thesis in a liberal music department. This would be to take the subject matter of arias (songs) written by master composers such as Bach and Handel and correlate these with the archetypal symbolism of the key in which the aria was composed. This would show whether the composer was consciously (or intuitively) using the system. This study could be expanded to cover even instrumental music where there was a definite descriptive or programmatic content.

The basic premise of this chapter, that there is correlation between the fundamental aspects of sound (through numbers, shapes and symbols) with similar aspects of the human being, has been proven to my satisfaction not only by my own ministry, but by the work of the Swiss scientist, Hans Jenny, ("Cymatics"). He passed different vibrations through various liquids and substances and photographed the patterns produced. These patterns provide convincing proof that underlying all creation are numbers and frequencies arranged in basic, understandable, and logical patterns. On these patterns are built variations leading to more and more complex and highly-evolved forms of life. Jenny demonstrates that it is through these basic configurations that we can correlate all life forms; and thus, that the universe exhibits Higher Intelligence, Order and Harmony.

"Music is the universal language of mankind."

Henry Wadsworth Longfellow

CHAPTER ELEVEN

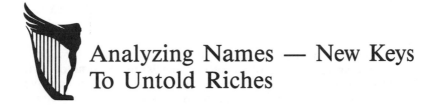

Analyzing Names — New Keys To Untold Riches

Can you imagine my excitement when, early in 1974, I realized I had learned so much about the meaning of the letters of a person's name that a recorded analysis of it might be of great benefit? By this time, the system of symbolism for each letter of the alphabet, revealed by The Sources, had become fairly complete. Remember that as I played the name under guidance at the beginning of each reading, I had the choice of going upwards or downwards for each new letter. I had been shown that the descending and ascending directions of the melody signified involution and evolution, and this could be added to a name analysis. I was intrigued by the possibility that such a method of analyzing names might add new dimensions to what has already been developed in Numerology (the symbology of words by translating the letters into numbers). This has proven true as we shall see. In addition, I found that a Name Analysis provides a client with "evidential" — a kind of cross-reference — proving the reliability of the clairvoyance as well as the symbology of the music. Patterns can be seen in the name which have already emerged in the music.

At this point, my friend, who has more of a feeling for what the average person might be thinking (and thus for what you, dear reader, might be thinking) broke in saying, "This name business is fascinating. But before you plunge into the details, could you tell me a little more about the general significance of a person's name? Why is a name important?"

I replied, "Thanks for that essential question." When I asked The Sources what was really happening when a person used their name, I received some surprising insights. First of all, you use your name in four ways: 1) you write it, 2) you speak it, 3) you hear it called and respond, and 4) you think of yourself internally as your name. According to the

Free Will Plan, we are, to a great extent, self-actualizing beings. This means that the words "I am" constitute probably the most powerful mantrum in the language! We should watch carefully whatever we associate with those two words. That which we affirm, we become. So we must realize that every time we use our names we are saying "I am this name." If someone says, "Who are you?", we answer, "I am so-and-so." You can see that if the letters for the sounds of a name have significance, their meaning is of vital importance since a person is taking on their significances constantly!

Because of this, there is much guidance from unseen forces (personal guardian angels and other karmic angels) at the time of birth. Should the ego of a parent get too much in the way, such a name will only occasionally be written and almost never spoken. I have been told that, where there was no name on the birth certificate, the word "female" or "male" contained the correct, although temporary, vibrations for the optimum growth of that child. Also, in the vast majority of cases, I have found that the nickname supplies letters and vibrations not found in the given name. So, the unseen forces can make corrections through the use of a nickname, especially where some vibrations of the name are to be reserved for a later time in life. Often, when a man marries, his wife encourages him to use his given name. Or, a client may say to me, "That name was given to me, but I have never used it." Then, too, people come to a time in their life when they're guided to change their name! If it is coming from Higher Guidance, they should. I can help them by telling them what vibrations various names are going to attract.

If names are this important, shouldn't we be most careful how we say a person's name? If it is so intimately bound up with who they are and are becoming, shouldn't we intone it clearly, positively, resonantly, and beautifully? And with the knowledge that a person gets the right name, containing the right vibrations, shouldn't we overcome our prejudices against certain names and stop intoning them in a derisive manner? In my work, I have found that many names I thought were hilarious turned out to contain very high vibrations. I will refrain from giving any examples of these, because I have found that tastes vary considerably in what constitutes a funny name. A short perusal of the telephone book will usually produce incredulous laughter in the average person. Yet, now I know that every name in the phone book is the optimum growth pattern for that individual. If they came for a reading from me, it would be exquisite. Laughter at names, then, becomes a study in one of our favorite pastimes, judging others, and is unmasked as release of tension when faced with the exotic unknown! Given, then, the intimate correlation between our names and who we are, the person behind a strange—seeming name could be just as strange, but we must train ourselves to remember that behind appearances is our brother or sister. To be sure, the more you can put this into practice, *the less strange you will seem to those around you!* Moreover, many people act strangely because *they think* they're strange; that is, they have accepted other people's judgement of them! You might be able to help them honor their own individuality without losing their status as bonafide members of the human race, with equal spiritual status under God.

Now let us turn our attention to what The Sources have revealed concerning the symbolism of your names. Bear in mind that these symbolisms have proven their veracity over an 18-year period in some 1,800 Individual Name Analyses, and in my analysis of the words of my world over this period. To this date I can only remember one or two clients who said the name analysis didn't fit them. I assume that these were probably cases where the clients asked for truth, and then resisted it, as happens occasionally during and immediately after readings by all psychics. Clients may change their minds with further study of the tape. Also, their names may have fit them earlier in life.

First of all, your full name, as you write it or say it, is a continuous sequence of letters, sounds and qualities. We are told that this is a progression of archetypal vibrations you are traversing in any natural time-frame. This means that you are experiencing the sequence of these qualities in a day, the 28-day moon cycle, the year, any cycle of years that is significant for you, such as seven or 28, and your whole life. At any given hour of the day, you could be expressed by a cord or cluster of archetypal qualities made up of the letters or pitches of where you are in your day, in the moon cycle, in the year, also in your birth year that starts on your birthday, in your other year cycles, and in your whole life.

Secondly, your name naturally breaks down into three aspects of you: your first name, all middle names and maiden names used as middle names, and your last name. A first name is your Essential Self, your Ego Projection into life. I sometimes call it the Outer Expression or the Personality, but the middle names (the subconscious) and the last name (activities) also contribute to these last two aspects. Do keep in mind that these three categories are all working toward oneness and harmony and you are trying to encourage all aspects of your being to work together. Your middle name is the key to your subconscious or what I prefer to call your Basic Self or Selves. Ever since Freud, who called it the "UN-conscious," we have been uncovering the rich intelligence of the subconscious. We can no longer call it "sub" or "lesser" in intelligence than the conscious mind, even though it may be more or less centered lower in the body, that is, in the general area of the abdominal cavity, and I am finding Basic Selves occupying a variety of other positions. Your Basic Selves take care of the 500 functions of the liver and this is just one organ among many! They carry the wisdom from the past that you might call "body consciousness" and this certainly includes some high forms of specialized intelligence. If you have more than one middle name, each one represents a different aspect of your subconscious and perhaps a different Basic Self. If you were given a middle name, but are now using a maiden name as a middle name, you are adding the qualities of a past Activity Pattern to the qualities of the subconscious that you already have. It seems fitting, doesn't it, that the name which is emblematic of the subconscious, the somewhat hidden part of you, should be found in the "interior" of your names, between your first and last names? If you don't have or don't use a middle name, it suggests that your subconscious is expressing itself through your first and last names.

We know that dreams are the language of the subconscious. Whenever I meet people who don't have a middle name I ask them how easy it is to remember their dreams. They almost invariably reply that it is difficult to remember them unless they make a great effort. Not having a middle name doesn't mean that you don't have a subconscious, but it can mean that this inner aspect of you is somewhat hidden and not so ready to make itself known.

Your last name represents your Pathway, your Activity Pattern, the sequence of qualities you go through when you are in action or at work. Coming at the end of the name, it shows, in a way, the result or manifestation of the first two names. We know from history that a person's last name often came from his occupation, such as Smith (a goldsmith), Tanner (a leather man), and Wright (a boatwright or playwright). Looked at in a slightly different way, your first name would represent your Conscious Mind, the Initiator, your middle name would represent the karmic patterns from your past that you're working with, and your last name would express the growing edge of what you're doing with these two. Many women have come to me with a number of past married names. When I told them what they meant they attested to how their life paths had changed with each marriage. This brings up a most valuable insight that has come through for all married women. YOUR LAST NAME IS JUST AS MUCH YOURS AS IT IS HIS. You are together for what The Sources call "sweet abrasion," because you deserve each other for "negative" and "positive" karma, so you have earned that name just as he has earned it. Now each of you might be drawing the experience that the name carries from different sources in the past. The melody might take on a different contour, and the Purpose of Growth of the name might be slightly different, and yet the last name is a general archetypal pathway, as well as skills, that you share. This has been a revelation to many married women (as well as men!).

The first letter of each name (the initial) is expressing the Purpose of Growth which you have chosen for this incarnation for that aspect of you. The music of the reading has shown us the path that you chose, at the beginning of this series of lives, or at the very beginning of your lives on Earth, as your pathway of soul growth toward God-realization. Your initials show us subpurposes of that soul-path that you wish to complete to achieve synthesis in this life, and possible ascension. The remaining letters in the body of each name show what you're drawing on from past-life experience in many times and places. The qualities in the body of each name characterize the aspect which that name symbolizes and are helping you to master your chosen purpose of growth in that area of your life.

One of the very significant contributions of this system is that once the letters of your name are translated into pitches, we can see the musical interval that one letter makes with the letter before it and the letter after it. If you can get a feeling for the relative consonance or dissonance of the musical intervals, you can easily feel the degree of tension, or of peace, that exists in how one quality relates to the quality on either side of it. Through the symbolism of each interval, we learn even more about these relationships. What we have in your name, then, is your *melody*. As you might have suspected, parts of this melody do appear in a person's channeled music.

People who have delved into metaphysical literature ask me sometimes if I can tell them their note. I usually answer, "Well, what would you do with it if I gave it to you?" To ease their consternation, I hastily add, "I might be able to give you your melody, some of your chords and some of your symphony!"

In my own studies, I have come across passages which say that if your note were sounded, you would reach instant enlightenment. I speculate on the number of souls who accidentally heard their note and were instantly translated to the shores of Paradise without much experience of what lay in between! Other passages state that, if you heard your note, you would instantly die. I suspect that the "notes" being referred to here, while they may be understood by Higher Beings, are not accessible to us on Earth as we are not evolved enough to use them responsibly.

The final chord of a Life Attunement Session expresses the client's potential to complete the deepest underlying soul-purpose. While there have been miracles of ecstatic upliftment and healing, no one, so far, has translated at the end of the session! On the other hand, a person's channeled music can bring them the uplifting ecstacy of who they really are, put them in touch with their highest purposes, and set them on the patient path toward their greater unfoldment in The Light.

Here's a phenomenon that took me awhile to figure out: at the beginning of a reading, after I play the birthdate and the name, the first life of the present series almost always begins with the same notes that end the client's name. Also, in almost every reading, we find that the last two or three chords of the music at the end of the present-life are the same as the last two or three notes in the name. Now remember that we said the last name represents the culmination or manifestation of the first two names.

What I finally realized was that these notes at the end of your name represent your potential to finish the soul-purpose begun at the beginning of this subseries of lives — the completion of a grand circle. Once in awhile, the last note in the name, and the last chord in the music, is the deeper underlying soul-purpose that goes back to the beginning of all lives on Earth. Occasionally, the last two or three notes of the name will be expressed in chords. Then comes a chord expressing the potential to complete the underlying soul-purpose going all the way back. Or perhaps I get just the E chord itself, which is pure Light. These final chords appear in the channeled music, in spite of the fact that I am not looking at the written name after I play it in the beginning of the reading. This is another "evidential" showing the internal consistency of the system and the presence of Higher Guidance.

Let us take a common example of two letters that create a good deal of tension between them if they are adjacent in a client's name, such as "C" and "O" (in pitches, the interval C-C#, a half-step). "C" symbolizes "ordinary survival-type challenges," whereas "O" symbolizes "ability to manifest artistic sensitivity in the physical when it serves others." Let's say these two letters are linked up in a woman's name, I will ask her if she is experiencing conflict between these two aspects of her life. Almost invariably, she will say that she is. Then I tell her that when she is bothered by this conflict, she might separate the two in space and time; that is, conduct her survival activities in one place at one time of the day or week, and pursue her artistic creativity in service to others at another. When she has eased the tension, then she can gently bring them together with the idea of learning how to harmonize them. I tell her that everything in her name represents her highest growth processes, and that there isn't anything which can't be harmonized — with God's help.

Another interesting creative tension is between the letter "G" ("how to go about survival-type challenges") and the letter "I" ("manifesting artistic creativity for self development"). These two create the musical interval of the Tritone or Augmented Fourth, G-C#. The Tritone expresses, since it is one-half of the scale, "polarization," and this interval can be one of the most difficult to resolve. I give the client the same advice as with C-C#, but this musical interval suggests a resolution (dominant to tonic) into the key of D (Human Love). So in any situation involving tension between these two aspects of life I suggest that the client resolve it into human love. Of course, any Tritone can be resolved either outwards or inwards, but it will be obvious which way to go since one key (in this case Ab) is much more esoteric and remote than the other (D).

Concerning the letters in the body of your names which show what you're drawing from the past, it has become clear that your name shows only the primary qualities that you are bringing to the fore in this present incarnation to help you with your purposes of growth. While you may carry in your subconscious the total of past experience, and might be able to recall any of it at certain special times, many of these patterns lie in a latent state. To activate them might be a temptation to digress from your chosen purposes into a familiar and easier path of repetition. I have found that these latent skills and sensitivities do exhibit themselves through understanding, sympathy, and appreciation of those around you who are similarly engaged. This gives us the key to understanding the lack of certain letters or qualities in a person's name.

I don't believe I have ever found a name that contained all 12 qualities of the system. Out of the 1,800, I would say the average number of pitches lacking in a name would be three; there have been quite a number lacking two, and just a few lacking only one. I have seen as many as six lacking, and occasionally seven. The more qualities that are lacking in a person's name, the more concentration of certain qualities you will find in the name (unless it is quite short) and the more the person is *focusing* on certain types of work to complete their purposes of growth. I tell clients that I should tell them about the vibrations that are lacking in their names so that they might understand themselves better. I explain to them that they may have experienced these qualities in the past (sometimes we can get an idea of whether they have from their past-life music), that this is according to a higher design, and that they will accomplish things in the areas of "lacking" with the skills that they did bring through. If it seems they haven't worked on a particular quality, I always say that all the qualities are present in God's universe, just waiting to be drawn forth and developed.

Quite often, I find that the client is not drawing forth past experience in the qualities of one or two of the initials (Purposes of Growth). They wish to learn new ways of dealing with these challenges. Also, some qualities are less common than others in the body of names, and I often find them missing, such as "F" (past direct contact with the angelic order), and "Z" (the equivalent of the physical plane on another planet), and "W" (attunement to life experience outside Earth). Often, it is already clear to both the client and myself, why they aren't bringing through a certain quality. They could have spent the previous incarnation entirely devoted to artistic productivity and so carry over into this life three, or perhaps four, F#'s (artistic sensitivity), but very few C#'s (the inclination or ability to manifest it physically). The C#'s could have brought them the temptation to repeat themselves. It is a revelation to realize that the people around you may be carrying highly developed skills and talents which they may only show through appreciation. It is also of great value to know that a person may be concentrating on certain things in this lifetime and is not supposed to be eclectic or versatile, and to be able to learn this fact just from the perusal of the name.

The way I check through a name to find missing pitches (qualities) is to go through the Cycle of Fifths, scanning through the whole name for each pitch—F, C, G, D, A, E, B, F#, C#, G#, D#, A#, E#. I don't normally expect the last three.

Another aspect of the qualities valuable to comment on, is the balance between the A's and E's in a person's name. Keep in mind that I'm speaking of qualities (pitches not letters). Here I'm commenting on the balance between attunement to the Divine Mother Principle (the letters "A", "N", and "T"), and the Divine Father Principle (the letters "E", "K", and "Q"). Since these two great aspects of God are equally Divine, each can be seen as a legitimate pathway toward God-realization. I often see a client pursuing one of these paths for a series of lives and then turning to the other for balance. One can grow by concentrating one's attention and sensitivities on the physical world, achieving some mastery of material things, then begin to look for the Divinity of that world, learning that matter is truly Light in form, that all dimensions of life on Earth have consciousness, from the minerals on up. The danger here lies in becoming so identified with matter that you lose touch with your own Divinity.

The other path involves attuning yourself directly to the Light, the Solar Logos, sometimes called the Christ Spirit, trying to achieve as direct as possible a union with the Father Principle, then trying to anchor this Light in Earth to bring it into manifestation in the physical world. The danger here lies in losing touch with practical physical reality here on Earth, as one spends so much time in meditative states, and risking being unable to maintain the body adequately. While it may be proper and valuable for a particular soul to follow one or the other of these paths for a few lives, the most complete, balanced and harmonious state is the holy wedding of the two attunements. And it is this "wholiness" toward which we are all evolving, especially in the present life where so many are trying to finish their series of lives.

An interesting dimension of the A-E balance is that it gives a rough indication of the male-female balance of the subject. We are all both male and female in some kind of balance, and carry with us memory of both male and female embodiments. In fact, my recent research into the nature of the Basic Selves, (and I will report on this in the next chapter), shows that the vast majority of us have Basic Selves that are male, and also Basic Selves that are female. Of course, our inner sexuality is always in flux, but I have found it uncanny how accurate an indication the balance between the A's and E's in a person's name can be. Early in the readings, the Sources kept saying that one of our most important tasks as evolving young adults, is to transfer our need for mothering and fathering from our human mothers and fathers, first to Mother Earth and Father

Sun, and then on to Divine Mother and Divine Father. Our mothers and fathers have been surrogates for these aspects of God. We should be grateful for the services they have performed and as soon as we graciously can, help them release these roles and return to the status of our brothers and sisters—fellow children of God.

I remember when my mother passed away, it took me some months to release her, and part of this was truly letting her go *as a mother.* When I was finally able to do this, I had the following experience. I was attending a workshop led by Kay Ortmans. We were asked to choose a colored sheet from a pile on the floor, and dance with it to the music. When I got to the pile there was only one left, and it was black, the last color I would normally choose. I accepted it, put it over my head, and not feeling like dancing, sat down on the floor. Here I was, sitting alone, enshrouded in black (which symbolizes the Dark Principle, or Divine Mother) and Earth Mother came to me.

She said, "Now that you have released your mother, I will be your mother. I offer you the abundance of the Earth and mothering whenever you need it. Come to me." Of course, years of work led up to this experience, just as it did before the experience five years previously when the Father came to me as my dad.

Once you know the pitches of your name, you could learn to play it on an instrument or even sing it. I'm sure that playing or singing your name calls forth the true you, awakening the skills and talents developed in the past and the pathways of evolution and growth embodied in your initials. If you have developed musical abilities, you can even improvize compositions on the themes of your names.

Can you imagine how valuable this new method of name analysis could be in the business world? Often, in everyday affairs, one receives letters from persons one has never met. They normally don't give you their birthdate, so you don't have any astrological clues about them, and they usually don't write you in longhand, so you can't do a quick graphological analysis. But they do give you their names, and thus reveal a great deal about themselves if you have learned this method of analysis and even more if you know numerology. If you were receiving applications for jobs, you would want to know what skills and talents a person was carrying from the past. It would also be of value to know what their chosen purposes of growth are. These two factors would largely condition how well they would do in a certain position. Knowledge of a person's name could even supplement what you have learned through working with someone. The applications are endless.

Let us return to an actual Life Attunement session. The first thing I do after the Affirmation is to play, under guidance, the birthdate, and the names which I have previously translated into pitches. This ability can certainly be developed by anyone with experience in improvizing who has developed also humility, dedication, clairaudient sensitivity, and relia- bility. The pitch of each initial could come through in any combination of the Levels of Being on the harp: Physical, Emotional, Mental or Psy- chic (the four octaves starting with A, first space in the bass clef). For most of the clients who come to me for readings, the Purpose of Growth of the Essential Self comes in all three octaves (Physical, Emotional, and Mental). The Purpose of Growth of the Basic Selves usually appears in one or both of the lower two octaves (Physical and Emotional). If the Mental octave is occasionally sounded, it usually comes just after the lower two. This symbolizes that the subconscious is carrying a past pattern of stimulating the conscious mind, because this octave is not normally its area of activity. Then the initial for the last name (Activity Patterns) usual- ly sounds in all three octaves. I assume I'm getting all three octaves on the first and last names because nowadays people are really trying to "get it all together," to synthesize and complete their series of lives. Keep in mind that the letter "W" might come through as the note E# if the client is trying to develop direct attunement with outer space. Or, it might come through as an F, if the client is enlisting the aid of the devas and angels to help make this attunement.

After the Purpose of Growth is played, there is the choice of where to play the next note and choice of going either upwards or downwards to each succeeding pitch. These directions are highly significant. Just as in the channeled music, if the melody goes down to a certain pitch or quality, it means that when you're tuning in to that quality, it is going to involve you in life for adventure and growth (involution or descen- sion); if the melody goes up to a pitch or quality, it means that quality is helping you to spiritualize yourself (evolution or ascension).

An interesting question just occurred to me: should the upwards or downwards direction that *follows* a certain pitch be considered the result of that quality? After some thought, I realized that the answer is "no" because, according to the nature of music, the arrangement of pitches in a melody does not create the next pitch. This is the prerogative of the creator of the melody. Although the arrangement of pitches in a melody creates anticipations for a certain note, or notes, the creator of the melo- dy is always deciding how much to satisfy these anticipations, depend- ing on the effect that is being created. Also, in the case of names, the next quality must be positioned in the correct octave. In an analysis, I don't usually go into the positions in the octaves of each quality the client is drawing on, but this would be a possibility.

Now I can comment on another of the tension patterns that appears in names. Where you find a half-step resolving upwards such as G#-A or C#-D, it suggests the completion of an octave of steps of growth in the scale of the last note. I explain to the client that life is often difficult at the completion of a series of steps toward a goal; that they should not avoid any challenge related to this completion, and that they should practice patience, seek guidance, and "hang in there" to complete the series. This explains the type of tension being expressed by this half-step in the person's name. If the melody returns to step one from step seven, this would symbolize the need to return to the original purpose of the steps of growth prior to completion.

Another interesting pattern is repeated pitches. Two pitches in a row, and sometimes three, imply concentrated experience and super-concentrated experience being brought through in a certain area of expertise. While these skills could be drawn from different lives, two of the same letters in a row suggest that it is from the same life, whereas different letters, (such as A, N, and T) suggest the possibility of different lifetimes, although I'm sure there are exceptions.

Internal words within a name have always interested me. I have found them to be significant for the client. I take them to represent a group of skills packaged together, and I have found them meaningful, even as words suggestive of past-life experience. The common one in those who come to me is the word "Ra" (Egyptian Sun God). The implication here is that the person is drawing on experience attuning to the sun from a past-life in Egypt, and usually we have gotten a life in Egypt or the client knows about past-lives in Egypt. (An interesting study here is to take a word such as "heart." Write down all the internal words that actually appear in that word, and then add to the list all the possible words you can make with the letters.)

Here, then, are the basics of a new, revealed method of analyzing names and words. It arose as a dividend out of 2,300 channeled musical past-life readings, together with channeled material from the Lords of Sirius and 15 years of analyzing words around me to corroborate it. To be sure, I found words which were "good words" where the vibrations of the chosen letters supported the meaning of the words, but I also found "bad words" where they didn't. Of course, one should look deep before judging a particular word.

I remember a man who came to me who had no middle name. I explained to him that it didn't mean that he didn't have a subconscious; that probably his subconscious was more hidden than people who had a middle name. I suggested that it was probably expressing through his first name and his last name: his Essential Self and Ego Projection into life, and his Pathway or Activities. He wrote me back three or four weeks later that in meditation he had received guidance that I was to give him a middle name. As I thought it over, I realized the karmic responsibility of naming someone! So I sat in meditation and reached out with love to his subconscious, saying that I had no desire to change it in any way, but that I had been asked to supply a name which would provide helpful vibrations for its evolution. I then selected some of the highest vibrations in the alphabet, and put them together in a very strong, positive sequence without dissonances, and mailed it to him.

In two weeks, I received a letter saying he was delighted with his new name and expressing his heartfelt thanks. It was a relief to get the letter, and I had the following fantasy: I pictured his grandson talking to his grandmother, asking where he had gotten his first name, since he hadn't heard of any ancestors with that name. I pictured her as an honest soul telling him that it was given to the family by a clairvoyant harpist. Then I tried to imagine the look of wonder that steals across the little boy's face! — and his decision that he better not tell his friends.

A Name Analysis usually takes between 20 and 30 minutes. (Incidentally, I have been told not to analyze the client's birthdate — I guess we'll leave that to the numerologists.) If the client has been given a spiritual name by a teacher, they often ask me to analyze it for them. I simply interpret the symbolism of the letters on higher levels in the light of what a spiritual name might be doing for them. On occasion, I have been asked to analyze the name for a projected organization. I explain what purposes of growth and what experience from the past this name would draw to the organization. It is also fun to analyze the meaning of names of places on Earth, especially as these are not usually whimsical. After I do a Polarity Reading (past-lives a couple have had together and music to harmonize the relationship) I compare the Purposes of Growth and see how they harmonize. If they have not had Name analyses, I often go ahead and do these, then usually make a graph showing exactly what each one is drawing from the past in each area. Of course, I feel moved to explain to them that this information is given in the spirit of greater understanding, cooperation, harmony and love, not at all in the spirit of competition. I explain that people are not drawing forth all of the skills they have developed. Also, that if one is bringing through more skill in a certain area than the other, that one should encourage the other to develop it; but that "when the chips are down," and they need to act quickly, or they need to express as a couple the highest possible quality, it is good to know who has developed this skill and to respect it. These charts have proven most valuable. Here I have to be careful not to use any names for the lady that she's not actually using, such as a maiden name, or she'll come out ahead.

At the close of the Name Analysis, I tell the client that we have been trying to shed some light on her nature through this system, which is one among many; that if she will look for this sequence pattern of qualities in her life, she will find it, and this will help to explain who she is and what she's doing in this incarnation. I suggest one of the best ways to use the Name Analysis: if she's having a hard time, she could try to locate this tension in the sequence of qualities. This will reveal to her whether she's going down or going up, getting involved in life for adventure and growth, or pulling out and ascending. It will show, perhaps, what has led up to this situation, and what quality she can expect to come into it next. Also, she will see in which of the three areas it lies.

I suggest that there may be other lives that she knows about, in addition to the ones that have just come through, from which she is drawing these qualities. And I suggest that at every important juncture of life, the patterns of her name can align her mind and her consciousness with the skills and talents she is carrying and the Purposes of Growth she has chosen. Then I extend to her a three-fold blessing in the Light.

"*Great music is a psychical storm, agitating to fathomless depths the mystery of the past within us. There are tones that call up all ghosts of youth and joy and tenderness; — there are tones that evoke all phantom pains of perished passion; — there are tones that revive all dead sensations of majesty and might and glory, — all expired exultations, — all forgotten magnanimities. Well may the influence of music seem inexplicable to the man who idly dreams that his life began less than a hundred years ago! He who has been initiated into the truth knows that to every ripple of melody, to every billow of harmony, there answers within him, out of the Sea of Death and Birth, some eddying immeasurable of ancient pain and pleasure.*"

Paul Elmer More

CHAPTER TWELVE

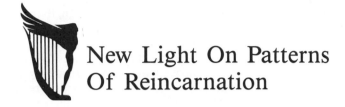

New Light On Patterns
Of Reincarnation

There are a number of incarnational patterns in these past-life at-tunement tapes which I found most interesting. I would like to share some of them with you now, not only to show their wealth and diversity, but also because I think they might make a contribution to the evolution of reincarnation theory. Let's begin with the premise that we are only start-ing to understand what we call reincarnation; later in the chapter, I will explain the reasons behind this theory. There are hundreds of cases of the standard types of reincarnational data in these readings. Since you might find them in many books on the subject, I will try to avoid them.

The paramount feature of these readings, which manifested in the first ten that I did, is that they are highly evolutionary and progressive. The subject is found to be in (usually potentially at the end of) a series of lives. Although we do sometimes take the person forward from the first life in the earth, in the majority of cases the series of lives we are portraying is a sub-series of the longer series. To be sure, the life sections are chosen for their maximum healing for the subject, but they are also selected to show the evolution of consciousness of the subject through the series. To my knowledge, the actual illumination of progression from life to life has appeared fairly recently in past-life readings. It is also rare to present a life in which the subject upleveled their Soul-Purpose, form-ing a new vision of a pathway toward God-realization. Yet we find this in every one of these readings. Isn't this pattern of renewal one we ex-perience in our everyday lives? Don't we become engrossed in a subject or activity, pull out, and then become deeply involved again, always work-ing on the same threads of evolution through different experiences?

In these readings, the present incarnation, during this special tran-sition time between the Piscean and Aquarian Ages, is seen as a time of synthesis, a time of bringing into harmony the many strands or facets of the original mandala of purpose on which the subject has been working. This potentiality, to "finish up," is extended even to the long series on Earth. In every reading, ascension is mentioned as a possibility. This means: the option of escaping the "wheel of karma and rebirth," and going on to higher realms at the time of transition. I will go into more detail about this a little later in this chapter. I have had the growing realization the last few years that this music presents to the subject what is essential for the transmutation and *completion* of these past patterns — the *releasing* of them! It seems to me that this process is more easily accomplished in sound than in words which have a tendency to fix the pattern. We must remember that in the first few months after I started the readings I asked that they be not only accurate "pictures of lives," but that as soon as so-called negative patterns were touched, these be raised into The Light and transmuted. I believe that this is what has been going on, since all dissonances become resolved soon after they appear in the music. In a way, they are "reincarnation readings to end reincarnation"!

Here are the cases I have chosen to show especially interesting patterns:

#13—John Paul Larkman. This was the fourth life reading I did and was interesting on two counts: it contained some strong evidence to spur me on, and also a musical quote — an occasional feature of a musical reading — of which I would have many. I knew beforehand that John had been given past-life readings as Henry the Eighth. A close friend of mine, who did not know this, was sitting in on the reading. She saw a clear picture of Henry the Eighth in her mind as I was playing the music. Then the section of the music (after which I saw him as Henry the Eighth) consisted of "Greensleeves." At the time, I did not know that the history books say he either wrote Greensleeves, or that it was his favorite piece. Afterwards, friends said to me, "Well, wasn't that his favorite piece?"

Later on, the quotes became more and more symbolic and significant. Of course, The Sources can activate any piece of music that I have in memory if they can count on me seeing the symbolism of it for the subject. (I might add that John looked the image of Henry and was married to one of the ladies in Henry's life.)

#14—An Anonymous Pilot. In 1973, when I was often being shown scenes taking place between lives in physical bodies, I saw part of this man hovering over a bird, learning the patterns and rhythms of flight. After the reading I learned that he is a pilot. Surely, whoever we are between lives on Earth isn't just waiting for the next opportunity to embody, but must be preparing for each new incarnation.

#15—Anonymous: a mother with a number of children. This session took place at the end of January, 1974. Picking her up between the previous life and the present life, I could clearly see part of her over-shadowing a tree as it grew. She was fully experiencing the roots drawing sustenance from the earth, the trunk stretching straight and strong toward the heavens, and the crowning branches spreading forth with fruit. This pattern was provided for her as a matrix for raising children in the present incarnation. What an inspiring model for the childhood of a new soul!

Before I tell you about the next case I should explain that a part of me has strong connections with space (has origin in Arcturus), but has experienced the Earth through a number of incarnations. For this reason, part of my ministry is to people who have space connections that puzzle them and make it difficult for them to adjust to life here on this planet. It has been given me to explain to them (or to the space aspect of them) that they come here voluntarily and for two basic reasons: to bring something to Earth that is much needed here and to evolve through adjusting to these vibratory conditions.

These "star children" must fully experience life and learn how to maintain themselves so they can offer their special message to humanity. It is not so true for them that their path to God lies in transcending the senses. Of course, like all of us, they must be constantly on guard that they don't become so identified with the material plane, the animal sensibilities, that they lose their connection with their home planet — and forget the special skills which are their gifts. If they haven't been here long, they may feel quite alien, afraid and vulnerable, and wonder what they're doing here. It has been my great pleasure to help many of these special souls on the path toward a truer and more comfortable orientation to Earth life.

#16—Peter Waphter. As soon as I had finished Peter's attunement music, I had the strong impression that he hadn't embodied on Earth too many times. He was still somewhat puzzled as to his purpose here. I began by asking him what his job was like, and he confessed that his work patterns were one of the greatest puzzles of his life. No sooner would he begin to know his place of work and the procedures of his job, than he would be let go. He said he would explore every aspect of his business, looking into every room, then something would occur to move him to another place, another job entirely. He was beginning to be somewhat depressed by the lack of recognition, especially of his sincerity.

At this point I broke in saying, "I'm so glad you told me about this pattern because I think I can explain it to you. What I see is that you have been sent by the people of your planet to record how these businesses are conducted on Earth so that they can study them and help us. When you're going into every room and looking all around, you are like a movie camera, photographing it all. When you return to your home planet, you are going to be the custodian of the archives. Don't worry about being moved along as soon as you've completed each assignment.

Just make thorough inspections, and be careful not to arouse suspicion because you are doing your real job — and it's important!"

When I finished he was shaking his head up and down saying, "Well, that's how it feels — that I'm photographing everything!"

I was go glad that he had responded to the prodding of his space brothers to come for a session, and that I had been able to help him understand what was going on. He was grateful also for additional information concerning star people on Earth.

17—A well-known clairvoyant, lecturer, and founder of a Light Center. One life-section of his music described his home planet. It was most unusual and beautiful. Toward the close of the session, I was moved to congratulate him on the success of his *simulated* human body. I know that this man has a mother, but there must have been something out of the ordinary in the construction of his physical form.

In the earlier years, when more star people were directed to me, I would sometimes get the first experience on Earth, that is, *before* embodiment. Instead of being born of woman, I would see them coming to Earth in a space ship, in simulated human form. They usually landed in a deserted place to the northeast of the Holy Land, on the edge of a desert. Here they had ample opportunity to adjust to the vibratory conditions of Earth. If they did well with this, then they could be born of a woman at the next opportune time — and I would often be given the next life.

In one case, the entity did so well in his adjustment he was allowed to walk into a village and take up life as a human. He successfully passed as a human for years, then walked out into the desert, and was picked up. His occupation was as a musician. While he was considered somewhat strange by many, there were those who put aside their prejudice, receiving much love and wisdom from him. Early embodiments of space people are usually male since a deeper attunement to Earth Mother is required to be a female capable of bearing children. The first time this happens is a milestone worthy of celebration.

Once at a party, I met a man from space experiencing his first embodiment on Earth. After some conversation, I told him that I felt he was not from Earth and he visibly cringed. He had been so afraid he would be discovered! I explained to him hastily that I could recognize him because I was from space myself, but that I had just been on Earth longer. We had a wonderful talk, he confessed some of his deepest anxieties, and I was able to help him feel better about many of them. His Crown Chakra was wide open and he wanted me to help him close it down. Of course, my guidance was that you don't close down the Crown Chakra; you try to help the lower chakras to live in harmony with this blessing.

18—Tim Jamison. In an earlier reading, I found myself playing

the folk song "Black is the Color of My True Love's Hair." The subject of the attunement tape was the girl for whom that song was written! I fairly wept with the love the young man who wrote the song bore for her. Mixed into the depths of this love was the sadness of parting. Three or four years later, Tim came to me for a reading. Believe it or not, the same song came through! I found myself telling him that he was the young man who wrote that song for his love. I felt bound to tell him of the previous reading, but left it entirely up to him whether or not to look her up. I told him she was married and had children. He didn't seem particularly moved by all of this and left in a few days for his home in the northwest. (She lived on the east coast.) Two or three years later, I heard that he had passed on. As far as I know, he never looked her up. I assume that either it wasn't time for them to meet, in terms of optimum growth, or that they had both fully processed the past liaison and learned all they needed from it. But I found it a fascinating cross-reference.

#19—Jerry Miradek and Mona Handley. This was one of the early Polarity Attunements (channeled to show and heal the past history of a relationship and to harmonize it in the present). Jerry ran a successful New Age business in a large eastern city and had done much research into modes of wholistic healing and paths of spiritual growth. He had asked Mona to come to the session with him because they didn't feel quite right about the relationship. They hoped to find out more about its history and true purpose so they could decide which way it should go. The first life that came through, which set the pattern for the series, was in the Temple Beautiful in ancient Egypt. They were working together under Ra-Ta, a past aspect of Edgar Cayce, to stimulate in people the sense of the Divine through the arts. They both realized that the primary focus for them in this life is to complete work together that they began in Egypt.

Many people have come to me who worked in the Temple Beautiful, some of whom I knew when I was there. Those were also times of great transition. The Higher Forces were helping people to align themselves with their true spiritual paths. We learned then that a person's taste for higher things can be stimulated by the sense of beauty and we are seeing in these times a spiritual renaissance in the arts — the arts used to raise consciousness. Certainly in my work, higher states such as universal peace, love, harmony and spiritual ecstacy have been stimulated in the listener — words can only *refer* to these states.

Now here is the story of the second complaint I have received among all the attunements completed to date:

#20—Sally Marr. Sally was very upset about her past-life reading because I had given her a life around 1830 — the same time as an incarnation given her previously by a well-known reader! She was so upset she couldn't listen to the music. She wrote me that she was going to ask the prominent reader (who was a friend of mine) to do a reading on me, presumably to check on the accuracy of my channeling! Again, I took this quite seriously since I had asked God to send me only those who I could help, and I wrote her a long letter. I explained that I had only received one complaint previously, and that this turned out to be under the direction of my Sources. Also, that everyone who used their tapes had seemed to benefit from them tremendously. I suggested she just listen to the music side of the tape, forgetting about the verbal interpretation, and see how it felt. She wrote me back that she was so confused and upset she couldn't listen to the tape at all.

Two weeks later, I drove from my home near Washington, D.C., to Virginia Beach and, upon arriving, entered a restaurant. There she was, sitting at a table with a friend. It seemed that I had manifested her! We discussed the matter again, to no avail, I became frustrated with her lack of open-mindedness and left her with a few less-than-soft words. Ten steps up the sidewalk, something stopped me in my tracks. I realized I couldn't do things that way anymore, and I went back in to talk to her.

I said, "Look, please forgive me. I love you and I'm just trying to help you. This is a new type of attunement being developed through me. We don't fully understand it yet. Can we take this gently, with some patience, and ask to be shown what's going on?"

She relaxed, and I left. As I tell you this story, I remember that she was moved to tears over this situation. It must have had deep subconscious significance for her. I can now say with assurance that the healer never knows quite what form the healing is going to take with the client — exactly what the Sources have in mind in terms of a response — or how long it's going to take. I didn't hear from Sally for a few months, but began to discuss with every past-life reader that I met the possibility of "multiple lives." Apparently right around that time (1976) many readers were beginning to get more than one life in the same time period. Then I was asked to come to Phoenix for a conference and while there I did a number of readings for clients who had had past-life readings from the well-known Bonita Brookshire. Two or three of them said that Bonita had given them up to four lives in the same time period! I was overjoyed with relief.

A few weeks later, I received a postcard from Sally. She had moved from New Jersey to the Los Angeles area and was excited over making an appointment with Bonita Brookshire.

When I looked up from the postcard I said, "Now that's the working of spirit!"

While there is probably more than one explanation for "multiple lives," my research into the nature of the subconscious (Basic Selves) suggests a most plausible explanation: that each of your individual Basic Selves could have been in a different body around the same time. I will elaborate on this later.

#21—Garvin Skalter. While doing healing sessions in downtown New York, I had an offer of a recording studio if I could transport my harp across town. My hostess kindly arranged for Garvin to help me since he was active in healing with the arts and had a station wagon. He had already scheduled an attunement session and I was looking forward to it since I had enjoyed sharing life experiences with him as we moved the harp. The reading went without a hitch until I came to the interpretation of the third life section. Nothing came. I sat there and waited as the tapes went around and around and I didn't receive a thing! Finally, in frustration, I asked the Sources why I wasn't getting anything and the cryptic answer came, "Because he was you." Part of me was thinking, "*Now* what am I getting into?" but I managed to keep my balance and finished the Interpretation.

Afterwards, as we sat discussing the reading, I decided honesty was the best policy: I told Garvin exactly what had happened. The explanation came to me in a later meditation and I wrote to Garvin about it. The first life of his series took place in Egypt. During his reading I got that he was a twin. What came later, was that I was the other twin! The reason I couldn't receive anything for the third life section was that, at that moment, my consciousness was recognizing the deep connection and oneness between us as having come from the division of a single cell. I hadn't met him since then and I was excited to see my long-lost brother! I suppose this was manifesting the principle, "That which has achieved a high degree of oneness seeks diversity." I have only appeared in seven or eight of the readings; this was one of the most interesting.

At the time of the reading, Garvin was working for one of the top cosmetic firms, utilizing computers to help raise the consciousness of a client through enhancing her natural beauty and self image. (It sounded to me like part of the program in the Temple Beautiful!) So in this present incarnation, when he and I are trying to finish our series of lives, we are pursuing similar healing professions.

There was an interesting sidelight in this case: I normally have such a high regard for people's free will that I resist the temptation to engage in matchmaking. But in this case, I felt guided. Garvin said he was looking for a mate. There was a girl who came for a reading the same week who was also looking. Because of the nature of their music and the skills, talents, and purposes of growth shown by their names, it seemed that they would be more than compatible. I took the liberty of telling him about her. I have never heard whether he looked her up or not.

#22—Peter Shelpher. As I often tell clients, I explained to Peter that all of his "lives" were going on in him simultaneously; arranging them consecutively on a tape in a reading was just a convenient way of seeing them and dealing with them. A few days after he arrived back home, he received in meditation the suggestion that he copy the life-sections of his music onto another tape so that they would all play at once! The result was remarkably harmonious with only a few places of relative dissonance and tension. He reports that it "gets him together" when he listens to it. Years later, when he arranged a series of concerts and workshops for me, I finally had a chance to hear this tape and noticed a few correlations of which he hadn't been consciously aware. As far as I know, he is the only one out of all the readees adventuresome enough to take me at my word in this matter.

#23—Wolfram Shuliman. This case illustrates that, as the conceptual capacity of the channel develops, the spectrum of what can be brought through expands. With this versatility comes an increase in the variety of clients who can be served. Wolfram's attunement music was normal except that there weren't any breaks between the life-sections. This hadn't happened before. What I have been calling a Healing Tape is continuous music and, although one or two lives may be discernible in the beginning, most of this music is not identifiable as lives in sequence. Of course, most of it is past patterns anyway, since much of healing is transmutation of the past. But Wolfram's was a life reading which would normally be in sections. During the interpretation of Wolfram's music, the point was made of how important it is for him to *synthesize* his various strands of experience, the different aspects of his life — especially in terms of smoothing out the continuity of them. I believe continuous music in a Life Reading has come through two or three times since Wolfram's.

I'll share with you now some of the general patterns worth noting in the readings. Following the time and place of the incarnation, I usually receive a feeling for whether the client was male or female. This most often comes from the quality of the music itself, but sometimes clairvoyantly. I would say roughly 20% have been the same sex throughout the series. I hardly ever find alternation of sex; the general rule seems to be to progress gradually from one into the other and then stay for awhile unless there is a more important karmic reason for making a sudden change. It is my theory that many cases of homosexuality are simply the Basic Selves (body consciousness) trying to adjust to a somewhat sudden change. Another causative factor here would be Basic Selves who were carrying patterns of recent homosexuality. (I have more to say about this interesting question in the section of the Basic Selves research, Ch. XIII).

Since every one of us is both male and female in some kind of balance, we need experience in both embodiments. And one life isn't enough before a change to the opposite gender. Where there is a great deal of balance between male and female in a certain life, I get a feeling for this and report it. I have had much training in my own past-lives concerning the nature and relationship of male and female, and have presented many workshops on the subject. Since the last 20 years have been a time of the rise of the female spirit, I have explored in depth my own female sensitivities. I am somewhat of a champion for women's rights.

Here is another fascinating pattern: after two or more lives in tropical climates, a life experience is usually arranged in, let's say, Northern Sweden, or even Alaska, for a "cooling off" period. The challenge is to see if the person can maintain the internal heat to sustain themselves. And, of course, the reverse sequence takes place. Here the challenge might be to see if the person can "maintain their cool" among the more fiery temperaments of the equatorial peoples. Then, too, occasionally people seem to need to retreat from the world. I see them in a monastic setting, spending much time in meditation, seeking more direct attunement with the Light. In these temples set apart, I see them in the solitude of the garden sanctuaries of nature, attuning to the Divinity of the Mother Principle, or equally focused periods in their rooms, seeking direct communion with The Divine Father.

Then there are many souls who walk the earth unhappy because they have, in a recent life, experienced a great love. I suppose this is why I say, when interpreting such a life, "Think of yourself here as developing the capability of loving in one of the greatest workshops life has to offer: the love relationship." I explain that an enduring relationship is a priceless seminar in the true love of self, of another, of life, and of the holy, creative wedding that takes place between the two aspects of God. But I suggest that the Higher Forces in charge of our optimum evolution arrange it so that we won't become too complacent in the harmony of human relationship with another, who is really our brother or sister. The supreme relationship is with God and Life. And so, rather than experience another almost perfect relationship, shouldn't we have the opportunity to experience the joy of service in leading a less-open heart into the fuller love that we can now offer because we experienced it.

*   *   *   *   *   *

My friend was deeply moved by this. He said, "What you have learned about love is so profoundly beautiful — it certainly speaks to what I'm going through in my life right now." Yawning and stretching, we realized we had been talking for three hours and the fire was going out! I suggested we finish the evening by listening to a few minutes of some music I had recently channeled from the star Arcturus. It turned out to be the perfect transition to ennobling slumber.

The next morning, as we were walking in the woods, he opened our discussion with a question . Slightly embarrassed, he asked, "I've been concerned about the average reader of your book. I'm wondering whether people who haven't had much experience with past-life readings ever ask if it's *necessary* to know your past-lives?"

I replied, "I'm glad you asked because it does come up from time to time. I don't think it is necessary — at least at most stages of a person's development here on Earth. Every day as you interact with life, you are experiencing and working with the patterns you have created in your past. As you look out on your world through the eyes of your past you see mostly what you expect to see. Rarely do you allow something truly new to enter your consciousness, unless somehow you have maintained the innocence of your childhood. Also, have you noticed that it seems so much easier to become *involved* in life situations than to learn the lesson they present and *release* them? We are definitely inexperienced in processing and clearing out our past so we can become empty vessels that can be filled with fresh, higher experiences. This is why the majority of holistic healing techniques have in common that they are various ways of transmuting a person's past."

"When you're nearing completion of the Earth experience, knowledge of your past-lives would, in one way or another, be opened to you as part of the summing-up process. Before that time, a past-life reading, if you are attracted to one, affords one method among many of shedding light on your past in a workable way."

I also felt moved to confide in my companion that I strongly suspected that the angels who give me the music of a life give it to me all at once; and that this makes sense to them in their space-time continuum. Then I, with special abilities that I have developed, express it in a musical continuity suitable for our space-time continuum. I have been told that I have special cells in the back of my head that enable me to translate a wide spectrum of vibrations from this world and other worlds in this manner. (I don't feel that this makes me a special person — everyone has the potentiality to develop the skills needed to pursue their chosen path of spiritual evolution.)

I told him that I thought we were living on a plane of existence where the quantitative aspects of life, time and space, are accentuated and slowed down so that we can absorb the qualitative aspects of life at a rate that we can handle. Later on, we'll be able to grow qualitatively much faster. So a past-life reading is simply a convenient way of laying out primary aspects of a client's evolving being so that they can be viewed more clearly. This is why I say to the client, "This life — or deep aspect of you — whichever you wish to call it.." Nevertheless, many more details and qualities can be communicated in a language of pure vibration, such as music, than a language such as words, which are *symbols for* reality.

How much more even than this can be brought to the client if the music is a precise language in which all of its elements have standardized meanings; that is, a language approaching a scientific language. And then, of course, in these attunements, music is presented for the present life to help the client, through the years, synthesize the aspects which have been separated out, and harmonize them in the light of the chosen soul-path toward God-realization. So I advise the client not to become too enamored with the details, the time and place, of a past-life, but to see what can be learned from them *as symbols* — to analyze the scenarios as one might analyze a dream sequence. You see, *this is the deeper reality and value of past and present experiences in the first place!* I often say that in 500 years you're probably not going to remember the details, but hopefully you will remember the life principle or lesson of which they were a dramatization. Remember Will Shakespeare's insightful line, "All the world's a stage and we be players upon it."

Another valuable characteristic of these musical "lives" is that they're like "windows" through which clients may look at various aspects of a past earthly sojourn. While fully experiencing the music, they receive impressions on any level of being: physical, emotional, mental, and even higher levels that were going on at the time. In fact, some clients have reported receiving glimpses of lives prior to the past-life! It is certainly true that in any life in your past you were resonating with a selected set of *prior* lives. Theoretically, there is no limit to how far back this could go. Again, we see that the music, of its very nature, establishes vibrational contact with past-life experience for further exploration. When it is channeled from High Sources, with love, it will guide that exploration to be positive, enlightening, uplifting, healing, and spiritualizing.

At this point, I wish to confess that I am sure I don't fully understand the deepest nature of this attunement music and the extent of its ramifications and consequences. Even though I have experienced and studied it for some 18 years, insights have come that the music's function is not quite what I thought — that its effect on people is more than I considered it to be. Even as I write, I am aware of guidance from the Sources as to what I should say about its nature and am receiving many new insights as to what I've really been doing!

Most of the great philosophers of history have commented on the nature of music, saying that it was a bridge, through the laws of vibration, from this world to higher worlds; that it was the language of the soul from its most mundane expression to its loftiest heights. They say that you could understand the heart of a people through their music; that music integrates the inner life with the outer life; and that music has the power to heal the various ills to which man is heir. Consider also that music exists on a level which is EXTRA-verbal. Then how can I, in these short (although expansive) years, possibly achieve a definitive understanding, and express it in words, of a musical portrait which really does seem to recreate the abundance, complexity, and subtlety of a human soul?

"Music once admitted to the soul becomes a sort of spirit, and never dies; it wanders perturbedly through the halls and galleries of the memory, and is often heard again, distinct and living as when it first displaced the wavelets of the air."

Sir Edward Bulwer-Lytton

CHAPTER THIRTEEN

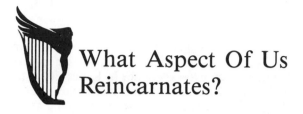

What Aspect Of Us Reincarnates?

Now, we can proceed to some recent developments in my thinking about the nature of reincarnation. I hope you will find them exciting, or at least stimulating, as I have. I mention these because I believe they may have bearing on a true understanding of the nature of these Life Attunements. In order to explain this new conception of reincarnation, I must invite you to follow me down two different paths of seeming digression until they come together at a later point. As I mentioned in the very beginning of this story, one of its themes is that we never know fully what we're doing, especially if we're listening to Higher Guidance. We just have to wait to be shown at a later date, often unexpectedly, how things fit together. First let me share with you a brief account of research I have been doing for fifteen years into the nature of the subconscious. (This is the material I have been promising you concerning the Basic Selves.)

In 1971, I experienced a "Three Selves Reading" from Bonita Brookshire. She is certainly one of the great clairvoyants, and the information that came through was most illuminating, especially as to the nature of my subconscious. She has developed the sensitivity to allow aspects of the subconscious of the client to speak through her. They give their names and comment on how things are going in the areas of their responsibility. When Bonita shifts from one Basic Self to another, the tone quality of her voice changes. I was moved to tears when first my female, and then my male Basic Self, spoke to me. There seemed to be no doubt that they were not aggregate "subpersonalities," but *actual entities* with various duties which were somehow marvelously integrated in my body consciousness.

After a few months of trying to get more consciously in touch with these two, and feeling better and better about the idea that they were entities, the most amazing thing took place. I was sitting with Nel, the clairvoyant with whom I had been working very closely, and our Basic Selves began talking to each other! I began the conversation by telling her about my Basic Selves and asking her if she had counterparts within her. Within minutes, we were having a six-way conversation between my male and female Basic Selves, her male and female Basic Selves, who gave their names, and the ego consciousness in our two minds, who went by our first names. What astonished us was that the voice would change, depending on who was speaking, and we knew who was talking to whom! We were so excited that we envisioned giving workshops to demonstrate it and to encourage people to experience it. I guess it wasn't time yet to give the workshops and for three years I just wished that Bonita didn't have such a long waiting list so that more people could have these revealing readings to improve the relationship between the conscious mind and the Basic Selves.

Three years later, I was studying kinesiology with a certified Touch-For-Health instructor, using the arm test to ask direct questions of the Basic Selves on a variety of questions. Incidentally, she provided some of the earliest outside testing of the music that was coming through me. She suggested we conduct a workshop in kinesiology and music. We taught the participants how to "muscle-test" each other in the areas of the body governed by three chakras. We had them tabulate the results (weak, semistrong or strong), then we asked them to lie down and fully experience the music channeled for the healing of the three chkras. After each one, they would get up and muscle-test each other. In my innocence, I didn't realize until the beginning of the workshop, that the authenticity of the music was "on the block." I was so relieved when we counted up the tally sheets and found that almost everyone had gotten stronger, and three or four out of 15 had gone from weak to strong!

For months we explored the general arm test and found that if you are sincere, you can access a great deal of valuable information about what is good for you and what's not so good for you: Basic Self knowledge about which your conscious mind is often wrong. It suddenly occurred to me, like a light being turned on in my head, why couldn't we use the general arm test to ask the Basic Selves direct questions about *their* nature to put people in closer conscious touch with these very present and highly intelligent aspects of their body consciousness? (Remember, Freud had called them the UNconscious!) I had never heard of this being done, and with great excitement I put together a one-hour muscle-testing analysis that I still call the Basic Selves Schemata. I have completed some 80 of these to date, and the technique has become expanded and refined. Just imagine how the following procedures could cut down the time and expense of any type of psychotherapy.

Now bear in mind that the answers to these questions can be achieved through two types of response that the general arm test will give you: 1) a YES or a NO (a firm or a lax response of the arm); 2) the DEGREE to which exposure to something from outside the body will strengthen or weaken it (degree of strength or weakness of response). You do have to tell the Basic Selves which kind of question you're asking. First I ask how many Basic Selves are present and get the answer. Then I find out whether each one is male or female.

From years of readings, Bonita says that male and female Basic Selves pair up and begin to work toward ambigenic harmony. She gives symbols for the three stages of this as follows: 1) male and female relating; 2) a male and female head on one stem; and, 3) one head on a longer stem with a male face on one side and a female face on the other (the Janus figure). So I investigate how they pair up, and how they're progressing toward ambigenic fusion. Then a Basic Self can be fundamentally of three origins: 1) beginning as the subconscious of an ANIMAL, and evolving to the point where it can be a Basic Self of a human; 2) having origin in SPACE (two or three different kinds); and 3) from the devic kingdom (rare). Each can develop attunement with the others and the more advanced ones embody all three. I check all of this out with the arm test and write it down. Bonita also gives the five areas in which a Basic Self might work. I ask each one for a relative strength response to show how much he or she works in each area. They are usually quite precise in their answers.

The next subject of inquiry has been almost mind-boggling: the phenomenon of "replacements." Apparently, when a Basic Self can no longer evolve properly due to free-will decisions made at the conscious-mind level, it can, as it were, apply for a transfer! At first the options seemed to be: 1) going back to the repository of Basic Selves to await re-assignment; or, 2) if another person can be found where growth would be optimal, an inquiry might be conducted by the Higher Selves involved, plus the karmic angels. Permission might be granted to be installed. I discovered this option myself: 3) if the evolution on the earth plane has been completed, an advanced Basic Self can pursue its own form of ascension. Anyone, with a little practice gaining the confidence of the Basic Selves, can corroborate these findings by muscle-testing!

First, I ask if there has been a replacement in the recent past. Then I go back through the months or years asking for a strong response for the year, and then the month, in which the new Basic Self entered. Once we find it, I ask the subject how they felt at that time. Invariably, they report some confusion in their identity, and some even remember a life crisis. Very often a loved one left them: relationships very much involve the Basic Selves. After all of this, I can explain to the subject what was going on, and this is always most enlightening. The Basic Self that is being replaced remains for a few weeks or months to "teach the newcomer

154

the ropes," then goes on. I encourage the person to welcome the new Basic Self, pledge cooperation, and to thank, bless, and release the old one to its highest growth. You can see how helpful this could be in facilitating the changeover. It has been most exciting the few times when a new Basic Self came in *during* the Basic Self Schemata session. Once I saw Dale Mathis, Bonita's conductor, officiate in the installation of a new Basic Self. Probably because, nowadays, the "name of the game" is *growth,* I have an increasing number of clients who are experiencing replacements. My first-hand knowledge of it grew immensely when I bid a fond and grateful farewell to "John," who had been with me since birth, and welcomed "Jonathan." Six years later "Robert" arrived.

The final thing I go for is the names by which the Basic Selves would like to be called. I ask the subject to make the mind a blank and say the first name that pops into it. Then I ask a Basic Self (by number) for its name. I immediately muscle-test to see if it is correct and ask for a spelling. Then I test the correctness of the spelling.

So in one hour, I have helped the conscious aspect of the person to understand a great deal about the subconscious galaxy of aspects, sexual polarities, degree of ambigenic harmony and job descriptions. We have arranged a first name introduction and "handshaking," as it were, between conscious mind ego (the client's first name) and each of the Basic Selves. It is somewhat analogous to introducing the executive director of a business to some of the key staff members. From now on, this director can say hello to these staff members as they "pass each other in the hallways." If there are blocks to the smooth-running efficiency of the "business," he can go *directly* to these key staff members and discuss it. It is quite possible he can come up with directives which will enable them to do their jobs better. All of this builds confidence.

Not only is this technique a breakthrough in a person's conscious/subconscious rapport, but as soon as a psychotherapist has worked out the client's Basic Self Schemata, he can begin to *speak directly* to the Basic Selves. At first, he will receive answers through the arm test; soon thereafter, answers out of the client's mouth. I have found that often the life challenges a client is facing can be localized in a certain Basic Self and his or her relationships. What are commonly called "subpersonalities" may be a Basic Self coming forth, or may be a Basic Self playing a role; but can also be composite "personalities" put together out of appropriate strands of past memory by one or more Basic Selves. I have definitely experienced both types. We certainly know that the Basic Selves are accomplished actors and actresses. As a matter of fact, if they are entities and have sex, we really should refer to them with personal pronouns rather than "it."

It would seem then that the Basic Self Schemata, which is not that difficult to learn, would be of tremendous value to anyone who works with people (counselors, therapists, nurses, doctors) if they wish to accelerate the healing process. Especially if they would like to help clients know themselves better and thus be able to explore self-healing between sessions. The Basic Self Schemata can cut down the time and expense of any kind of psychotherapy and so I consider it a breakthrough in psychology. Everyone is not ready for this knowledge. Some might think that they were "possessed," which is not at all the case. We must realize that we are triune beings. It is wise to know the aspects we are trying to harmonize.

Now the reason I have shared with you this Basic Self research is that it provided a vital key in my growing conception of the nature of these past-life attunements. This is the fact that *the Basic Selves are the parts of you that carry the karmic record of your past.* These are not records that a Basic Self looks up in some kind of archive, when a situation comes up, but *living patterns* which a Basic Self *actually remembers having experienced.* This explains why their reactions and responses are so instantaneous. These patterns are not stored in the conscious mind, which has the role more of a *processor* of responses, and an *initiator* of actions through thought-forms, and a *mediator* between the superconscious and the challenges of life. With the premise, then, that your Basic Selves as entities embody all the experiences from your past, let us take up my second story: the account of a "training" I have been taking which will place this premise in a larger context.

Early in 1975, as I have mentioned, The URANTIA Book came into my life, and it has profoundly deepened my understanding of many aspects of life. This book contains over 2,000 pages. Since I spend roughly one-third of my year on tour, I have only just recently completed the first reading of it. This book commanded my respect when I first browsed through it. Then came seven years of study in weekly discussion groups, and application of its wisdom in my life. Now my respect has deepened into an admiration bordering on awe. Please understand, dear friend, that I am not attempting to sell you on this book, because I understand full well that only you can do that. However, information in this book is germane to our story. In this book, Urantia is given as the correct space name for our planet. It is stated therein that The URANTIA Book is the Fifth Epochal Dispensation to the human race, and the previous four are also described. This remarkable revelation comprises 196 papers authored by many Higher Beings and all brought through one of the clearest channels the world has known. His identity is completely played down by the URANTIA Foundation so that the revelation might make its way based solely on its contents. The material is written in the most perfect and precise English (the book does not contain one typographical error!) and covers the widest possible variety of subjects deemed essential to understanding life on Earth. It contains an entire cosmology of the universe and the Ascension Plan for evolutionary will creatures of our type. It is a monumental testament to the grandeur of creation. The book begins with a detailed description of primary aspects of the Triune Deity at the focal point of the Central Creation. Then it proceeds outward, describing the major types of beings, their natures and activities, who inhabit this Central Creation, and the seven superuniverses which revolve around it. A long section follows, describing the origin and evolution of our local universe (one among thousands). The middle third of the book consists of a detailed history of our planet, Urantia, beginning with the formation of the Solar System and coming right up to the present. The last one-third of the book consists of a week-by-week, sometimes day-by-day narrative of the life of Jesus, written by a panel of angels. Some of them were actually present during these events and all of them have access to the true and complete records of planetary history. This commission was under the supervision of a Melchizedek (a high local universe teacher.) It is clear to those who study this book for any length of time that it has come to us from higher dimensions as a powerful beacon of light, help, and hope in straightening out the confusion in the world about what's really going on. I have found, as have growing thousands of people, that this revealed material really does answer the basic questions: 1) What is the nature of this creation and how is it organized? 2) What is the nature of The Source, or Creator, of it? 3) Where and how does our world fit into it? 4) What kind of being am I, and what is my potential destiny? and 5) What is the process and meaning of life?

A friend told me once that the primary criteria for a philosophy of life were: 1) Is it internally consistent? and 2) Does it provide simple and effective solutions to the challenges of life? For me, The URANTIA Book satisfies these requirements far better than any system I have come across, and I have studied in many paths. While I have found glimmers of varying intensities of truth in a number of systems, none can compare with the blended spiritual wisdom and love combined with historical, philosophical, logical and scientific approaches that are integrated in this work. I could go on and on about the supernal wisdom that can be found here, as well as the information that is presented for the first time, but perhaps I have made my point, and presented enough of a background for our purposes. Let me just add that, if you have a true thirst for truth, and if you persevere in your study of this book, it will more than satisfy you. I know of no book like it to be found at this time.

The parts of this book that pertain to our present discussion are the direct comments on the concept of reincarnation; the detailed description of the process of death, or what they call, "terrestrial escape."

I was already developing trust in the truth value, consistency, and reliability of this material, when I discovered its first cryptic commentary on reincarnation. I had been doing past-life attunements for five years at the time, and they were impressively healing for the clients. They included the usual kind of reincarnational patterns, so it was quite a shock when the Higher Beings stated that there was no reincarnation as we understand it! I quickly got out the Concordex (index) and looked up other references to reincarnation, of which there were not very many. These were even stronger! One of them went so far as to say there was only one type of being in the universe who experienced what we term reincarnation, where the *essential whole* of a being is enabled to lay down one body and take up another; and this took place on a planet farther up the ascension series. After I read these, I almost exploded with frustration and wonder.

I said, "Now wait a minute!" Then I said, "We had better take this very gently and patiently."

There wasn't any question about the readings helping people in major ways, my guidance was quite strong to continue doing them, and I was afraid if I swallowed this new information too quickly, it might make it difficult to continue the work! For four years I struggled with this question. Keeping these two departments of incarnational theory somewhat insulated from each other in my mind, I searched diligently for a way of synthesizing them. I knew from training in logic and scientific method that I was looking for a hypothesis that was broader than each one of them and which could include them both. My Geminian nature provides a built-in ability to embrace dualities. This must have helped me because, as I look back, carrying this schism didn't seem to upset my life much, even though most of my URANTIA Book reading friends had no background in reincarnation and simply accepted what the book said at face value. In my lonely moments, I would "plead" with the authors of the papers as to why they couldn't have added a page or two more of explanation on this subject. When I discussed it with others who had made the same plea concerning other subjects, we would come to the conclusion that this revelation was written for all peoples in a wide gamut of stages of growth and for a period of centuries or even some longer time cycle on Earth. We agreed we could not expect The Sources to speak to a concept which might be undergoing tremendous changes and even might, in the long view, be enjoying only a temporary popularity.

Finally, in 1981, on January 1st, a time of year when I often receive my greatest insights, the answer came. I had gotten some pieces of it, but now it was reasonably complete. It resolved the dilemma, integrated the book's description of death, my research into the nature and function of the Basic Selves, and the Past-Life Attunements. What a relief! Here's how it goes: In the vast majority of cases, when a person makes transition, these are the aspects that go on: 1) the High Self — that undiluted fragment of Deity which has been assigned to you to lead you back to the Source and Center; 2) the Personality, the Book's name for your individuality, the quality of vibration about you that makes you not quite like any other created being, (and these first two are gifts from the Universal Father of all), and 3) your Soul: what you have built of enduring soul qualities, your acquisitions of permanent spiritual value, learned through the interaction of your High Self, your conscious mind (the mediator), and your experience, your past. Here the word "soul" is used in a different sense than the usual way with which you may be familiar. In the metaphysical literature, the word "soul" is much overused, having a wide variety of meanings, but I have found that most often it refers to the eternal spiritual essence of a person which would designate the High Self. In The URANTIA Book revelation, your soul is an aspect you are building and the process goes something like this: As your mind tries to figure out and help you solve life challenges (a great many of which are called forth by your past "unfinished business"), it reaches out from time to time to the High Self for a higher, more universal, principle to apply. If the principle works and really helps to resolve the situation, then the conscious mind says, "Ah-ha! I have demonstrated that this is a valuable principle. Let's remember it and make it part of our permanent collection." At this point, the High Self (and this is one of its primary functions), translates the mental thought-form of the principle or law into *spiritual substance* which actually causes the person's soul body to grow in proportion and quality.

These are the three aspects of you that go on when you make transition: your High Self, your Personality and your Soul. *Nothing is mentioned about your body consciousness going on with you, and nothing is mentioned about your terrestrial-type mind going on with you.* In the Book's rather precise description of your arrival in the resurrection halls of the "mansion worlds," they speak of a body of higher-realm substance and a new, comparable type of mind being provided. This corroborates what I was getting from the Basic Selves who confirm that the three paths open to them are: 1) back to the pool for reassignment; 2) transfer to another human; or 3) progression along their own line of ascension. Also, I never found a conscious mind that said it reincarnated. (An interesting note here: whenever I ask a conscious mind whether it is this or that, such as animal, devic, space, male, female, I get an afffirmative response. This is because the mind is whatever it can *conceive of being.*)

Since all the High Selves are fragments of the Father, they are all essentially, qualitatively, the same, differing only in how much experience they have gained from indwelling humans. Each one hopes to attain Personality (individuality) through taking a human on up through the ascension. We, as individuals, attain divinity through the High Self.

Because the grand scheme is a Free-Will plan, some humans elect not to take on the great cosmic adventure and the High Self has to be reassigned. This might explain reincarnation were it not for the fact that the book makes it quite plain that a High Self is not allowed to indwell two humans on the same planet. True, if you have an experienced High Self, you are benefiting from life wisdom garnered on another planet. However, it is unlikely that the High Self would present to you a scene from a former indwelling, but adapt that experience to your life here in the form of principles. *The past sojourns of the High Self are not sufficient to explain the vast body of literature we have describing human past-life experience, and the "proofs" that frequently appear.* It is also definitely stated that if the High Self has to be reassigned, the Personality (individuality) becomes part of the Supreme Being, the aspect of Deity that is in the process of manifestation in the seven superuniverses.

Let me hasten to underline once more that we grow in many areas of our being through our free-will choices. For this Plan to work at all, there must be an option *not* to choose God. When you fully understand this Plan, you realize that to not choose God is to choose *nothingness.* Those who continually refuse to choose God for long enough eventually, *by their own choice,* choose spiritual suicide. Of course, God does not want this and provides every possible help toward the choosing of God, or life. It is described how thorough the investigation must be before permission can be given (by an extremely High Being) to erase even the most backward of one of God's creatures from the census rolls. I understand this is a concept which may take much time and thought to accept. Finally you realize that it's the only way the free will plan could work.

For the purpose of our discussion, we have arrived at the crucial question: What part of us is it, then, that reincarnates? And we are left with one aspect: the Basic Selves. So the resolution of my dilemma could be expressed thus: The more essential parts of you have the capability to go on after this *one life.* The part of you that is providing the body vehicle for your growth in consciousness may experience many, many embodiments in the earth, and is capable of its own form of ascension. This is why the book says you don't reincarnate, because *the "you" to which it is referring includes parts that can and parts that don't.* It would be incorrect to say that you, *as a whole,* reincarnate.

We should also keep in mind that one of the major purposes of the URANTIA Book seems to be to free us from the "wheel of karma and rebirth"; to open up the vistas of The Ascension. In the light of this new concept, we might describe an incarnation in this way: a one-time only combination of aspects is assembled including a High Self, a Conscious Mind (taken from the pool of human mind essence), a Personality (the gift of individuality from the Father), and a set of one or more Basic Selves (drawn from various sources: animals or devas on this planet, humans on this planet, animals or "humans" or devas on other planets).

We don't require that this hypothesis be the final truth, but if it is truer than what we had heretofore, it will explain more of our experience than we could explain before. The Book says "Truth" evolves. For myself, over the past four years since this insight came to me, it has seemed more and more correct. When we are born, we are given a body consciousness comprising skills gleaned many life experiences. These probably include some specialized talents such as fire-walking, plant cultivation, and harp playing, but also, disharmonious patterns from the past which we will use as "grist-for-the-mill" to develop higher consciousness through demonstrating that higher principles work.The Basic Selves have the amazing ability to hold unprocessed past patterns until you have developed the higher principles to transmute them into lessons. This is one deep meaning of the "lead into gold" of alchemy. The lead-filled bags which people carry on their backs may seem heavy but they are God's way of guaranteeing that not a moment of our experience will be wasted!

Also, I have found in the readings that "service to life" is one of the primary ways we grow toward God-realization. It is one of the contributions of this theory that we "leave the world a better place to live in" by taking some of these past thought-forms and emotional patterns that didn't work, and are still "hanging around the place," and clean them up by bringing them into alignment with higher understanding and transmuting them *for the Earth,* as well as ourselves.

So the Basic Selves are the parts of you that have experienced the past-lives and are carrying the karmic patterns from them. (And, to be sure, most people identify rather strongly with their Basic Selves.) At this point, we remember that one of the five areas I check out in a Basic Self Schemata is how much each Basic Self is working with the karmic records. Bonita Brookshire says that you shouldn't think of yourself as having been a certain person in history, but that *a part* of you was part of that person. And it follows that two or more of your Basic Selves could have been part of different people at the same time in history. I think you will find, with some study, that not only "multiple lives," but other aspects of past-life readings, especially those since 1975, will be explained by this new conception of reincarnation. So a past-life attunement accelerates your evolution by speeding up the processing of your past.

Very soon after I formulated this theory I realized with great pleasure that it explained something which has always been a great puzzle to me: the Eastern idea of "transmigration of souls," that a human might be incarnated in an animal.

Let us say that a Basic Self has been evolving quite well through the higher animals and is now ready to be a member of the subconscious of its first human. And let us say that, for various reasons, it doesn't quite make it. (Wouldn't it be normal to assume that they all don't make it on the first attempt?) It would make sense that the karmic angels in charge of such things might send him or her back for another life or two in the animal kingdom — and most probably in close proximity to humans, as a pet. I now believe it is a strong possibility that our Basic Selves are training the Basic Selves of our pets for possible upcoming human embodiments. After this neat explanation of transmigration of souls, I suspect that this is another case of a doctrine that lost its original meaning as it was handed down.

To close this chapter, I would like to tell you about a reading I did some two years after the foregoing hypothesis was formulated and which corroborates it.

#24—During a series of Life Attunements in Jamaica, a young boy of 16 was brought by his father and sister. He was considered to be retarded and was mute. I had finished the initial life section of the series and was waiting to be shown the details. After a pause, I received telepathically the words, "There are no human past-lives here: this is his first embodiment in a human. The music you have been given expresses the creature's love for his Creator when offered the opportunity to evolve." The music was in the key of D, Human Love, and was charged with deep, poignant emotion. Then followed a single, long section and I was told that this provided vibrations to help his success in this initial installation. After I gave the father and sister this information, they still kept asking what the karmic lesson was that explained his condition. They had had some exposure to metaphysics which led them to believe that all difficulties in life are due to past misdeeds. I hastened to explain that with the boy this was not the case — that he was doing just fine considering where he was in his evolutionary path. I told them also that another possibility is that the High Self, or other Higher Beings in charge of our development, place in our path a challenge designed to accelerate our growth. I explained that he had been given a rudimentary type of mind since a more evolved mind would have been a burden to him, considering what he was dealing with, just adjusting to being human. I said he needed a lot of love and would be happiest relating to interesting rocks, plants, and animals, in addition to the humans in his environment. I told them that he was simply not ready for speech, but that this was a possibility later on. Also, that he was oftentimes puzzled and fearful with the antics of the humans around him, and that they should be simple, direct and free of ulterior motives in his presence and play with him. I encouraged them to remove from their minds completely the idea of karmic punishment and consider it a privilege that they were chosen to officiate in "Grade One" of this Basic Self's "School in Humanity." The boy responded to the music positively, but during the discussion that followed, he got up a couple of times. He seemed to be frustrated with the talking and appeared to be trying to go outside.

I am grateful for the privilege of hearing and playing the music expressing this creature's deepest feelings concerning this major step in his evolution. My gratitude is even deeper for the corroboration of the validity of my expanded conception of how reincarnation actually works, and the resolution of my four-year dilemma. I continue to check out this new hypothesis and I welcome reports by anyone who finds it of potential value and worthy of research.*

*Mr. Andrews presents lectures and workshops on the subjects discussed in this chapter, as well as other aspects of his work. Please see the last page for where to address inquiries. You will also find, in the Bibliography, more information about The URANTIA Book.

CHAPTER FOURTEEN

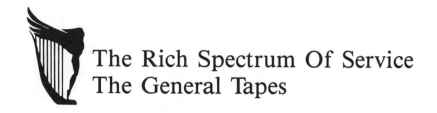

The Rich Spectrum Of Service
The General Tapes

The unseen team working with me enjoys a highly developed versatility. Over the years, these Sources have come through with a wide variety of channelings. Every sincere, legitimate request has been honored and fulfilled beyond expectations. The following is a list of the principal types of channelings I have produced over the years:

INDIVIDUALIZED OR SPECIFIC HEALING TAPES FOR:
Individuals (Past-Life Attunement or General Healing tape)
Couples (the Polarity tape)
Plants (especially trees)
Animals (of many kinds)
Parts of the World
Political Situations
The Channel (myself)
The Work (my ministry)
Certain Maladies
Background for an Artist's Studio

TAPES FOR AN INDIVIDUAL HEALER to use in a specific room or at a specific address.

TAPES CHANNELED FOR USE BY ANYONE IN THE SAME TYPE OF WORK FOR:
Healing Sanctuaries
Doctor's Offices
Psychotherapists
Counselors

Body Therapists and Masseurs (of a number of modalities)
Movement Therapists
Childbirth (doctors and midwives)
Infant Massage
Art Therapists
Weight Loss Therapists

Ambient healing backgrounds for:
Meditation Groups
Study Groups
Yoga
Meditation
Birth

Tapes for chakra balancing

Tapes to promote creativity (Especially Children)

Channelings:
that deal directly with pain
directly from spiritual teachers such as Yogananda, Sai Baba and
The Christ
from masters in ascended planes of being
from angels, devas, space beings, etc.

Verbal channelings on the subjects found in this book

I suppose this wide gamut of tapes could not have come forth had I not been interested in seeing how much of life could be served by this new form of healing. It will be my particular pleasure to recount for you some of the highlights of this spectrum. But first, I must shed a little more light on the difference between the two primary types of healing channelings for individuals.

Very early in the development of the Individual Attunement readings, it became clear that there were to be two types: one for the client whose mind is open to the concept of past-life embodiments, and the other for the person who is not. Type I is called an Individual Attunement, Past-Life Attunement or Reading, or Life or Life Path Attunement. It presents two to four (usually three) sections of music, comprising past-lives of a series, followed by the present-life section of music; all of these being separated by pauses. The past-lives range anywhere from one to three minutes in length. The present-life section, the life of potential synthesis, is of longer duration, usually three to five minutes. The gaps between sections occur as I am pausing to receive impressions after each life. They are left on the tape so that the client might be inspired by this vibration of clairvoyance, but also so that fantasies stimulated by the music can have a chance to play out. Even though these life-sections are spaced out to facilitate concentration on them, I always make it clear that they can also be viewed as deep aspects of being and that the client might prefer to work with them as such. It is the qualitative significance of the details of life that are important for one's growth in consciousness. The Past-Life Attunement emphasizes the stages of growth more than the Healing Tape and contains more verbal information about who the client is.

The Healing Tape does not pause between sections. It is still progressive, moving from section to section, and the sections may be drawn from past lives,since, to present healing patterns, the music must be a portrait of the client, but there is no mention in the Interpretation of these past-lives. Once in awhile, the Sources ask me to give information from one or two. In the Interpretation I present the symbolism of the elements of the music, correlated with whatever insights the Sources give me. Emphasis is on the optimum sequence of phases of development which the client can apply to life in different time frames (day, moon-month, year). Of course, the music is quite similar in both types of readings. The Healing Tape might be somewhat more generalized and the Sources might have slightly more latitude in terms of synthesis. For clients who have a great faith in their ability to learn from experiencing art, who really know that much more can be communicated through the arts than with words, the Healing Tape is indicated (and there can be slightly more actual music on a Healing Tape). Also, with this type of tape, you have the option of not having an Interpretation. Some clients prefer not to have the vibratory realities of the music limited by even the words that I might bring through, wishing to stay entirely open to whatever they might receive at any time from the music. Some clients have felt very strongly about this, even though the Interpretation is on side 2 of the cassette. Personally, I find this attitude admirable, but the purpose of my ministry is to serve as many as possible.

Here is a resume of the rest of the major types of sessions which I have offered for several years with notes on their variations:

(1) The POLARITY ATTUNEMENT (which I used to call a Couples Tape) traces the series of significant past-lives that two people have shared. I play the two birthdates and names, then we pick them up in the first life where they made some kind of commitment to each other; often, where this commitment also included spiritual redirection. The lives in between show the evolution and deepening of their relationship; then the present-life section is both a portrait of their relationship and music to illuminate, heal and harmonize it. This last music is only roughly chronological and might be aptly described as phases of growth through

which the relationship has passed in this life and would follow for optimum growth and fulfillment. These Relationship Attunements are most interesting and valuable and, of course, any two people can have one. If I analyze the names, I erect a chart comparing their sub-purposes (from their initials) and also what they're drawing on from past-life experience (body of the names). This has proven quite helpful. I have grown a great deal through relationships in this life, and I've developed a workshop which I give on tour entitled, "The Holy Wedding—Reconciling Male & Female." I really enjoy these counseling sessions with couples. We live in a time of highly-polarized opposites, (Edgar Cayce called it a "time of division"), and it is natural that relationships are challenging at this time. I try to help couples understand that a relationship is a supreme workshop for developing the true love of self, love of another, love of life, gratitude for spiritual principles and love of God. Even if it's not a love relationship, the information is helpful in understanding why the clients behave the way they do toward each other.

(2) The OFFICE TAPE is channeled for professionals to play as background in their working space. Doctors, chiropractors, therapists, counselors and especially practitioners of massage have found these tapes most beneficial adjuncts to their work. They provide a soothing, relaxing and healing atmosphere conducive to all the healing arts. Usually, they are channeled for a specific person's work at a certain address. Of paramount importance here is how they quickly put people into meditative and receptive states. The two most common adjectives used to describe the music I produce are "meditative" and "healing."

(3) A SPECIAL PURPOSE tape covers a wide variety of applications. I have co-created tapes for plants, animals, communes, towns and cities, the San Andreas Fault in California, and larger geographical or sociological areas. At least one channeling ("The Heart Chakra") was broadcast by a group of special angels over the entire planet and I will be relating this story. Another interesting variety of this kind of tape is the channeling I do for a newly-forming business. We can channel for a group of the founding members, and we can also analyze the prospective names for the business, finding out what vibrations these would attract from the past, and what purposes of growth would be set into motion.

(4) I also do a PAST-LIFE REGRESSION WITHOUT MUSIC utilizing the Multi-Level Awareness Technique. This is a regression without hypnosis where I use simple deep relaxation techniques, make suggestions and then go along as a friend and guide as the subject explores one or two past-lives, experiencing them in fantasy. The account of the odyssey is recorded for further study.

(5) The BASIC SELF SCHEMATA, as we have described, involves the use of kinesiology (the general arm test) to ask questions of the Sub-

conscious or Basic Selves to build a model of its nature and introduce the conscious mind to the body consciousness. This new type of reading combines disciplines from my experience over the past 10 years and is a most valuable tool in any kind of psychotherapy.

The excitement I feel as I share with you now the Attunements and Disclosures that stand out for special mention seems to come from three sources: 1) my personal destiny-fulfillment represented here, the satisfaction that comes when you feel you're being used properly—to your full potential; 2) the knowledge that in these readings I had a golden opportunity to serve my fellow humans and life; 3) and the deep amazement and gratitude I feel as I remember the unbounded ingenuity, skill, knowledge, and creativity exhibited by the Sources. Right after they happened, most of them seemed like miracles. So, I am also thankful that I was, especially in the early stages, open-minded enough to imagine that they were possible. In some cases, like the first one, I probably had to be maneuvered into a position of no escape in order to show me something new.

#25—For all the Attunement sessions up to June 1973, the subject was present in the room. During that month, I was doing a series of readings set up by a well-known doctor in the mid-West. I had done tapes for a number of his patients with special pain problems and for members of his family. The last taping was for a colleague in his office. He must have forgotten the appointment and had gone on vacation to Louisiana! The session was to take place in the offices and the receptionist had gone home for the day, locking his office, so I couldn't even use his home address. All I knew about him was his name and that he was on vacation in New Orleans. My friend, the doctor, had flown to London the day before, so with my promise to do the reading, I was really stuck.

I appealed to the Sources, reasoning that I would be able to tell from the quality of the music whether we had "brought him through" or not. I went through all the usual procedures, except at that time I wasn't yet using the birthdate, and the music came through strong and clear. It felt just as particular as any other reading, and I knew we'd channeled him. What a relief! Again, I was impressed with the Sources' abilities. I had heard of other psychics doing long-distance readings and decided I, too, could do them—especially if I had the exact address of the subject.

Nowadays, I probably would accept a client's office address as sufficient, but I didn't think of this at the time, I suppose because his personal office was locked. Over the years there has been a gradual increase of "in absentia" sessions, and now they constitute roughly one-half of the readings. The music comes through exactly as if the client were sitting before me, the only difference being that we can't discuss it and help with the application to life.

#26—In the fall of 1973, I attended a conference at the Association for Research and Enlightenment (the Edgar Cayce Headquarters) in Virginia Beach. A young man walked up who had had an Attunement Tape the previous year. In the course of conversation, he said he was disappointed because something had happened to his tape—his dog had been so attracted to it he'd chewed it up! I told him that was not the kind of nurturing we had in mind with the tape, but this was only met with slight amusement. Then I told him I had kept a file copy and would be happy to run him off one. He was overjoyed! I have received a number of reports that animals are fascinated by this music and often try to get as close as they can to it. This I take as another corroboration of the special power of its vibrations.

#27—It was in early January of 1974 that I did the first "reverse channeling" (one of only two or three). I thought I had lost $650 and I wondered if the Sources might help me find it. Since I wanted words from them, I thought if I channeled a melody and then translated the pitches back into letters they might be willing to give me a clue. All I got was "LERN—LERN—LERN"! At the time, this was a little disheartening, but as I mulled it over, I realized the situation could be seen as a spiritual lesson. I approached it on that level, forgiving all people I could blame, and found that I had hidden the money in a "safe place"—in the inner pocket of a little-used coat in my closet! It is interesting that there have only been one or two others like this. I assume that it is not considered valuable to use the special qualities of music to provide mere words, especially when words themselves can be channeled.

#28—On February 16th, 1974, I was playing one of many concerts for a light center in Atlanta. Marietta Khounal, the co-director of the Institute, has been a long-time student of the angelic order and she could see a shining presence over my harp. At intermission she said, "Why don't you channel for the angel over your harp?"

At that time, I suspected that angels were involved in my work, but I had never channeled directly for one. I said, "Do you think I could?"

She replied, "Of course! Why don't you do it tonight?"

At the end of the program, without saying a word about it to the audience, I silently said an affirmation asking to be able to bring forth music from the presence over the harp. What took place, I still remember as one of the highlights of my life.

The music opened with a section of tremendous power in the key of F. (This confirmed my growing suspicions that this was the note of the Angelic Order in the system). Then followed a section of plaintive, sliding notes created by the tuning key held against the strings. I know this to be the angel pleading with us to take care of our Earth. Rich chords followed, and melody in the left hand accompanied by a very high, sustained vibration—the rattling of the metal shank of the tuning key between two of the higher strings. At times, I sang in a high, pure falsetto which people said sounded like a being from another plane. This complex, subtle music taxed my nervous system to the utmost. When I finished, I bowed to the presence over the harp, bowed to the audience, and went off stage in semi-hysteria. I was weeping tears of joy and ecstacy at the extraordinary beauty of what had come through. It was 15 or 20 minutes before I could get myself under some kind of control.

In the week that followed, I realized this music was for everyone and, as other general channelings came forth, I began to make "An Angel Sings" available to the public. I remember that I copied these first tapes myself, selling them for $7 per channeling, $12 for both sides of a cassette. The purchaser could choose another from the list of titles for side 2 (prices have come down since then). The angels are the builders of form on the planet, and their language is vibration—they are the artisans of much of what we see on Earth—so it is little wonder that an angel with some experience in music could bring forth a piece of such magnificence and rapture.

#29—While doing some attunement tapes at Lake Junaluska, N.C., in August of 1974, some most interesting music came through. My client had had a life as a Wagnerian tenor. The music was unmistakably in the style of Wagner, with the richly-textured chromatic harmonies rapidly changing, under soaring, expressionistic melodies. My feet fairly flew on the pedals of the harp as its tonal possibilities were pushed to the utmost. I was astonished at how these shifting harmonies, which I had certainly heard but never played before, could be lifted out of my memory. There was also a section about a sojourn on Jupiter which I found most transporting.

#30—Channeling from the Ascended Master Kuthumi (I am including dates here so that you can see the frequency of these special events.) On February 29, 1975, with support from this side, and I'm sure a great deal of help from the other side, I accomplished my first musical disclosure directly from an ascended master. I had met a circle of young people dedicated to the Light in Daytona Beach, Florida, and they wanted me to channel from their master, Kuthumi. Assuming it was successful, they planned to produce the music as an LP album. This most important and beloved Master was then serving the planet as a Chohan (custodian) of the Second Ray (Love-Wisdom) and World Teacher. An afternoon was arranged at a recording studio and I was taken to a clairvoyant in order to consult this Master as to how to proceed.

Christine Stacey (she has passed into spirit so I can use her real name) was one of the clearest and most technically refined channels to the masters that I have ever experienced. I loved her after the first session, and discovered three years later that she had been my mother in my last life! She seemed to be in almost constant contact with the Master Serapis Bey (Chohan of the Fourth Ray, Ascension). Through him she was able to get other primary masters "on the line," providing they were not too preoccupied. It was all easy conversation and most impressive. The Master Kuthumi gave his approval of our recording project, saying that it would be his great pleasure to give me music if I would attune myself in meditation to his vibration. I would recognize him by his "persistence" and a "finely-tuned electric blue." The session was the next afternoon, and the only place I could find to attune to Kuthumi was under the billiard table in my father-in-law's house! I did see a column of beautiful blue light descend around me and it seemed to be permeated with the quality of definiteness of purpose.

After we had made our preparations in the studio, I discussed with the engineer how long the music should be. We decided it shouldn't run longer than 25 minutes per side. I gestured toward higher planes as if to put in that request. It was taking a little while to arrange the ideal conditions for such an important channeling and the engineers were getting a little "antsy" about the time. I realized that most of the rock groups they record take the best version of many renditions and can take all afternoon to get on tape two good tracks. So I told them we would be ready soon and once we started there would be no retakes. Of course, they looked at me with incredulous humor.

We placed a picture of the Master on my music stand and the group of dedicated young people arranged themselves in a circle around me. After some "OM" chanting, Scott Livingston, the focalizer of the project, said some affirmations and decrees. Then I said my affirmation and the music came forth. This was the first time I had channeled in a studio, and just as a precaution, I asked three of the group members to watch the time. If I approached 25 minutes, they were to give me a sign.

When I finished the music, I was guided to put up my arms to keep the tape rolling, capturing the vibratory ambience in the studio. When I gave the cutoff, I looked down at the group around me. They were all "out cold" in meditation. Each one had lain down backwards so that the circle resembled the petals of a flower. Of course, no one had an eye on the time! I brought them out of meditation and they were all ecstatic. Someone thought to ask the control room how long the music lasted. The studio clock said 25 minutes and 8 seconds (including the ambience time at the end)! At first, this seems miraculous, and it did at the time. But, when you consider that music is the art of time, you realize that if masters can bring through music at all, the overall length is no problem. On the other hand, if Kuthumi gave me the music all at once, and I translated it into time, then the overall length must have been accomplished by a different technique.

The day before the session, Nel, my wife at the time, and a very fine sensitive, had seen the music coming through in a new scale. As predicted, the majority of Side I is in the Locrian Mode, the rarest and strangest of the Greek scales (from B to B on the white keys of the piano). The keynote B symbolizes persistence, patience, organizing yourself in space and time (and in its higher aspect, the Actualizing Principle for The Light, and thus, Service to The Light).

We returned to Christine the next day to ask the Master Kuthumi how he wished us to handle the details of production. He seemed pleased, saying that this music would be of great value to new metaphysical organizations who don't have their music yet to help them organize and manifest the Light work. He left production to us, saying that we would be guided, and made his exit with many blessings.

Imagine my satisfaction when the following October brought the first shipment of what we called the Kuthumi record. We felt that it wouldn't be right to use his name on the album, so we put his face on it without a title. He works very closely with The Christ and so his picture emanates a Christ-like vibration and is often mistaken for The Christ. The repeated note B at the beginning of this music promotes deep centeredness and peace, and has helped thousands into meditative states. Harried mothers tell me that when the din of the children rises a few decibels beyond reason, they simply sneak in the room and put on the record and the effect is magical, gradually bringing the sound level down. Side II takes us on flights to various higher planes and then helps us apply to life what we learned there. The effect of this music is the opposite of focusing and centering, and helps us to open up, expand, and fly.

#31—"Healing Music for the Whole Earth." On the way back from Florida, we stopped in to see Joe Garnor in North Carolina. Joe is a fine color healer and lecturer on spiritual matters and has since built a temple for healing and awakening on his property. He leads meditations to disperse the negativity surrounding Earth, and he invited us to take part in one. We sat in silence for a time, then I channeled on the harp and this was followed by a spontaneous channeling by Nel. The meditation was especially vibrant and the music was extraordinarily powerful. Through Nel the Sources explained that there was a political situation brewing in the Near East. The music was used as a carrier wave for our peace, love and harmony through certain key people in Washington, D.C., to other key figures in the Near East. Important work had been accomplished, significantly helping to resolve the situation. They also asked me if I would channel for the United States Government in the nation's capital. Now most of my life I have felt frustration at having any effect on the government. It is so difficult to find out what's really going on. So the possibility that I might, in some way, have a positive influence on the United States government was exciting!

A little over a month later, on April 3rd, a concert was arranged at the Church of Humanity (Russell James) in Washington. There were about 40 dedicated souls present in the sanctuary. I asked them to offer themselves in meditation for the government as I channeled on the harp.

We directed this concentrated energy toward the White House. Again, the music was extra strong, and the sanctuary became charged with a powerful resonance.

In the two years that followed, I often took part in the "Biocosmological" healing conferences put on by Joseph Kantari at American University, situated right behind the White House. Each time I played, I would ask the entire audience, sometimes as many as 300, to beam positive thought-forms and emotions to the President and his staff. We would invoke the Master Saint Germain, since he was so instrumental in founding this country, and, as a primary custodian for the Flame of Freedom, he is our mentor. ("Uncle Sam" was undoubtedly patterned after Saint Germain.)

#32—"The Heart Chakra." On May 11th, 1975 ("Mother's Day"), there occurred an event which was a milestone in this musical ministry. Certainly, it was one of the most remarkable experiences of my life. Here's the story:

For some months, I had been wanting to channel healing music for the Heart Chakra, but it had not been forthcoming. On this particular morning, I went off to my studio to do some work. When Nel, my partner, arose, she took a shower. Her Sources, the Lords of Sirius, came to her in the shower asking her if she would go right over to my studio for some important work.

I was playing the harp when she appeared at the door, saying that the Sources had sent her. She sat down in a chair, going directly into full trance. I hastily grabbed a tape recorder and started it. She began to speak. The voice was one of power and authority, (but one that I didn't seem to recognize), and it began with seven repetitions of "I AM the Violet Flame." Then, it continued along these lines: "Many forces are present on this chosen day—an optimum day out of many time cycles. You are the proper channel for this work, and if you will assume the lotus posture, we will prepare you for the channeling." As I had been trained, I said, respectfully, under my breath, "If it be God's will." The voice said, "Indeed!" I had developed the utmost respect for Nel's Sources, but this voice was new to me. I was somewhat anxious as I surrounded myself with the Light of Protection, and assumed the lotus position. The voice certainly hadn't said anything negative, and as it intoned mantrums of purification and alignment to prepare me, I gained some confidence. My chakras were aligned and energies of great power were brought into my being. Mighty cosmic forces were being invoked for something momentous. Whatever human part of me was still conscious was saying, "You mean you expect me to play the harp after this?" The strange thing was, in spite of all the power being accumulated, I felt balanced and at peace. Finally, the voice said, "You have been wanting to bring through music for the heart. Did you think you could do it alone?" (This referred to Nel and I working together.) Then followed more invocations of cosmic forces and acknowledgement of the presence of the broadcast angels ready to disseminate the music, and other decrees. The Master said simply, "The action of the Heart Center is vital at this time as it balances the lower three chakras with the upper three. Now you may bring through the music for the Heart Chakra."

I was in such an altered state (one of the highest I have ever experienced in my life), that I didn't notice that one channel of the tape recorder was set slightly too low. The music that came forth was of such deep, profound love and exquisite loveliness as has not often touched Earth. The first section seems to gather up all of our misunderstandings, anxieties, and disharmonies connected with love. Then, the second section begins the sensitive unraveling of all of these, and the raising of them into the Light of Universal Love. It is imbued throughout with intense radiations of The Violet Flame for transmuting past patterns. By the time the final notes are reached, one can touch the Holy Christ Love if one is open to it.

All the time I was playing, Nel sat in full trance. When I finished, the voice spoke again, "On this day your love has covered this planet. Through the ministry of the angels, this music has touched every heart chakra on Earth. This day marks the beginning of your true work. I leave you with my love and with signs and symbols."

When Nel channels in full trance, they take her conscious mind to another place where she is shown scenes and symbols so when she returns she has some idea of what took place. On returning, she said, "I don't know what this was, but they were showing me beams of light going out all over, entering people in the chest."

When I told her what had come through, all we could do was hold each other and shake our heads in awe of having served the purpose and power of Universal Love. When we could talk, we realized that, yes, this planet did seem to be going through an initiation of the Heart Chakra. We felt so blessed to have been chosen to play a part in it. We also remembered that the Higher Forces need us as much as we need them; for the greatest work a co-creation is required. It is often not as effective for them to give humans spiritual concepts about human love, as it is to inspire a human to express spiritualized human love to another human. In 1971, I experienced an opening of my heart chakra. I had been steadily developing the awareness that everyone on the planet was my brother or sister, so I guess I was ready to express this universal love through my highest means of expression, the vibrations of harp music. I will forever be grateful for this unusual opportunity to serve my human brothers and sisters on the earth.

Now remember that the Source's last words were, "I leave you with signs and symbols."

As we were talking, Nel looked under my table. Her gaze became fixed on a cardboard box on which was written the name Roger Bacon. This immediately reminded us of Francis Bacon, who, according to a number of esoteric sources, is considered to be the main author of the Shakespeare plays. He is said to be either an "embodiment" of the ascended master St. Germain, or to have been strongly overshadowed by him. When we went home for lunch, we checked the mail. There in the box, to our gleeful amazement, was a violet envelope containing a channeling from St. Germain! We knew he is the Chohan (custodian) of the seventh Ray, the Violet Flame energies of Transmutation, so when he said, "I AM the Violet Flame" seven times, it should have been a clue to his identity.

Another observation I would like to make about this dispensation: notwithstanding other dispensations elsewhere in the world, does this not strengthen the visions so many have had about the destiny of America? That the people of this country have a special role to play in carrying Light and Love to the rest of the world? And if you study the American renaissance in spiritual healing, you see hundreds of dedicated people studying a hundred different modes of healing, (most of which involve Love and Transmutation of the past), and taking these techniques to other parts of the world. There they give workshops to help people heal themselves. I wonder how many of these practitioners are working under St. Germain, or his students, without knowing it consciously?

My last question is why was Mother's Day chosen? Was it perhaps a gift for Mother Earth? To be sure, on this day, in the countries where it's celebrated, people would be thinking about mother love and would be more receptive to the qualities of heart-love. I must confess to you that when things didn't seem to be going well, I would sometimes entertain the stupid human thought that this day was a pretty hard act to follow! Fortunately, I can report that there have been many miracles in my life and work since May 11th, 1975.

#33—"Meditation No. 2" November 11, 1975. A good ten years before this date, at an Edgar Cayce conference at Asilomar, California, someone asked me, in all seriousness, if I could create an album of music for meditation through the chakras. After thinking it over, I told him that I was intrigued, but did not feel ready for the karmic responsibility of creating music for everyone's chakras. The chakras are basic transformers of energy for hundreds of uses in at least four of our different "bodies." They are fine-tuned and complex in the way they work together, and should not be toyed with by someone who isn't experienced, unless the work is under the guidance of a Higher Being.

Ten years later, while I was in New York doing a series of Individual Attunements, time was arranged for me in a recording studio owned by a friend of my sponsor. He was worried about the strange things that were happening at the studio. She thought there might be dark forces at work, and asked me to channel some music to exorcise them and heal the space. In return, I was to have an hour or so recording time. Just on awakening, I often receive guidance for the day. It was very clear that morning that I was to channel general healing music for the chakras and I was given the key-centers for each section.

There were some problems in the studio, but they were eventually ironed out, and the musical transmission went quite well. The opening section is in the key of F to provide a vibration for the angelic forces to come in wherever the tape is played. These forces enlist the aid of the devas and elementals present, stabilizing and harmonizing the space. After a pause, music for each chakra follows in ascending order with pauses in between. I had a number of chakra experts check out this tape. The consensus was unanimous: each section does bring purification, regulation of spirallic flow (acceleration or retardation), and general healing to the appropriate chakra. It also helps to balance and harmonize each one with the other chakras. This was most satisfying, and I could see the great value of this tape. Also, since it works on all the chakras, it's an excellent tape for general healing. In addition, it has been successfully used in color healing where slides of the basic colors are projected on a person, going through the spectrum, starting with red. Conveniently, there is a pause between each section where the slide can be changed. It is also an ideal background for various kinds of therapy, especially body work.

#34—In the spring of 1976, I moved from Virginia Beach to the area just west of Washington, D.C. Upon arrival, a woman by the name of Jean Keyes asked me to participate in a psychic fair she was producing at a local junior college. During the course of my lecture, I was telling the story of how a woman stood up in the audience of the A.R.E. and asked me if I could improvize music on a person. Jean was present at the lecture, and at that point broke in, saying, "I was the one who asked you to do that." What a miracle! As the years had passed since 1971, my curiosity had grown and grown about who that woman was. I had suspected that the Sources, who knew I was ready to do this new kind of work, must have asked her to speak up. But I had wanted to meet the lady who was so open to that guidance.

Jean later arranged a workshop for me at her home and, getting to know each other better, it became clear that part of Jean's work is to encourage new psychics and lightworkers. I was certainly grateful to the Higher Forces for this meeting, and especially to the angels who have a lot to do with getting people together. You can see from the letters of her last name that the Purpose of Growth of her Activity Patterns is to seek greater attunement with the note E (the letter K), the Father Principle, the Light. She also draws on past direct attunement with the Light, the two E's.

#35—On May 13th of that year, I was asked to take part in an unusual meeting of light-workers. The full moon in May is celebrated by esoteric metaphysicians, especially those following the teachings of the master Djwal Khul, through the writings of Alice Bailey. It is known as the festival of Wesek—a time when the Buddha sends his radiations and communications to his followers and to thousands of others who are listening all over the world. A devoted light-worker, whom I had met by the name of Ben Fuller, called me to set up a five-way telephone conference call at the exact time of the full moon. I was to channel for about ten minutes from the Buddha, and Ben and three other clairvoyants would be listening in.

It was both intriguing and exciting. Half an hour before the appointed time, I had my harp tuned and set up next to the telephone. Ten minutes ahead, I had said my affirmation and was sitting in meditative anticipation. With only slight difficulty, everyone was on the line. The phone rang, and Ben said I could begin the channeling. The acoustics were excellent in my dining room and the music was truly resplendent. The comments that followed were most interesting. Although there was some variety in what they got, there was much similarity. Esther McVeaney is a well-known sensitive in the Washington area. She's a wonderful woman from whom I had received readings and for whom I had channeled a Past-Life Attunement. She gave her impressions last, and her interpretation of the music was extensive and exalted. Ben knew it was important for me to make a living with my new work, and he paid me for this service, even though I probably would have done it just to take part in it. It gave me a special twinge of pleasure to be recompensed for such esoteric work as channeling music for a conference call! Yet, Ben's idea was also grounded in practicality—it would have been difficult for all those psychics to meet where the harp was, 50 miles out in Middleburg, Virginia!

Since then, I have channeled four times for the Buddha on Wesek, and also on the other two esoteric Festivals of Light: the full moons of April and June. It is always a peak experience for me and two of the Wesek channelings are on tape. They help one attune to the masters and places on the earth involved in the Festival.

#36—A tape to harmonize a family. August 26th, 1976, found me doing readings in Phoenix, Arizona. The Kaynors were both deeply involved in work for the Light. They were working with a group to purchase a tract of land outside the city for the development of a Light community and retreat center. This intense activity was, of course, extracurricular to their jobs and family responsibilities and there had been some strain in the household and with the children. So I took the full names and birthdates of every family member, asking for music that would

take all their karmic connections into account and provide vibrations conducive to understanding, cooperation, healing and harmony. It went very
well, and they were pleased. Since then, I have done a number of these
channelings for family harmony.

Two days later, Bill Kaynor returned for another first request. He
said the group would very much like a channeling and a name analysis.
They were forming a corporation to buy the land and to plan and administer the retreat center. Again the channeling was strong, and the analysis most revealing. I explained the vibrations that the name would attract,
the Purposes of Growth that would be set by the initials, and what the
organization could draw from the past through the personal past-life experience of its members (and also from the history of similar organizations). Members of the group found it valuable as to possible areas of
disharmony, as well as areas of service to the Light and the magnificent
future potential.

Since then I think I must have done six or eight analyses of business
names either existing or projected. It was gratifying to see a whole new
area opening up for the use of the name analysis; that is, a consultation
before an entity is named. We can go over possible names to see what
patterns of purpose and past experience are going to be attracted. If you
are convinced, at this point, of the importance of a person's name, perhaps
you can appreciate how important the name of a large organization af-
fecting thousands of people might be!

#37—My first long channeling. Up until November of 1976, I had
not channeled on the harp for over 20 minutes. The first half of a concert would usually consist of written music by other composers. After
Intermission, I would improvize for around 20 minutes, discuss with the
audience their responses, and then close with a short improvization. When
I projected my work into the future, it seemed that one day I would be
able to improvize an entire concert. I had some anxiety about this, and
needed a little nudging.

On November 7th, I was slated to play for a banquet in Detroit. The
previous week was taken up completely with readings in New York, and
I had no time to practice. I thought that at some point, I would have
an opportunity to go over the pieces, but logistics were tight and there
was absolutely no time. As I lay down for a few moments of meditation
around five o'clock, I appealed to The Sources for help. As I came back
to consciousness, they gave me a plan for a long channeling. It consisted
simply of going through the Circle of Fifths (C, G, D, A, etc.) and improvizing in each key (tied in with the chakras). At the banquet, I helped
the audience into a receptive state, said my affirmation, and settled down
to explore each tonality and its archetypal meaning in the system. This
challenge was a stimulating one and I rose to it. The tape I was recording
on ran out at 45 minutes, but I was getting deeper and deeper into the

music and played on for at least 10 minutes!

After that, I knew I could do it and began to improvize full concerts. This was actually a relief since it was becoming increasingly difficult to change from the state required for accurate recall of a written composition, which calls for mental alertness, to the optimum state for the reception of the higher music, where the mind is much more diffused. These two, quite different, states require changes on a number of levels, and each one was acting more and more to the detriment of the other. Sensitive people in the audience were beginning to comment that the channeled music was much more moving than the written music. I gave it up soon thereafter and, as much as I love the music of certain composers, I have played very little of it since that banquet.

This direction has been recently confirmed at a concert at Findhorn, Scotland. I was taking part in their Earthsings Festival (October 1981). Chungliang Al Huang, the well-known Tai-Chi dancer, with whom I have worked for a number of years since the Alan Watts days, had asked me to accompany him on his concert. I was to play a rather difficult piece by Bach. I found the possibility of revisiting the former Joel Andrews, who played written music, thought-provoking. I was interested to see what the effect might be of adding to his musicality the experience of improvizing channeled music for ten years.

I practiced diligently for five weeks on the long, iridescent, E Major Prelude, but the long-awaited, and single, performance was a mild disaster! The harp they had procured from London had a pedal that would get stuck in the "natural" notch. I worked on it for two days, trying to free it up, but sure enough, right at the beginning of the piece, it decided to get stuck! There I was, trying to maintain the nervous equilibrium that is required to play Bach, while my left foot was kicking frantically to dislodge the recalcitrant D pedal! Finally I had to stop, make an explanation to the audience, and free the pedal with my hand. I was able to be humorous about it, and since it was not an audience of concert-goers, but a group of enlightened, Aquarian-Age souls, they laughed and took it in stride. I managed to get through the piece, but not without a few strange chords involving the stubborn D pedal.

As I thought this over on the flight back to California, I came to a sober realization. If I was going to depend on the vagaries of rented harps around the world, I couldn't be playing chromatic, written music with any assurance of success. If I had been improvizing, and a pedal got stuck, this would only be an interesting limitation. It would stimulate my creativity, and I would accept the event easily, saying to myself, "All right, we're now going to have a section of music revolving around this note (whichever note got stuck)."

#38—Recording "The Violet Flame." I remember this session took place at the Winter Solstice of 1976, and I think it was December 22nd.

I was on tour in Florida, and the same group that asked me to channel for the master Kuthumi asked me to bring through music for the Violet Flame, the 7th Ray energies of transmutation. They booked an afternoon at the same studio.

The Violet Flame is most important and valuable for the transition into the Aquarian Age. Everyone who is responding to the upleveling of vibrations and the spiritualizing of human destinies is anxious to call forth past experience, learn its karmic lessons, and release it. Invoking The Violet Flame, and visualizing it passing through oneself, or a past situation, can be most effective in transmuting so-called negative patterns into positive ones—ones that work for everyone. It can also be flamed through a space, room, or another person. It is the equivalent of what is called "The Law of Grace," which says that it is not always necessary to "walk through" or act out past patterns, in order to transmute them. You can, with the help of God, accomplish this on the level of consciousness. Lessons can be learned by reliving unresolved situations in reverie—sometimes with the help of a guide. If we don't meet them this way, for sure we *will* meet them eventually in the physical world because we outpicture them there, attracting situations to us expressly for the purpose of this work on ourselves. It has been said that this is one of the primary advantages of having a life in a physical world. It helps one to see what one is working on *because* it seems to be "outside."

Many Masters and Higher Beings work with The Violet Flame, but St. Germain and the Archangel Zadkiel seem to be its primary custodians. They have been given responsibility for keeping it flowing to us. Anyone can call on it just by saying, "I call on the Violet Flame and see it flaming through _____, transmuting all negativity into positivity." This is why we felt it so important to channel it through musically. We suspected that music might be a superb carrier for it. Of course, as it turned out, we were under guidance and there was no question about this.

Just as the group had settled themselves around me in a circle, and were ready to begin, a friend came rushing in from outside saying we had to come right out and see something special over the studio. There was on that day a low, continuous cloud cover over the town of Edgewater. As we looked, directly over the studio we saw a perfectly circular hole in the clouds and what looked like rainbows in the opening! I looked at it and said half-jokingly, "It's the cone of energy—it's burned a hole right through the clouds!" I had come to know that when The Sources are transmitting high energies they will create a vortex, stepping down the energy gradually so that we humans can handle it. Those of us who have thought about it agree that it was this energy cone that separated the clouds directly over the studio.

Little did we know, at the time, that this valuable music would be distributed all over the United States and to many other countries as well. As we once more arranged ourselves, chanting "OM" together, and entering a meditative state, Scott Livingstone began the decrees, in a medium voice, to invoke the presence of The Christ, the Masters and The Violet Flame. Every time he would make a direct call, I would hear a hum which would quickly rise and fall. I said to myself, "Why do they build these recording studios close to railroad tracks? Or could it be a nearby airport?" The hums got louder and louder, and when Scott asked the Violet Flame to pass through the sound equipment, transmuting all negative vibrations, a loud "framp!" came over the loudspeakers—much louder than his voice. The music that came forth was quite different from anything I had ever played, and the first third of Side I expresses various flame-like patterns. It explores the Dominant harmonies built on the note Bb (suggestive of the seventh Ray).

When we had begun to recover from the music, we asked the engineers about the strange sounds. They explained that they were definitely not sounds from outside the studio, but power surges that occurred inside the equipment, which they could not explain.

They said, "We don't know what this was, but when your leader asked that The Violet Flame pass through the sound equipment, our needles went all the way over into the red, which would normally register a loud sound."

Just as this incomparable music of The Violet Flame must be fully experienced to be appreciated, Side II, "Violet Joy," must be danced to, or moved to, to be fully known. It is gentler and lighter than Side I, and works on more mundane levels helping us to transmute and spiritualize the daily tasks of life. It is more rhythmic, and I always play it in workshops when I want people to experience the healing power of joyful movement. It begins simply, but in 20 minutes those who are willing have become accomplished ballet and contemporary dancers! We are dancing with the angelic orchestras and choirs to hosanna's of Love from glorious cosmic realms.

The "hums" of The Violet Flame, as Scott called it forth, and especially the loudest one, are clearly audible on the master tape. Sometimes I ask a friend, "Would you like to hear The Violet Flame? I have it on tape." Of course, what we are hearing is probably not The Violet Flame, but all the dissonant musical thought-forms that had become lodged in the equipment by all the confused, or even satanic, groups that had recorded in that studio. We're hearing them scurrying away before the powerful Light and Love and Purity of The Violet Flame.

#39—Past-Life resonation with the name Miklas Doulos. (I hope Miklas won't mind my using his real last name—it is essential to this story.) During his past-life Attunement, he was given a recent life in France where he had a toy business. The name I heard for his business was

"De l'Anz(e)." Now in French "de" is pronounced something like the English "do" and the N is nasalized without the tongue touching the roof of the mouth. The "Dou" of "Doulos" is also pronounced like "do" and the "o" like "oh." There was a great deal of similarity between the name of his toy business in France and his present last name. When I did his reading, I didn't know what "de l'ans" meant in French, and was pleased to discover that it means "of the years or ages." What a perfect name for a business which sells toys for children of different sizes. This is only one case, out of many, where the sound or spelling of a name, or internal words within a name, show a connection with a previous life.

#40—"Pan Solstice" Summer Solstice, 1977. While playing concerts in Atlanta three years before this date, I struck up a friendship with a most interesting young man by the name of Elfrik Newman. He had followed a number of spiritual paths, and had studied Aikido assiduously, but his special interests were working with the subtle energies of the body for healing. He had also studied the secret power of sound and music. He seemed almost more "devic" than human, and we would spend hours in the woods looking for power spots, attuning ourselves to tree and water devas. Early in 1977, he arrived in the Washington area to spend a few months and we played some concerts together.

He had assembled some of the sounds that he liked in an instrument which, I thought, resembled more than anything an insect-type creature who had just beamed down from a rather strange planet! It stood about the same height as the harp, and the top third, which was a set of Montessori bells, looked like a set of vertebra. Just below this was a bar, suggesting shoulders, from which hung two cymbals (breasts); then a small table for smaller instruments (hips), and just under this, two tunable drum heads called "rototoms" (buttocks). The harp also appears to some people to be other-worldly and, since there are few other instruments that stand up to its height, when we put the two of them together, it looked as if the harp had finally found a suitable companion! Elfrik and I would go out into the woods and talk about music, and then create for our audiences some of the most interesting aural spaces that I have ever been in.

As the Summer Solstice approached, he said to me, "I know what let's do, let's channel for Pan! And let's do it exactly on the Solstice." We had both heard the cassettes from Findhorn about Roc's confrontations with the angel Pan. And having spent so much time in the woods attuning ourselves to his kingdom, we hoped he might bless us with some music. I also have a basic self in my subconscious with developed devic connections, and was "turned on" by the prospect. Then, too, my house in Middleburg, Virginia, was right on the edge of some undisturbed woods. Ten minutes before the appointed time, we were out in the middle of my lawn, chanting and invoking Pan, when two unexpected friends arrived: a young girl who had had a reading from me and the 80-year-old man for whom she worked. He was dressed in a heavy, dark suit (on June 21st!). There was nothing for it but to welcome them into the circle, and the five of us completed the invocations together. We went directly into my studio, started the tape recorder, and began to play.

What took place there was absolutely extraordinary. I had tuned the harp to an Overtone Series (the untempered, pure scale of nature), and I began with this chord as a musical invocation. Its sonorous proportions surged and pulsed, expressing The Law of Resonance, throughout the music. It turned out to be a 26-minute journey into the heart of Pan's kingdom.

After the invocation, Elfrik sings some words channeled from a deva, inviting us deeper into the forest where we find ourselves in a clearing. Many of Pan's creatures are about to have a festival celebration. There follows a series of dances, each by a different group or soloist, so the style of the music we are channeling changes accordingly. There is a laughing dance by a group of fauns, and then a more lyrical, graceful, ballet solo by a water deva. You can hear the laughing of the fauns on the tape and the water sprite solo is quite an experience, especially if you're dancing. As soon as the dancing is over, Pan, who is sitting on a rock nearby, takes out his pipes and begins to play a haunting melody to call them all to him. Until that time, I had not whistled in a channeling, but it was the only way to capture the clear, shimmering quality of the tune Pan was giving to me. It is reminiscent of Debussy's "Afternoon of a Faun." Pan speaks to them, and then he leads them all off, single-file, into the deep forest. Next a storm comes up, but Pan's merry band seems to enjoy this display by the elemental forces. Finally, the storm subsides and peace reigns once again in the devic kingdom—a peace full of love for God and the grandeur of creation.

Truly, as the music swelled, my studio dissolved and we were present in the scenes I have described. It was a journey into the power and beauty of nature—an experience to dispel the fears many of us have about these forces. Pan gives us a deep lesson here by allowing us to enter his world and partake of some of the unalloyed joy and beatific artistry of his creatures. In addition, he gives us his own music. He reassures us that all things are working for good (or God) if we could but understand them and dance with them. Once more, he shows us what a gross and childish mistake it was (and costly!) to associate him with the devil. Fully experiencing this music can take you to places seldom experienced by man, and can help you overcome fears normally locked deep within the subconscious memory.

#41—While I was in Virginia Beach, I met a couple that came over from Holland to study the work of Edgar Cayce. She had a radio program in Amsterdam, where she interviewed people in the New Age field, and she had a special interest in wholistic healing. In 1977, she invited me to Holland, setting up a number of concerts and workshops. A close friend of hers arranged an appearance at a healing conference in a small town north of Brussels. The only harp they could find was 90 years old, and the mechanism was so far out of adjustment, it was unplayable as a chromatic harp—some of the pedals wouldn't even work! This is the kind of nightmare that I sometimes have: I'm supposed to go on stage in an hour to play a concert and my harp is impossible to play. Fortunately, in real life, we are usually prepared ahead of time for these exigencies— often by dreams.

For at least two years, I had been retuning my harp to the Overtone Series. I would select a fundamental note for its appropriate symbolism, and tune the entire harp to that Harmonic Series (through the fourth octave). Then I would improvize without pedal changes, (the mechanism is adjusted for the *tempered* intervals). So this I did with this aged, but noble, instrument. It sounded wonderful! The older and drier the wood of a harp becomes, as long as it isn't cracked, the finer its resonance.

This may have been the first time I channeled in the Overtone Series before an audience, but it went quite well and I got positive feedback from a few of the listeners. One man did come back and ask me if I had some difficulty tuning the instrument. There are differences between the two tunings, especially in certain notes, but for the average, lay, listener they are not enough to notice consciously. This man, however, was a musician; and I have found that musicians who play a keyboard instrument, do notice the differences. Until they relax into the new scale, and flow with it, it sounds out of tune. Our hearing has adjusted remarkably well to Tempered Tuning (which came in around 1680), but it would be impossible for us to forget pure tuning, because it is The Law of Resonance itself. Its notes are the result of how a vibrating body (or, for that matter, everything in the world) reacts to being "played" or set into motion. You can imagine how overjoyed I was to be able to rise to this challenge. It seemed like another case set up by The Sources to push me into using what I had been given.

The Overtone Series is obviously the most healing scale to use, and I have been increasingly guided to use it through the years. At concerts, I often do one channeling in it, retuning the harp during Intermission. It appears to me that the more people become healed and open up their sensitivities, the more they will be irritated by the dissonance inherent in the tempered scale. Eventually, they will be ready for some tuning based on the pure intervals of the Harmonic Series.

#42—A tape for use in a healing sanctuary. In October of 1977, I received a request from Ellen and Benson Nicholsen, who had founded a healing center in Miami. Through its doors flowed a constant stream of clients coming for hands-on healing, and they wanted me to channel a tape that they could use. They wanted it to create an ambience conducive to relaxation, centering, calling forth the dissonant patterns, transmutation, and release. I channeled the tape, and then realized that even if I made up the usual C-90 extended-play cassette, they would still have to keep flipping it over, as their sessions sometimes lasted for hours. I hit on the idea of using an Endless Loop cassette. The longest one available was 12 minutes, but this was practically the length of the original channeling, so I copied it for them and sent it off. They sent me a check with a note of thanks, saying that the tape was working fine and then I didn't hear from them. I ran into them recently at an American Indian ritual dance in Santa Fe. They said they had just closed the sanctuary in Miami after serving some 50,000 healees and training many healers. They said the tape lasted for years. Since then, I have channeled six or seven tapes for healers to use in this way.

The popularity of endless-loop tapes has also grown, and I'd like to tell you a wonderful story about one in particular. This happened to a close friend of mine, and I trust she won't mind my telling it as long as I don't mention her name. I had brought through some music called "Ambience" for the healing of love relationships. And this soon became her husband's favorite music for love-making. After a few weeks, she confided in me, "Could you possibly put that music on an endless loop tape? Because I have to keep getting up to turn the tape over!" As soon as I could, I sent off the new tape. In a week or so I received a note from her which said, "Oh, thank you so much. You have done us both a great service—especially me!"

#43—The 1978 Festival for Mind and Body. Many of my family are broadly educated, and my friends would say that I was more European than American. Naturally, for many years I wanted to go to Europe. It just didn't happen and I finally gave up the idea, consoling myself with the knowledge that I had spent the last two lives there. In May of 1978 I flew to London. I had met a well-known color healer from England, Rose Gladden (real name), at a Festival for the Esoteric Sciences in Phoenix. Within ten minutes, we had recognized each other as Lightworkers having special rapport with the devic and angelic realms. She asked me to collaborate with her in a demonstration of her healing work with an individual. It was highly successful, and corroborated some of my growing theories about the equivalence of pitches and colors. Later on I will report to you on this research.

Rose enjoyed the intensification of the healing energies so much that she flew me to London to play in her booth at the Festival for Mind and Body. It took place in Olympia Hall. It was a huge exposition, with probably 100 booths, presenting every imaginable approach to New Age consciousness. There was an open sound stage on the main floor for larger productions. The roof mainly consisted of panes of glass in the shape of one half of a huge cylinder. The sounds of some 2,000 people, mixed with a number of tape recorders in the booths playing different music, as well as lectures, and the louder sounds coming from the open theater, all rose to the roof. There, they were thoroughly mixed in the cylinder, and sent back down as cacophonous pandemonium!

Now when I channel, I'm in the habit of expanding the sensitivity of my hearing tremendously, and this includes my surroundings. After the first 45 minutes of playing, I started to get a headache and some nausea. By two o'clock, I had to go back to my hotel room with symptoms approaching the flu. As I rested my ears, I asked the directors of my ministry how I could meet my responsibility. It was one of the most difficult assignments I have ever had. Three or four healers took turns so that there was a steady stream of clients and Rose was hoping I could play more or less continuously! While there are instruments on which you can play for long hours, a harpist can get blisters rather quickly unless he has the callouses that come from playing five hours a day. Of course, since I had been improvising for some years, I had not been in the habit of playing more than one hour a day, and I started to get blisters.

When I came back early the next morning, I told Rose I was ready to try it again if I could have one-half hour off for every 45 minutes of playing. I knew that I would not be able to open myself up at all to the environment, and I asked the Higher Forces to help me out. After two or three hours, I asked Rose how it was going. She said that the colors were coming through strong and clear. What a relief! The Sources had come through again, working out a new method of transmission so that I didn't have to go into an altered state at all. All I had to do was play the harp. I have to hand it to Rose and her staff who kept the hands-on healing energies flowing from 9 a.m. to 9 p.m. for five days! My heart would have kept it up, too, but my fingers would have been bleeding sores. An interesting lesson.

#44—Another incident that showed the amazing versatility of The Sources took place on tour in Florida. I think it was 1977. My harp was literally coming apart at the seams, and great cracks were appearing between the sounding board and the base of the instrument. This affected the operation of the pedals, and it was getting more and more out of tune. On the last concert, the gaps were growing wider by the moment, and more and more chord combinations were noticeably out of tune. The channeling kept taking more and more interesting modulations into remote keys and finally ended up on just two notes—the only notes which were left in tune on the instrument! I came off stage in a state of awe that The Sources could have had such precise knowledge of which intervals would be in tune as the mechanism went rapidly out of adjustment. Some pedals finally stuck and were unable to be used.

#45—Trip to Dornach, Switzerland, to find one note. The day before I was to leave London, a fellow Light-worker said that I really should go to the Goetheanum and meet a lady who had studied music with Rudolph Steiner. I borrowed $200, and flew to Dornach. The lady was most interested in my work and then began playing me notes on her monochord. This instrument consists of one long string (actually she had three) stretched over a sound box about six inches by six inches by three and a half feet. She had many marks underneath the strings, and began to play for me the same musical interval in different tunings, some of them less tempered than others.

Then she played me two versions of the same note "C." She asked me how I responded to them, and when I told her she asked me how I had arrived in Dornach. I said I had flown from London the day before, whereupon she replied, "I see. Let's try this again tomorrow." We continued our discussions, and she warned me against using electricity in my music.

The next day she asked me again to tune deeply in to the two "C's." The first one, the higher one, seemed to have a brilliant and "flashy" exterior, but when I went into the heart of it made me uncomfortable, seeming dissonant and empty. The second one, seven vibrations per second lower, lacked the "flashy" beginning, or outside, but seemed sweeter, rounder and more natural. I liked the center of it, and it seemed more life-giving and harmonious with its surroundings. It actually seemed to almost increase in volume and to last longer. She was pleased as she explained that the higher C was the one found on the keyboard, and the lower one was a more ancient C, called the "Philosophers' C". She gave the frequency of the upper note as 263 with two decimal places and the lower pitch, 256. Frankly, I was mystified and I asked her if it could be the materials of the two different strings. She obliged me by reversing the strings she was using for the two notes and I still had the same responses. What mystified me was that, in all my training about the nature of music, I was never taught that one frequency was any better than another. We did not have time to discuss these two notes further, but I did have the presence of mind to buy from her a tuning fork for the lower C. She said I could also find it in a standard medical supply house.

As soon as I returned to America I gave a workshop. I played the two C's for the participants and asked them how they felt about them. It was not a group of musicians and I was most impressed that roughly three-quarters of them could sense the qualitative difference between the two pitches—just using different words to describe it. Since then I have repeated this experiment with all kinds of people—always with the same results. I have thought deeply about the difference and have received two insights:

(1) Since the higher C is our reference point for Western music, and most instruments are built in the C scale, including the piano, this pitch

reminds the subconscious of the dissonance inherent in the tempered tuning and also of all the music (much of it quite dissonant) of the past 300 years.

(2) I began descending by octaves from 256, dividing by 2, and arrived at the following number series: 256, 128, 64, 32, 16, 8, 4, 2, 1. So our C is a multiple of 1 vibration per second! I wonder how many music students know about this and that we are tuning our instruments 7 vibs/sec off! Another related revelation was that this number series follows the number of notes in each successive octave of the Overtone Series itself, the Law of Resonance: one note in the first octave, two in the second, four in the third, eight in the fourth, etc.

Soon after this, I met a friend who was studying computer language who said, "Oh, we're familiar with the number 256 because we work with sets of eight". As you know, I have been retuning the harp for some five years to the Overtone Series through the fourth octave which has eight notes in it. I realized, also, that this explains why we use C as the primary reference note for tuning our instruments.

A few years later, I was meditating on the word Overtone Series, and I read it in a different way so that it came out Overt-One. I realized that coded into this word is the concept: the overt or outer manifestation of the Law of One. (Note to musicians: In the name of everything that's sacred, do take the responsibility of never tuning your instrument to C-256 unless your heart and your motives are pure, and you wish to add the most beautiful sounds to the New Music.)

So this is the story of how it cost me $200 to get one note. But what a note! It has brought an added dimension of healing to every note I've played. I enjoyed so much a brief tour of the Goetheanum, the center Rudolph Steiner built, and named after his great teacher, Goethe. I also had the pleasure of attending an authentic production of Eurhythemy Dance.

#46—Power failure at Eckerd College. Around 1981, I was on tour in the vicinity of St. Petersburg, Florida, and was playing an evening concert at this college in Tampa. Halfway through my first channeling, all the power went out. It was a real test of my improvizational ability, to be suddenly, without warning, plunged into darkness. But I am happy to say that I didn't stop playing for an instant. The harp is an instrument that you need to watch to play, since it does not have any features that distinguish one string from the next (such as the piano with its raised keys). Consequently, sudden darkness required quite a shift of consciousness for me *and* the audience since they suddenly had no visual stimuli to distract them from the experience of pure sound. It was exhilarating for all of us and the music that came through was quite extraordinary and transporting. We all learned that when you're hooked up to "Universal Power and Light," you don't have power failures—you're not dependent on the local power company. Also, if I had been playing an electric-powered instrument, it would have been the end of the concert!

This calls to mind another similar occurrence at a concert in Jamaica. There, the power went out before the concert, allowing time for volunteers to gather together about fifty candles which they lit around the hall. This simple, ancient lighting created a relaxed, home-spun atmosphere...a timelessness that was appreciated by all, especially me.

#47—"Ematana," a sacred cedar in the Sierras. (December 13, 1978). As part of a tour of the San Francisco Bay area, a concert was arranged for me at the Ananda Community in Nevada City. The acoustics in their 50-foot dome sanctuary were rather extraordinary, and I channeled that evening for their master, Yogananda. The entire tour was recorded professionally, but the recording engineer for that particular evening had another engagement and requested that we record the next morning. He may also have wanted to tape me in that unusual space without the audience sounds. I developed a mild case of food poisoning later that evening and was up half the night pressing and massaging various acupressure points, and trying to remember other special exercises.

I felt much better by morning and made my way through the snow to the kitchen for some coffee. There was only one member of the community there, a young girl. She asked me to come with her down the path to a spot where some of the members had been playing volleyball to see what kind of vibrations I might pick up. She and some others had felt that it was a sacred space and should not be used for sports.

I asked her if I could come after the recording session, but she was insistent, feeling that I really should come before I went into the session. So down the path we went.

We came out of some small trees to the edge of a flat, triangular area about 50 feet across. She was behind me, and I immediately went into a meditative state that I often use when I am asking my body to be used as a dowsing instrument for earth energies. Right away, I found myself rushed forward about 30 feet, then turned around 90 degrees, and rushed about 30 feet to the right. Then, turned again, and rushed back to my starting position, inscribing a triangle. The force was strong, and as I stood on the original spot, I experienced a powerful line of energy coming from directly behind me, and extending across the little meadow. Turning around, I beheld a magnificent, old cedar, six or seven feet in diameter, with just a few gnarled branches at the top. I walked slowly toward it, and when I was about 20 feet away, I asked respectfully if I might enter its aura. I distinctly heard it say, "Come to me." As I approached, I realized how much I needed some healing, and threw my arms around the base of the tree. This embrace could not have lasted more than two minutes, but its deep peace, grounded lifeforce, and lofty ascension did much to prepare me for the coming session.

As I backed away, I gave it the *Namaste* salute (palms together at the level of the heart, symbolizing the "Divine in me salutes the Divine in you") , and I asked the cedar its name. As you might guess, I have had some experience receiving names from planets, beings, and entities of nature, and I heard clearly the name "Ematana." I quickly analyzed it. The E symbolizes its Purpose of Growth, to seek more direct contact with the Light, then the rest of the letters symbolize the experience that it's drawing upon: the M (intuitive approach to survival), the A (the Divine Mother Principle itself), the T (the form aspect of the physical), the A (Divine Mother Principle), the N (physical energy), and the A (Divine Mother Principle). I noted, also, that it had T, A, and N, all in a row, which represents the successful coordination of the three aspects of the Physical Plane. I did this analysis in a matter of seconds, gave great thanks to Ematana, and went on up the hill to the dome. I explained to the girl what I had gotten as we walked.

I still did not know, at this point, what the subject of my channeling would be. But I was guided to tune my harp to the Overtone Series of F (the devas and angels). The music was most distinctive and filled with the qualities of power, beauty and dedication. It covered the whole range of the harp, and seemed to emphasize the deepest register and the very highest octaves. When it was over, I announced to the six or eight people present that we had just channeled for the old cedar tree at the foot of the hill. The parts of the music in the bass symbolized the roots going deep into the earth, and the high parts symbolized the highest branches reaching to the sun and to the Light. I asked them if they would like to go and see Ematana. As we walked down the hill, I had a wonderful surprise. The first time down the path I hadn't noticed the top of this tree, and, of course, didn't see it as I walked back up the path. What I saw now stopped me in my tracks! Above the branches at the top of the tree was a fifteen-foot spire, silver from having been struck by lightning, shining in the sun. Here is one tree who certainly had achieved its Purpose of Growth: to make direct contact with the Light! I told my new friends my experience before the session, and we gave our love and wonder to this "warrior of the difficult path," and now, "carrier of the Light."

The engineer, wishing to capture the unique sonority of the space, aimed the microphones directly at the top of the dome instead of toward the harp. The effect is as if the listener is on top of the dome listening through an opening and provides an unusually erie and devic quality.

#48—Jamaican Light (Fall 1982). During my concerts and workshops in and around Kingston, I stayed with a Jamaican family. I had been looking forward to demonstrating my growing assurance that all peoples of earth are my brothers and sisters and was enjoying living in the heart of this family. I was surrounded by dark-skinned people, and on the third day I looked into the mirror in the bathroom and said, "Man, you're really white, you know! You're actually kind of pallid."

Then we drove downtown to the theater for the concert, and out in front, on a kind of marquee, a Jamaican artist had made a large copy of my publicity photo. As we passed it I exclaimed, "He's made me look Jamaican! How wonderful. I've made it." The dedicated sponsors had decorated the stage with natural greenery. The theater was filled with some 600 people, and I began by accompanying an American singer in the beautiful Jamaican national anthem. (Of course, they all rose.) Then I played a piece by Bach with a very fine Jamaican flutist, and proceeded right into a channeling for everyone present. It was a peak experience for me and the audience, and I am sure a large factor was the warm, open-heartedness of the Jamaican people, their natural musicality, and the fact that they had accepted me. There were some clairvoyants in the audience, and at least two of them said that at one point I became wrapped in violet flames and shortly thereafter disappeared entirely into White Light.

*   *   *   *   *   *

I hope these experiences, highlights of many, will speak for themselves. Taken along with the other cases in this book, I hope they will provide some picture of the unbelievable variety of richness, beauty, knowledge, and spirituality I have been privileged to experience. These joys await the one who can genuinely, with the heart, suspend the ego's necessity to say, "I did it," and open up co-creation with Higher Forces. I hope that what I have offered here will be an inspiration toward that opening for all who read this book, from the would-be music healer, to the person with a general interest in the process of channeling in the Spiritual Renaissance; even to the dear soul who picks up this book by mistake (?) and becomes caught up in the far-out vicissitudes of a fellow-seeker on the Path—one who has chosen the sound wings of music to bear him to God. To all of you I offer my unconditional love and a harpful of stars.

CHAPTER FIFTEEN

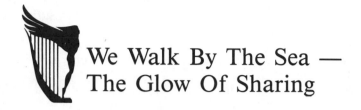

We Walk By The Sea —
The Glow Of Sharing

When I finished recounting the Jamaican experience, my friend and I sat in a highly-charged silence for some minutes, gradually becoming aware of our surroundings. We were sitting at the edge of a circular plot of ground covered with green grass, occupying the center of a large outcropping of rocks. From our position, with our backs against a tall, slanted rock face, we looked out across a 30-foot pool of green grass to the rugged, moss-covered boulders beyond. We could see the stately redwood trees surrounding the outcropping set against the rich blue of a clear sky.

Finally, he turned slowly toward me and said, "These cases you have reported represent such an almost unbelievable spectrum of experience—some of them have come almost nine in the same year—it's a wonder that it all hasn't aged you tremendously!"

I replied, "I was just thinking the same thing. I haven't had the opportunity to remember them all at once, and I am amazed how I could have done it. I think the answer lies in two facts: that I was in a state of meditative relaxation when most of them took place, and that I was co-creating with Higher Forces at the time. Their energies are a lot more efficient than mine in the normal state. I guess it shows a glimpse of what we can do when we let God do it through us. In fact, I can certainly say that I am in better condition physically, emotionally, mentally, and in terms of sensitive awareness, than I almost have ever been!"

"Here's another thing I've been meaning to mention to you: In recent years the Sources with which I co-create have shifed from individual masters, space beings, and angels to a "higher level" of Truth and Light. This focus is still very much under the protection of the highest of the Light in the Solar System which I term the "Christos" or "Christ Spirit". But again any suitable name could be used to denote this level. I feel also that at times I'm working more directly with the High Self assigned to me. Since this is an undiluted portion of the Godhead it would be certainly comparable to the Spirit of the Christ. Of course, we 'judge by the fruits.'"

He somewhat laboriously got to his feet saying, "Well, I'm feeling a little bit stiff. What do you say we go down to the beach for awhile?"

I got myself up (which wasn't easy since we'd been sitting on the ground cross-legged for two hours). I said, "I don't think it's possible."

He said, "We can't go over the cliffs, but I know a path that goes down where the river empties out, and I think it's only a few minutes from here."

We made our descent in about 10 minutes, and the beach was absolutely glorious! The gentle shock of the cool water sent our thought-forms scurrying, and at three o'clock the sand was still deliciously warm. We slept for twenty minutes, opening ourselves to the life-giving rays of Father Sun. When we awoke, we took a quick dip, then started to walk up the nearly deserted beach.

After awhile, my friend pulled some scraps of paper out of his pocket and said, "There are two things that I would like to know more about. I jotted them down two or three days ago when you mentioned them in passing. The first is the Order of Orpheus. Wasn't that the group you got together to study the art of improvization and channeling from Higher Forces?"

I replied, "That's right, but actually I didn't form it, it came together under guidance from Spirit. I'll tell you how it happened."

One evening in October, 1974, during meditation, I found myself sitting in the audience at a most unique concert that was taking place in the morning. The concert about to begin would be devoted to specific healing. There were about a dozen "patients" sitting some distance apart from each other and sipping herb tea, quietly preparing themselves for the music. On stage were five or six musicians, dressed in white, tuning their instruments. Some of these were traditional instruments and some I didn't recognize, which were yet to be discovered or invented in the West. When the music began, I found myself on stage playing with the consort.

The next moment, I distinctly heard a voice which said, "You have been shown a meeting of the Order of Orpheus doing their work. We have been working very hard to bring this into manifestation. You will be guided."

It was a remarkably clear vision which I filed away in gratitude with a number of other visions I have been given, hoping that I would be ready when this began to manifest in a number of years.

At the time, I was renting a room at the beach in an old broken-down, condemned motel in Virginia Beach, Virginia. Two weeks after my meditation, musicians began arriving at my door! First a guitarist appeared, then a flutist, and then a mandolin player. By the end of the month, we had invited a percussionist to join us and were collecting all manner of strange-looking objects that emitted interesting and beautiful sounds. We decided it would be a leaderless group, quickly falling into the practice of meditating together before playing, then chanting "Om", the accepted name for God as pure vibration. The improvization would come right out of the "Om". This music was completely without predetermination of any kind and the music that came forth was fresh and exciting. Most of the time, the room would become highly charged with uplifting vibrations. I was inspired to develop some games to help us refine the art of improvization quickly. The games were fun and developed our ability to listen to each other, and to play and listen at the same time. We also explored the various roles one player can take in an ensemble. We learned much from this as an exercise, especially when NOT to play, we soon developed one of our favorite games: setting up a fantasy in which we all took part and then performing it. These were powerful and dynamic musical psycho-dramas. Often, one of us would have a deep transformative experience. I still use these games, and others, that I have co-created, when I give workshops in the art of improvization.

After a few months, a schism developed over whether we should begin to incorporate words into our music; and whether we should see ourselves as priest-musicians and healers. I think, actually, two of the members had received what they needed from the experience for their maximum growth, and were ready to take it out into the wider world. A replacement came forward, the group continued to meet, and people began to come seeking healing.

Through the months, we channeled music for individuals, couples, communes, two cats and a geranium. We put on three concerts and produced two cassettes. We developed a curiosity as to whether the Order of Orpheus was a name that was given to our group only, or whether it was some kind of organization on the inner planes that embraced a number of groups. So we did a channeled improvization on this question and the results were far beyond expectation. Quite early, we developed the habit of comparing notes on what pictures and ideas we had received during the music, as well as listening back to it. On this afternoon, there was much agreement that the sections of this music tuned in to meetings of the Order of Orpheus in various periods of history, where one or more of us were members of the group. We came to the unanimous conclusion that the Order of Orpheus has existed for a long, long time, has many members, and that we might meet some of its other members if we were to travel. This was corroborated by a reading I did for a young man who, in a past-life in China, was playing in such a group. I saw him as part of an ensemble of musicians who rehearsed in a cave, high in the mountains. And I saw a priest coming to work with the group, to bring through higher concepts with the music. After the reading, I told him that I had seen myself sitting with this group.

For years after the members of this group went their separate ways, many of us would meet just to play a concert (with no rehearsals, of course). It was fascinating that we would learn more about what the other members had experienced in the interim through improvizing with them than by talking. After two of these impromptu meetings, I had a vision of future concerts being arranged by a sponsor who would gather together master improvizers and introduce them for the first time ON THE STAGE. Of course, this would only work where the ego could be offered up to the group, and to the Higher Forces.

I'd like to share one special story taken from my many rewarding experiences with this group. We were meeting for the last time, formally, in August of 1975, to wish "bon voyage" to a member who was moving away. Naturally, we decided to do this with the musical blessings of the guides of our ministry. We also wanted to give thanks to our friends in spirit. We had come to feel strongly that we were working under the "Nimmo Cone", a group of spirit doctors working in an astral hospital over Virginia Beach, and working also through an organization called A.D.E. (The Association for Documentation and Enlightenment). The other members present were Richard Rice, flute; James McBryde, guitar and sitar; and John David Saltzman, percussion (real names). Richard had just purchased a stereo cassette tape recorder and set it up to record the session. I was also recording on my Sony reel-to-reel.

I played my copy first, and we were gratified to find, as usual, that while there was a high degree of disparity among the separate parts, they were synthesized and harmonized into a very interesting whole, arranged by our unseen friends. But when we heard Richard's copy, we were astonished. An expanded space dimension had been added, somewhat like the electronic Echoplex sound, and we were transported by the overall beauty and power of the composition. We had some electronic knowledge between us, yet couldn't account for this unique effect. After consulting the experts, we came to the conclusion that it was an extra gift from the guides in spirit who had been working with us over the months: their way of saying, "job well done!" — their blessing of the new paths on which we were all embarking.

Some months later, we wanted to make an L.P., and we chose this channeling for Side two. Now, you don't go into a recording studio with the idea of making a master from a cassette! We planned to take the Sony copy, and the cassette copy also, just to show the effect that we wanted. We had to wait a few weeks, because Richard had carried the cassette to California in his knapsack, and was gradually making his way back to the East coast. The fidelity was still good, so I took it with me to the recording studio. The engineer processed my Sony tape with all the echo and "reverb" effects he could, and still could not achieve the sound of the cassette which literally put us in a cathedral-like space. The engineer was chagrinned, and finally had to make the L.P. from the cassette! Of course, this confirmed our feeling at the session, that the space dimension had been added by The Sources. So while the fidelity falls somewhat below professional standards, it captures a sound which was truly a miracle; a sound conferred upon it by beings in the next dimension— not only the sound of an expanded space, but the vibrational qualities of that space. My heart will forever be grateful for those experiences with the Order of Orpheus. I am proud to be a member of that organization, and as I travel and improvize with other experienced musicians, I often feel that I meet other brothers of the Order.

My friend, who had been grinning, shaking his head from side to side toward the end of this story, said, "I suppose there's a reason for everything, but I love these 'miraculous' happenings, and I certainly would love to hear a concert by the Order of Orpheus now that you've been apart for five years." Then he took another scrap of paper out of his pocket saying, "A couple of days ago didn't you say that you had done some research into the correlation between colors and pitches? I should think many of your readers would like to know more about that. I know it piqued my curiosity at the time."

Yes, this is a question which has fascinated creative people for a long time. In the United States, the "light shows" started in the '60's in San Francisco. Colored dyes were spontaneously dripped into a shallow bowl of water and then projected onto a screen or a wall at a Rock concert. Ever since then artists who are aligned with the Spiritual Renaissance have been exploring the blending of art forms for the intensification of effects — and sometimes upliftment. I improvized a number of film scores around that time, and felt the excitement of translating visual images and patterns into music. When one becomes immersed in this process, one seems to touch into a higher or deeper strata where archetypal patterns exist which are then translated into the particular designs peculiar to each art form. These designs differ because of the nature of each of our five senses upon which the art forms are based. Since I've been developing higher sensing, or psychic sensitivities, I've had the suspicion that on these levels, when you've transcended the organ through which the stimuli came, these patterns are more universal or, you might say, translatable one into the other.

We must keep in mind here that it is not the eye that sees. This organ merely transmits the visual information to centers in the brain which actually cognize their meaning. When one develops the ability to see without the aid of the eye, then one has clairvoyance. So the term "Extra Sensory Perception" doesn't mean "outside the senses of the body." Since the sensing is still happening inside the brain, it should be understood as "Extended Perception", where the brain center that is receiving the impression is reaching far beyond the confines of the body and bypassing the sense organ entirely. The same is true of clairaudience, clairsensience, and all the other varieties of what is called E.S.P. They might better be called "higher octaves" of sense perception, transcending the organs.

In the reports we have of life on higher planes, it is often said that there is never color without sound or sound without color. And in the work of Edgar Cayce, undoubtedly the most well-known American psychic, he was always saying (in trance) "this tone or color," "this color or tone or vibration." In spite of this evidence, we seem to run into real problems when we try to make *exact equivalents,* or translations from one art form into another here on this plane of existence. I have met a few experts who claimed they could translate pitches into colors mathematically, but I have never found it entirely convincing, although I remain open to this demonstration. I will attempt to explain some of the problems involved with such proof.

These understandings I brought to a project initiated by a chiropractor in Virginia Beach in 1973. He could see auras, and worked quite effectively with color healing with his patients. He wanted to add the dimension of tone, and had been working with a set of cassettes which provided one note for each color. The tones were somewhat strident and not pleasant to listen to. He had heard of my work, and asked me to channel a short piece on the harp for each color. He was especially interested to see what key or predominant note I would come up with, and thus to arrive at a color-pitch scale. I was intrigued by this challenge, but told him before I started to work that I couldn't promise to find precise equivalents for the colors.

First, I pulled out several books containing color-pitch codes. There wasn't much agreement among them, especially regarding how to fit six basic colors (three primaries: red, yellow and blue; and three secondaries: orange, green and violet) into seven notes (C, D, E, F, G, A, B). Every chart had to repeat a color in various shades to make it work, and almost every one repeated a different color! The most official-looking one, the Rosicrucian, had more shades of red than any of the other colors. I said to myself, "What's going on here! You would think that at least they would repeat the violet band because we do hear about purple, indigo and violet." Actually, if you go to a printer, he will tell you that it takes at least three colors to make indigo, so I consider it a tertiary color.

The next thing that struck me was that most of them would give the same change of color value for the half-step change from E to F as they would for the whole-step change from C to D, or D to E. Where some of them did agree, they gave C as red, and continued: D-orange, E-yellow, F-green, G-blue, etc. How wrong it seemed that it would increase half as much from yellow to green, from E to F, than from red to orange, from C to D. (E to F is half the increase in pitch frequency of the increase from C to D.) My question was, "Don't these people know anything about music?"

Another basic confusion that arises from this lack of knowledge, is that the people who make up these charts seem to think that it is a God-given fact that there are seven notes in the scale. In actuality that is a compromise on the Overtone Series (the natural Law of Resonance) worked out by man around 1650. It is called the "Well-Tempered Scale", but I call it the "Ill-Tampered Scale"! To be sure, The Law of Seven is a great law that operates throughout the universe, and we often see symbolisms given to the musical scale according to this Great Principle. As long as we're using a seven-note scale, I suppose its fruitful to ascribe the symbolism of seven to it. But, the fact is that music is an eight-system — at least on this planet! If you generate the Overtone Series of the note C, the first time anything like a scale of whole steps and half steps appears it starts on C, and there are 8 notes in it: (in terms of piano notes) C, D, E-, F#-, G, Ab+, Bb-, B⎮ — eight notes. And here's another evidence of the number eight in music: if you take one vibration per second, and keep doubling it to get the next octave up, you arrive at C, 256 vibrations per second, which we call Middle C, and use as reference point for all our music, tuning most instruments to it. As we have mentioned, 256 is used in the computer industry because it is a function of sets of 8.

Just after I realized this, I attended a New Age Festival Show in London. Theo Gimbel (real name), one of the world's foremost color healers was there. In his booth, he had put his color wheel on the wall. There were eight colors! Still another problem we encounter in color research is that those who see colors on the inner planes, say that green is a primary color there. And I have seen systems where there are four or five primaries, and the corresponding number of secondaries!

So I brought many of these considerations to my research with the chiropractor. I decided that first I would meditate and ask The Sources for some information concerning pitch-color scales. They said, "F#— green..". I waited for them to continue and nothing more came! As I found out, that was the only clue I needed. Later that day I wrote out a six-note pitch-color scale for use with the Tempered Scale (12 half-steps): C-red, D-orange, E-yellow, F#-green, G#-blue, A# (or Bb)-violet (please note that it's one more whole step up to the octave C). This is called the Whole Tone Scale, and divides the octave equally into six whole steps. At least it's logical, in that each of the six basic colors is represented by an equal increase in the number of vibrations to the next pitch. Also, it leaves room for more colors since there is a note between each two of these notes which can represent the color combination of each pair of adjacent colors: C#-red-orange, D#-orange-yellow, F-yellow-green, G-green-blue, A-blue-violet, and B-violet-red.

In my own work, I had started channeling music for the chakras. I had completed the Solar Plexus Chakra, and it came through mostly in the key of E. A few days later, I went into my studio to channel for the Thyroid Chakra. As I was meditating on it, I realized that it might come through in the key of G# (according to this new code). Now you can't play in the key of G# on the harp, you have to play on the Ab strings, and since I got started in my channeling work using the sharp keys, I was not familiar with the key of Ab. There was so much going on in my head that I couldn't channel, so I put it off until the next day. Then, as I often do when I have gotten too mental about something, I decided to just ask The Sources what to do. They came through clearly, saying, "Why don't you practice a little in the key of Ab, just in case, then channel. You'll know whether you brought through the music for the Thyroid Chakra by the quality and strength of it." So that's what I did. The music was definite, powerful and beautiful. It did come through in Ab and I had no trouble playing in that key. The by-product of this was that it corroborated the new system of color-pitch equivalents.

I have used this code successfully for a number of years and I feel that it is probably the best one, *in cases where you feel you need a code.* It is not completely accurate, because the tempered scale is not accurate according to the natural scale, the Overtone Series. Actually, the colors produced by these notes, for those who see them, will be slightly different than if you played tones from an Overtone Series. Also, keep in mind that we don't use a "tempered system" of colors. If it is possible for highly color-sensitive artists to perceive precise intervals between colors, as is possible in music, then the tempered intervals produced in the tempered tuning are going to produce color intervals equally out of tune with natural law.

While I was doing my research, the chiropractor engaged one of the best psychics in Virginia Beach to seek information from his Sources on our work. So often the "voice of truth" casts a whole new light on one's project! They said that, first of all, unless I took all the strings off my harp but one, I would be producing all the colors through sympathetic resonance with other strings, and that even with only one string, many colors would be produced through the overtones of that one pitch! They advised that we might get better results if we just had the harpist concentrate on green, for example, and play under guidance! They were saying that consciousness is on a level much higher than a *system.* What a turnaround! But, in a way, this was satisfying for me, because I had intuited it at the beginning when I told the chiropractor we might not get anything like exact correspondences. I completed the project by recording short sections channeled on the harp for each pitch in the new code, while concentrating on each color. He found them to be quite helpful.

I was most grateful for what we had learned along the way.

When I first met Rose Gladden, the English healer, she asked me to channel on the harp while she did color healing on patients. She said that when I played she could see the colors coming out of the harp. I asked to be used as a channel for the patient (consciousness), but I also used the new code whenever she requested a certain color (system). Afterwards, I asked her how it was working. She said it worked very well all during the session, the colors kept pouring out of the harp, and she would direct them into the patient's liver or spleen or whatever. This seems to indicate that at least this system isn't wrong. I do believe that it might have worked as well without the system, since the intention of mind on high levels of consciousness plays such a prominent role in the process of healing.

When I finished, my friend said, "Thank you so much. Those are penetrating insights into the relationship between different art forms and more specifically pitches and colors. I suppose this is an ongoing area of research, but this report will give people some important things to think about."

"Say, we must have come down the beach a couple of miles; shall we turn back?" my friend asked. "There's a spot I want to show you just past the mouth of the river. I had a rebirth experience there once."

Retracing our steps, we spent the next twenty minutes exploring the teeming life in the tidepools, marveling at its busy-ness. It seemed completely oblivious of us. Then, taking a deep breath, he said, "The other thing that you mentioned that intrigued me was your world anthem. I hope there's time for that story since it seems to be six o'clock."

Looking at my watch, I said, "I only have five. Did you remember to set your watch back for Daylight Saving yesterday? By the look of the sun, I think we'll have time, and if you like we can run back to the cabin."

One morning in the spring of 1975, as I emerged from the meditative state between sleeping and waking, I brought with me a grand fantasy: with my understanding of the symbolic meaning of the letters of the alphabet, I could write an anthem for world peace and harmony in a new language. The letters of each word would support the meaning of that word, and would be combined without dissonance, creating a powerful mantram that could be sung all over the world in the same language. No one on the planet could say it was in a foreign language. I could see an audience of 6,000 intoning it together, accompanied by full orchestra, and creating powerful thought-forms on the inner planes surrounding the earth. We know that when people can align themselves physically, and emotionally, behind the same idea, the strength of the effect is increased tremendously, exponentially rather than arithmetically.

After I was fully awake, I asked myself, *"Is the world ready for this?*

Is it time for a universal language? And what words would I use? And how could I disseminate it?"

So I wondered how I, who am not in the least involved in politics, could accomplish such a grandiose scheme, and filed it away with the stuff of dreams. This was in Virginia Beach, and a week later I invited some dedicated Lightworkers to the house for the evening. In the course of the conversation, I mentioned the idea of the anthem. There was much excitement and the consensus was that I should definitely do it.

I said, "How could I ever introduce it to the world?"

And they said, "Well, perhaps if you do your part, God will do the rest."

I said, "Of course, you're right!"

For sure, the idea of creating the words had fired my imagination, and I opened myself to the project. One week later, I was on the way to the Blue Ridge Mountains for a weekend of rest, and the poem began to come through. I asked my wife to drive, and I wrote it down in about 45 minutes. There were five stanzas of four lines each. I only adjusted two or three words later, because I had used the word "never", and it seemed that it should contain only positive words. The following week, I set to work translating it word for word into the new language. I had to work slowly because, in the first few days, I realized that I was co-creating with High Forces; that it was just possible these words might be expanded into a complete language, the truly universal language that is one of the prerequisites for world peace. Not only did I have to select the most appropriate letters for each word, but see that the root syllable for words with similar meanings had a family resemblance. But this wasn't all that dragged it out. I must confess to you that I usually have so many interesting "irons" in so many "fires" that, along with my need to make a living at the "far-out" work that I do, I have had a hard time finishing projects unless I could improvize them in the moment! Months would pass by, and I would feel guilty that I wasn't carrying out this project given me by the Masters. I remember one year of heavy touring when the only time I had to work on the anthem was in airline terminals, waiting for my flights. Then I would worry that I would lose my briefcase with some inspired word of the anthem in it.

At last, a heaven-sent miracle spurred me on at a particularly low time. I had worked out the word in the title which means anthem, "Eanokee." (Let's analyze it. The Purpose of Growth the word attracts, the E, symbolizes direct attunement with the Light, the Father Principle. Then the rest of the letters draw on past experience in: A, the Divine Mother Principle; N, mastery of physical energy; O, ability to manifest creativity when it serves the whole; K, the spiritual teacher; and the two E's, concentrated experience from the past in direct attunement with the Father Principle.) I was asked to play a concert at a psychic fair at George Mason University, a small college west of Washington, D.C. I was walking in the lobby and ran into an old friend, Leonard Blue, a Kabbalist. I was delighted to see him, not having had the pleasure for over a year, and asked what he was doing there. He said he was giving a lecture, but hoped he could come to my concert.

I said, "What are you lecturing on—maybe I can come."

He said, "I'm giving a talk on the Enochean language." (I had never heard of that language but "Enochean" sounds just like "Eanokee," even though it has its origin with the Enoch of the Bible.)

I couldn't believe it! I walked around in a circle, and when I arrived in front of him again, I said, "Leonard, what is that language?"

He answered casually, "Oh, it's an ancient, angel-given language." (I knew I had been guided by the angels!)

I was playing my concert at the time of his lecture, so I suppose my mind was not to be cluttered with already existing information; but the five minutes with Leonard was the powerful reinforcement that I needed and it spurred me on with renewed energy.

There were a number of revelations connected with the co-creation of this anthem; one of the high points was a new name for God. Under normal circumstances, I wouldn't have the audacity to create a name for God. But, since my task was to translate the channeled poem, word for word, it just didn't seem right to leave one word untranslated. Also, when I analyzed the meaning of the letters G-O-D, I found that their symbolism, while fairly good, was not the most appropriate for our Deity. The Purpose of Growth (the guttural sound G) is to learn "how to solve survival-type challenges with the mind." The name draws from past experience the qualities of the O, "ability to manifest creativity in service to the whole" (good), and then D, experience in human love. One can fairly easily translate the qualities of the O into cosmic dimensions, but it's a little more difficult with the G and the D, which have to do more with the creature level.

So, I called forth the highest inspiration, and set to work. After much deliberation, I came up with six of the most appropriate qualities arranged in a logical sequence. It began with the S, the highest-pitched sound you can make with your mouth, and ended with the same sound grounded by the addition of the vocal chords, the Z (represents ascension). In the middle is the I, the individual creature or entity. An arc is traversed, coming down from above, reaching an extreme degree of physical manifestation, and then rising back into spirit. This is an expression of the Grand Circle of Creation. One way of dramatically appreciating the difference between these two words for God, is to chant "GOD" continuously for awhile, and then chant the word "SOHIEZ" (So-Ease) continuously. Soon I noticed that the first two letters, SO, are what God is always saying: "Be it SO!", and the "Lo, Behold, and So be it," of the Bible. Often, in workshops, as we're chanting this flowing name, we lapse into saying "SO-EASY, SO-EASY, SO-EASY." One can imagine God saying, "It would really be so easy if you could try to see creation as I see it. I've given it all to you and if you could just trust me, and flow with me, it would all be so much easier." There have, of course, been many names for God down through history; I think somehow we inherited one of the lower ones. Start chanting and using "SOHIEZ", and see how you feel about it (and please see Appendix II for a fuller description of the higher symbolism of these letters.)

By 1978, I had finished translating the poem and had added a first word, "Unitas", meaning "coming together for unification", to the title. I presented the poem, "Unitas Eanokee", to the world in Amsterdam at a conference called "World Symposium on Humanity", which took place simultaneously in six other major cities of the western world. In August of 1979, I moved back to my place of birth, Santa Barbara, California, and as soon as I was settled, began work on the melody and the chords for the accompaniment. I realized immediately that I should translate the letters of the words into pitches and embody these in the melody. When we sing, we emphasize the vowels much more than we do the consonants. So, under guidance, I composed the melody for each stanza in the key suggested by the vowels of that stanza, and incorporating as many of the pitches of these vowels as possible in it. Then, when I set the melodies to harmony, I used as many as possible of the notes of the consonants. IN THE MELODY AND CHORDS, THE MUSIC CARRIES THE SAME MESSAGE AS THE WORDS, AND THE TWO WORKING SYNERGISTICALLY TOGETHER CREATE A MUCH MORE POWERFUL EFFECT. THEY ARE BOTH SAYING THE SAME THING. It was in this way that the melody and chords came right out of the words, and consequently, as a bonus, I discovered a scientific way of setting words to music and of selecting the proper key for a song.

Finishing the accompaniment for the harp in the spring of 1980, I invited a close friend to hear it. I had probably played and sung it a hundred times, but when it came time for its first performance, after five years of work, I "choked up" and couldn't get through it. Part of this was the depth of emotion and power of the anthem itself: what it could mean for the planet, and the almost incredible fact that its 60-month pregnancy was over. It was actually being born! In July of that year, it received its premiere performance at the Seventh Human Unity Conference in Chicago. My daughter, Myra, (real name, rhymes with miracle) has a rich and universal voice (she really sings for the Mother) so I took her to Chicago with me to sing the anthem. I passed out lead sheets, and 600 people from 25 countries sang "Unitas Eanokee" together, many of whom could not understand each other's languages. Myra put her heart and soul into it, aware of the momentousness of the occasion. It was one of the most deeply moving moments of my life.

In the weeks that followed, we recorded a cassette of the anthem, which serves also as a learning aid, and I began to present the anthem at every concert on tour. I would work with a local singer, and in spite of the fact that it was in a new language, two or three hours of rehearsal was usually sufficient. I would briefly tell the story of how the anthem came through, read it in English, read it in Eanokee, ask for audience response to the new language, and then perform it. Often, we would go through it line by line, and then all sing it together. In terms of a finished performance, the success would vary from town to town, but thousands of souls have been introduced to the new anthem, and the new language.

Almost everyone comments on the power and beauty of "Unitas Eanokee". At a Unity church in Austin, Texas, where there happened to be a number of professional singers in the audience, they sang it as if they had been practicing it and knew it quite well! What a gratifying surprise. At a Unity church in Oakton, Virginia (30 miles west of Washington), two highly-trained singers showed up—a woman and a man. There was a little professional bristling around the idea that I might choose one over the other; then I suggested that, because of the nature of the anthem, I would be delighted if they sang it together. They did a beautiful job, and I have it on tape.

I feel that I have finally done my part—as far as the creation of the anthem is concerned—and that it is up to the people of the world when they are ready to start using it. I have copyrighted it only so that no one else can copyright it and control it, and I have pledged all proceeds from it to be used for further dissemination. I have recently arranged it for choir so that it can be sung around the world. It was sung first at the Peace Meditations, December 31, 1986, in Santa Cruz, California. I am looking for conductors who tour a good deal as "guest conductors" to introduce the anthem to other countries. My guidance is to translate the words into other languages only so that those peoples can understand the meaning of the new words. I feel we should discourage singing the anthem in other languages so as not to perpetuate these barriers between peoples. A friend has come up with an excellent French translation coordinated with the music so that it can be sung. Another friend, who has a publishing company, has offered to have it properly printed.

Now you can see that what began as a fantasy on awakening has come to fruition (in seven years) in what could turn out to be my major contribution to the harmony of life on my planetary home and to all my beloved brothers and sisters. Certainly its qualities of universal love, co-creation between all life forms, and the dedication to work and play with the Light, go forth in a powerful way every time this new world anthem is sung.

My friend was visibly moved and he said, "I had no idea it was THAT kind of anthem. I can't wait to hear it; please send me the cassette as soon as you return home. I am in touch with a number of new Light-centers who might like to sing it."

We arrived shortly at the mouth of the river and waded across it, finding my friend's favorite spot in an inlet of sandy beach between some rocks.

CHAPTER SIXTEEN

 Postlude

We positioned ourselves where we could see the setting sun and sat in silence for a few moments as the plumes of soft fire developed. We had touched into so many higher levels of awareness that the progression of colors, sensitively interpreted by the artistry of the cloud devas, on at least three levels of cloud formations, seemed extraordinarily exquisite. We looked at each other and each could see in the other's eyes the gratitude that comes from deep sharing.

He murmured, "I can't thank you enough for these four days—they have opened up vistas that I feel will change the course of my life." I said, "I salute the genuineness of your curiosity. You have played a significant part in bringing these revelations from the privacy of my life into the lives of countless souls who can use them, check them, expand them, and grow with them. Please let's come here again sometime and I will listen to your story."

And then the strangest thing happened. As I looked at him a gentle turbulence came over his face; he began to gradually disappear, and over his face appeared one face after another! They were all different and yet with some indefinable quality linking them all. Then the speed increased and there must have been a hundred faces before I came to my senses and realized that they were all you dear readers for whom this book was written, and for whom my friend was a surrogate focus. I realized that I had created him so that I could relate to you more intimately, and that, unless I released him back to the Source, I could be carrying him with me and probably be looking for him in the real world! I gave thanks once more for him and asked that his release back into the world of imagination be final. As I watched, your faces accelerated into a blur and finally, as exciting as this was, faded. Finally, I could see only the sand and the rocks where he sat.

Turning back to the sun, which was setting into the Pacific Ocean, I was overwhelmed with thankfulness that somehow I had been able to complete this gift for you which has been thirteen years in the giving. And I was profoundly moved by how much I love you all.

P.S. I should perhaps explain why, in spite of the fact that I enjoy the company of women so much, my friend had to be a man. Well, you see, tomorrow my vacation is up and I return to my wife and home. Now I couldn't be carrying a satchel of cassettes all about four days sharing my deepest work with another lady, could I?

Appendix I

THE CIRCLE OF FIFTHS

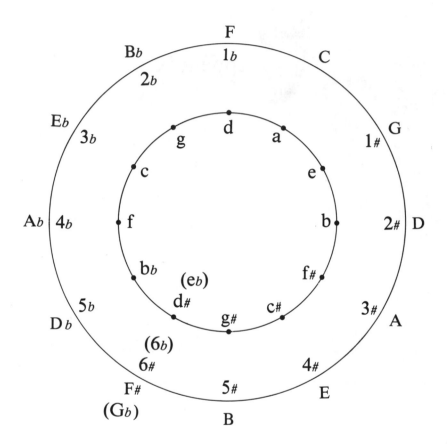

NOTE: The outer ring shows the Major Scale keys, the inner, the relative Minor Scale keys. F# and G♭ are the same pitch but different strings on the harp but the same "key" on the piano.

LETTER-PITCH EQUIVALENTS

This code has been used by composers for 250-300 years. In German, the note B is written as an H. J. S. Bach used it, Haydn wrote a composition based on the name B-A-C-H. More recently, to name just two, Brahms and Ravel both derived themes with it. At first this code may seem strange, but further study will reveal the soundness of its logic. There probably never has been as detailed a proof of its value as the research into music healing reported in this book. However, much corroboration would be brought to light by more detailed studies of the use of the code by the above-mentioned composers.

a	b	c	d	e	f	g
A	B	C	D	E	F	G

h	i	j	k	l	m	n
B	C#	D	E	F#	G	A

o	p	q	r	s	t	u
C#	D#	E	F#	G#	A	B

v	w	x	y	z
D#	E#	F#	G#	A#

The key to memorizing and erecting this table is to notice that the pattern of the natural minor scale is set by the first line, each succeeding line consisting of a natural minor scale starting a whole tone above the first note of the preceding line. It could be described: four natural minor scales starting on notes of a whole-tone scale beginning with A and ending when A# (Z) is reached.

NUMBER-PITCH EQUIVALENTS
(from my Sources)

Numbers 1-22 coincide with letters 1-22

23 = 2 and 3 or B and C

24 = 2 and 4 or B and D

25 = 2 and 5 or B and E

26 = 2 and 6 or B and F

Thus, for any number over 22, each digit is translated into its letter of the alphabet and then into a pitch.

Note: Some work has been done to correlate this system with Numerology with some success. I suspect that, as with all forms of divination, the two systems provide different points of view of a person which could be complimentary.

THE SYMBOLISM OF MUSICAL INTERVALS

OCTAVE — Higher significance of the qualities of the lower note. Transition from one cycle of life to a higher cycle, level, or phase. Ability to build on the past. Finishing and beginning (elision).

PERFECT 5th — Creation, actualization, manifestation. First "skeletal" building blocks of material reality.

PERFECT 4th — Mental concepts, thought forms. Rising from material reality of four dimensions to a higher plane (mental), toward transcendence.

MAJOR 3rd — The sense of beauty expressed in the external world. "Color tones" in music. Expansive (Yang). The completion, fullness and synthesis of the 5th and 4th (through the inversions of a major triad, such as C-E-G. E-G-C, G-C-E.)

MINOR 3rd — The sense of beauty felt in one's inner world (Yin). More emotional and intuitive than the Major 3rd.

MAJOR 6th — and MINOR 6th. Same as the 3rds only more ambitious; a larger leap, traversing and embracing more space.

MAJOR 2nd — A building block of life, a patient step toward a larger goal (up the scale toward completion at the octave.) A physical, outer connection or relationship between two things or beings. A detail of daily living. Caution. Deliberation. (Yang).

MINOR 2nd — The same as the Major 2nd, but *within*: emotional and intuitive. The psychological aspect of a step. Relations between persons. (Yin) Somewhat dissonant by itself and wants to be resolved, either into the Major 2nd or into the unison.

MAJOR 7th — One's relationship with the group around one through thought, material things and works. (Yang) Somewhat dissonant by itself and wants to be resolved, usually upwards, but downwards if approached from above.

MINOR 7th — One's relationship with the group through feeling, sensitivity, awareness, psychology. (Yin) Resolved down unless approached from below.

MAJOR 9th — and MINOR 9th. Same as the 7ths, but one's relationship with the larger group: nation, race, humanity, etc. This meaning comes from the building of chords in 3rds. The 9ths would also carry the qualities of the 2nds, but much expanded into a higher octave: patient steps leading to goals involving the larger group. The Minor 9th is somewhat dissonant and wants to be resolved probably downwards.

DIMINISHED 5th or AUGMENTED 4th or TRITONE: The relationship of polar opposites. Halfway up the scale symbolizes reaching the furthest point away from home before beginning the return. If alone: the most dissonant interval ("sweet abrasion"); if harmonized within the Dominant 7th chord, resolution of duality and the richness of completion and synthesis of Yang and Yin, male and female. Still wants to be resolved, usually upwards.

Note: — Tension/release, (dissonance/consonance) is a necessary part of life and provides much of its poignancy; it is also a constant process in art and music.

THE SYMBOLISM OF THE ENGLISH ALPHABET

This chart includes information channeled from the Lords of Sirius which they called "The Symbolism of the Mystical English Alphabet." I realized that they had brought it through in past ages but that it was being updated for the transition into the Aquarian Age. These significances have been corroborated by the 2,300 Individual Past-life readings and 1600 Name Analyses, other healing tapes, and concerts I have completed, beginning four years before the channeling from Sirius and extending to the date of this writing. The Sirius channeling in 1975 confirmed my work and provided some "lower" and some "higher" symbolisms for the letters. Any set of symbols, (such as numbers, astrological signs and aspects, or designs), must be clear and definite. Yet, they must be abstract enough to be applied to a number of different levels of being in a number of different contexts. This system has proven itself with these criteria and has, in my work, culminated in the co-creation of the new world anthem, "Unitas Eanokee," in a new language, for the peace, unification and harmony of the peoples of this planet.

Over the years I have found it logical and usable to arrange this chart in the order of the Circle of 5ths with the pitches first and then the letters to which they correspond. In this way you can see immediately that a pitch (and letters) is the Actualizing Principle for the pitch (and letters) that precedes it and a pitch (and letters) is *actualized by* the pitch (and letters) that follows next. Bear in mind that even an individual letter can be viewed in a number of ways: 1) physically; that is, purely as design-graphics. I realized that Sirius was using a system of symbols for each stroke that makes up a letter and I will give these meanings first in the chart. I have found that they are most valuable in analyzing the meaning of ANY design. 2) Then a letter can be responded to emotionally; the sound of the letter (and possibly the universal emotions a letter might evoke in people as they were making that letter with the body; of course, ruling out personal associations with that position. (This should be researched.) And finally 3): Looking at the letter as a human being with chakras.

It is obvious that this system was given for the *capital letters*. It would be more difficult to apply the symbolism of the strokes to cursive writing with its curves, but this might yield some interesting results.

Keep in mind also that some of these qualities, especially the polarized ones, such as A and E, overlap a little in life, and so are difficult to find in their pure state.

In the symbolism of the alphabet I have put the information from the Lords of Sirius first, then the symbolism which came through in the musical past-life readings.

SYMBOLISM OF THE STROKES OF LETTERS

INDIVIDUALITY, a discrete entity in any form of life, an item, an event in time, the spine, the channel of wisdom, indestructible consciousness, specificity, focus. The human "I AM" or personality. The connection between heaven and earth or a higher frequency plane and a lower frequency plane. A HUMAN AS THIS CONNECTION. The vertical axis of the cross. When repeated: a group of individuals or the measuring of time by events. Also implies the ability to separate one entity from another. (See Sirius material under the letter "I") (B, D, E, F, H, I, J, K, L, M, N, P, R, T, U).

CONTINUITY IN TIME. Flow. Eternity. A line between planes of differing frequency (and the ability to perceive such divisions.) For an individual: the potential to be eternal, to be an "eternaliter". (A, E, F, G, H, L, T, Z)

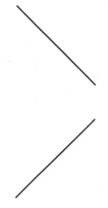

INVOLUTION. Descension. Deity, lowering frequency into the world of manifestation to realize or manifest its creativity, then to return: the first act of the Grand Cycle (Circle) of Creation. (K, M, N, Q, R, V, W, X, Y)

EVOLUTION, Ascension, the raising of frequency toward purer levels of Divinity. Deity taking back toward its center its outer manifestation for greater completion (an eternal process). The "return" of the Grand Circle-Cycle of Creation. An individual pulling up out of the world of matter and moving toward the Source. (K, M, V, W, X, Y, Z only seven compared to the nine Involving letters!)

(These first four strokes are equally important to the scheme of things: you could picture an "I am" entity sliding down the INVOLUTION line, crossing some planes into life, selecting a plane, experiencing Reality through CONTINUITY IN TIME, then earning ASCENSION back through the planes to a closer and closer embrace with the Father/Mother. Of course, there is a certain amount of CONTINUITY implied in INVOLUTION and EVOLUTION.)

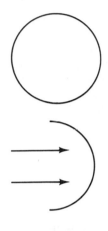

WHOLENESS, TOTALITY, COMPLETENESS, all inclusiveness, Universality, Unity. Perfection, the Universe, the Cosmos, God. And yet also condensation of the All-One into a concept of Itself, or an expression in form of Its Wholeness (condensation and contraction into a ball or planet), or balanced and harmonious expansion out from a center.

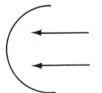

GATHERING FROM THE PAST and SWELLING FORWARD INTO THE FUTURE. Building on past experience, but not open to the future. Not using spontaneity or fresh guidance except as to how to apply the past to the future. (B, D, O, P, Q, R, S) (Two more of these than C's.)

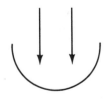

GATHERING FROM NEW EXPERIENCE, FROM THE FUTURE. (Of course, the shape and size of a person's "C" is somewhat conditioned by their past. (The same is true of a person's "B," "D," "P," and "R.") (C, G, O, Q, S)

GATHERING FROM ABOVE. Open to guidance from Higher planes, Beings, God. (J, O, Q, U).

GATHERING FROM BELOW. (It makes sense that we don't use this shape. The Great Law is, "As Above so Below", not the reverse.) (Not that the physical plane isn't spirit in form, and thus spiritual.)

THE ARCHETYPAL SYMBOLISM OF
THE ALPHABET AND IT'S CORRELATED PITCHES
FOR THE EMERGING AGE

PITCH	LETTER	SYMBOLISM
F	F	An individual's organized expression in thought (will) (throat chakra) and universal love (Heart Chakra) without grounding in action or application in the physical. When lower-evolved, can be lacking in practicality, common sense, or humor. Could be fanatical. Look for C's, G's, and H's and B's and other signs of grounding.

In the musical readings: THE INDIVIDUAL'S ABILITY TO ATTUNE DIRECTLY TO THE ANGELIC ORDER (including devas and elementals). Then, hopefully, the inspiration can be brought into manifestation on the physical plane. The initial F: the desire to develop attunement to the angelic order of life. Within a name: past experience in this direct attunement (somewhat rare in the body of names). Earth knowledge apart from its manifestation. The angelic order can come in on this note, in this key.

C	C	GATHERING. The half-completed, never-ending circle of consciousness. Open mind, heart and body. Questioning, receiving. When low, may accept without thought of discrimination. May have trouble closing down. May become constipated and confused if there is not enough time to process what has been taken in. could have the need to collect. When high, open to a "cosmos" of experience— eagerly seeking the Ascension Adventure.

The readings: ORDINARY SURVIVAL-TYPE ACTIVITY. Experience in maintenance and perpetuation of the physical plane, and the desire to add to this. Accumulation of life skills from the ground up, from the simple and mundane, to the complex and sophisticated. To evolve, it's important what consciousness we bring to these acts of survival. We can struggle, or we can realize that every act is a spiritual act, and co-create with God in our simplest tasks (the philosophy of Zen). A "taking on", "eating" letter. (Note how many words describing this letter contain the letter "c".)

G		PRACTICALITY, METHODOLOGY OR TECHNOLOGY OF GOING ABOUT OR MANIFESTING C — ordinary survival-type challenges.

G   G   Open, receiving letter (like C) but focused in a particular area or areas on the material plane (the horizontal "continuity" line). The Yang or masculine approach through the mind, logic and science. Open to all ideas related to a certain project. The student or researcher. When low, not open to other aspects of self and the outer world, such as artistic and spiritual. When high, is open to seeing the practicality of everything.

PRACTICALITY: HOW TO GO ABOUT SOLVING SURVIVAL CHALLENGES. Gaining experience through the logical, scientific approach (male) to "how to get things done here on the Earth plane"; especially in regard to the needs of maintaining one's self. (The note "sol" or Sun.) Usually indicates experience with money.

G   M   Contains Involution and Evolution, Descension and Ascension, supported on two legs (the Plane of Duality). Also contains the V of Universal Love planted firmly on Earth. The M of Earth Mother, also the M of matter. We use this letter when we say "MMMM" to express physical pleasure.

INTUITIVE PRACTICALITY. How to solve survival-type challenges by just "knowing" rather than figuring them out logically. The Yin, or female, approach. This intuition includes: 1) Drawing on past-life memory, 2) Tuning in psychically to whatever is involved, 3) Calling on the angels and Earth Mother for guidance, 4) Asking the High Self or The Source for the answer, and 5) Tuning into other minds that might have the needed information.

D   BUILDING ON PAST EXPERIENCE IN HUMAN LOVE. One-to-one commitment, physical love, sharing and growth.

D   D   MOVING (or swelling) into the future based wholly on the past. When low: bound by dogma, or convention, or established structure, or any "scientific" or "religious" system which claims it has "the truth." (Illness: digestive; if too bound up with self, having also G's, B's and I's.) The presence of a P, Universal Love, would suggest that the love nature is expanding. 1 x 1 relationships are so often subject to dogma and powerful social customs.

HUMAN LOVE COMMITMENT. Sharing space together in love, especially the nitty-gritty aspects. Growth in personalized love, dealing with yours and another's needs, self-expression, etc. A supreme workshop in these times when the whole world is so polarized, and when the institution of marriage is undergoing such reorganization and renewal. Growth in learning the true love of self and another and often, also, love of family, of life, and of aspects of God.

D   J   The "I AM" expression combined with the qualities of the "U" (the lower part of the letter). Individuality seeking spiritual guidance in the growth of the lower chakras. The desire to be open to God and to have union with materiality without action (the U is meditative). Thought tends to be systematic—the "ceiling" like the letter T (please see). Inspired development of the lower centers. The spine. (Illness: back trouble, if there isn't enough flowing exercise and physical activity. C's, D's, A's, N's, and H's, possibly E's will help for their horizontal lines.)

SPIRITUALIZED HUMAN LOVE. Idealized Christ love expressed to an individual. Bringing spiritual concepts into all aspects of the love relationship symbolized by the letter D. Practicing the Golden Rule. Unconditional Love. Giving without thought of return and total acceptance of another's evolution through love relationship.

A PHYSICAL MANIFESTATION, DIVINE MOTHER PRINCIPLE. Materiality, Four dimensions (three plus time), Earth Mother, The Planetary Being, Yin. Receptive, Dark, Yielding, Fertile and Nurturing.

A A The beginning of all action, Alpha. A solid physical structure (resembles a pyramid) for the collection of energy or for the physical manifestation of the Divine Father Principle (Pure Pattern). The love of structure, form and order. A neutral letter, the energy of which is influenced by the letters around it. Will tend to bring into manifestation the qualities of the surrounding letters. An Evolution line and an Involution line connected. More balanced and also less individual than the other letters for the pitch A: N and T.

DIVINE MOTHER, the physical plane of materiality, four dimensions, Earth. Physically manifested Light, Light in form. The ability to see that everything in this world comes from spirit. Physical consciousness. Spiritualized Physicality. (N is Physical Energy, T is Physical Form.)

A N A "hope" letter. The overcoming of the low self, of karma resulting in alteration of consciousness, opening up the possibility of ascension. Action. Drive or impulse to move and become involved in life. If you make an N with one continuous stroke, you see that it is two upward strokes connected by an involution stroke. But you have a choice which way to make the vertical strokes, just as you have a choice how you want to qualify and direct your physical energy: to take you down or up. The N looks like lightning on its side, or energy applied to life.

PHYSICAL ENERGY. The energy that comes up, Earth energy. Kundalini. Survival impulse. The energy, or vibratory aspect, or expression of, the qualities of the A (see above).

A   T   LIMITATION OR FOCUS OF THE INDIVIDU-
AL OR AN EVENT IN TIME. Limits set on physical expression. High goals, ideals and purposes, but
limited by circumstances and Karma of a group nature. "Trapped." Repression. The "I Am" limited
by laws or dogma of the mentality. This letter has
a ceiling on it. But the horizontal line does keep
the individual moving with the stream. When low:
inability to see that the physical is of the Light, not
open-minded to spirituality. When high: the ability to channel the Divinity of the "I Am" into
materiality with steady purpose and to accept temporary Earth sojourn. Looks like the beginning of
"cross hairs" — a sight that focuses on a point, or
physical details.

PHYSICAL FORM. The shapes and patterns that
Mother Nature uses to express herself and the patterns of Light. Solid geometry. Clock time, meas-
urements. The most disciplined, applied, and
conditioned of the A letters. (See the basic qualities of the A).

E   PURE DIVINE FATHER PRINCIPLE. Creator,
Light, Power, Creative Pattern, Heaven. Yang. The
Sun.

E   E   A symbol of the individual at his/her best, reaching out on three levels: Will (Throat Chakra, top
line), Love (Heart Chakra, middle line). and Action (Root Chakra, bottom line). In a way, the
highest letter for us since it shows the "I Am" individuality evolving through time, combining mind,
heart, and application.

CONSCIOUS SPIRITUAL ATTUNEMENT
WITH THE FATHER PRINCIPLE, THE LIGHT,
THE CHRIST SPIRIT, and the ability to channel
what is perceived into the outside world, through
application of higher principles to life and physical reality. Triune expression of individuality. When
high: manifested spiritually; when low, just the ability to receive energy from the Father, the sun, and
use it in life.

E K Ability of the individual "I Am" to channel the ancient (and contemporary) wisdom and apply it in a practical manner. Ability to harmonize the principles of Involution and Evolution with Love. (These lines come out of the Heart Chakra.) (Illness: Heart, when there is confusion between Descension and Ascension.) When high: Cosmic Consciousness and wisdom of the heart.

THE SPIRITUAL TEACHER. The ability developed from the past to organize one's spiritual experience into concepts, or other patterns, that one can teach. Must avoid the ego temptation common to gurus: that they own the wisdom, or that they are the only channel of it, or that their version of it is the purest to be found. An opportunity to learn that "truth" is evolving, and changes according to a number of variables, and that we are only co-creators of it, filtering it through our individuality.

E Q The perfect circle of Cosmic Consciousness, broken and tied to Earth. Past or present practice of grey or black magic. Manipulation of others by power of mind, or knowledge of the law. Tapping into universal knowledge directly with an ulterior motive. Tapping race collective wisdom, but often tampering with it or limiting it in the process—often leaving out the love part of it, the wholeness of it (in contrast with E). Also not necessarily interested in *applying* the knowledge. The occultist, or magician, or the psychic interested in phenomena without spirituality. Love for self rather than co-creation.

B ORGANIZATION IN SPACE AND TIME, BASED ON PAST EXPERIENCE, TO MANIFEST IN, OR MANIPULATE, PHYSICAL REALITY, SELF, OR ENVIRONMENT. Its higher octave is PEACE.

B B Reaching out on two levels of consciousness from the solid, upright base of the "I Am" individuality—the central purpose, the "One". Self expression as the past expands or projects into the future. The first step, or steps, of building on self. Without other open letters like C, G, or E, could be self-centered, preconceived-purpose-centered, or narrow-minded, especially if lower evolved. When low, could be manipulative, reaching out only for that which reinforces self. When high, pressing forward with the assurance of experience and "know how," combining head and heart, and also heart and root' or thinking and love, and love and action.

B   B   PATIENCE. One step at a time. Knowing what *the* next step is. "Looking before you leap." The quality of caution, deliberation, circumspection. Awareness of the passage of time, especially minutes and hours (the letter H would be longer periods of time). Also awareness of units of space, and what could fill it. Through mastering this kind of patience, we transcend time and space, and achieve peace.

B   H   CONTINUITY AMONG TWO OR MORE ACTS OR STEPS OF PATIENT ACTUALIZATION ON THE PHYSICAL PLANE. Connecting two upright structures in consciousness ("I AMs" or events in time) to form a sturdy foundation. Combining attunement upwards with attunement downwards for balanced manifestation on Earth. Also depicts two people holding hands in cooperation. The only letter you can't make with the body without another person. A cross expanded horizontally through time. "Love-Wisdom" in its highest use. The Christ letter.

The sound of this letter has been thought to contain the magical power of the breath. The H in "HU" and "Huna." We also say, "Hu are you?", wanting to know what's behind the name.

Patient organization in space and time to complete long-range projects, especially those that require physical acts. Also the ability to coordinate others carrying out such a project. Attunement with the materials involved. Cooperation with others. Leads to making your peace with time and space.

B U Openness to God. Desire for direct union with Higher Forces. Ability to receive guidance and hold it. Gathering from above, waiting for help and inspiration. The listener. Without other action and manifesting letters, could subordinate physical expression to contemplative states and would wait to be shown. When low: the beggar (with his bowl).

THE MEDITATOR. The ability to quiet the mind, the emotions. and the body, to listen to Higher Guidance. The ability to "Be still and know that I am God." The presence of mind to stop and seek inner guidance before acting. Capability of higher attunement. Tends to listen to advice.

F# CREATIVE, ARTISTIC ABILITIES. KNOWLEDGE OF, AND SENSITIVITY TO, FORMS, THEIR CONTENT, SIGNIFICANCE, AND GRADATIONS OF QUALITY. THE CREATIVE PROCESSES.

F# L First steps and actions to build physical structures or systems of thought (thought-forms). Ability to understand and recreate basic life forms (root chakra), and their archetypal symbolism.

Sensitivity to THE QUANTITATIVE ASPECT OF ARTISTIC CREATIVITY: the lines which enclose or circumscribe forms, patterns and structures. Ability to create designs. The geometric aspect of solid, physical objects. Outer form as separate from content—pure idea as separate from its manifestation in the world. The yang aspect of artistry. In music; pitches as points, form.

F# R As an individual: EXPANSION OF CONSCIOUSNESS THROUGH LOVE—WISDOM. Evolution of the letter P. Both feet on the ground, but capable of being a visionary, a Rabbi, a Reverend, a spiritual teacher (more traditional than the letter K). Building on the past in the areas of thought and heart, and combining these, like the B; but adding to this the desire to get involved with the challenge of fresh experience in the chakras of love and action (Heart and Root).

THE QUALITATIVE ASPECTS OF ARTISTIC SENSITIVITY that an individual can bring to the creative process as the pure pattern is manifested in the physical: that which fills the form. Body, content, texture, color, etc.. The Yin qualities. In music: the spaces between the notes, tone quality, timbre, the qualities of chords sounding together, inflections that call forth emotions.

F#   X   INVOLUTION AND EVOLUTION, ASCENSION AND DESCENSION, AT THE SAME TIME, AT CROSS PURPOSES. Cancellation. (The most natural sequence is one after the other as in the letter V or Y.) Could possibly be handled in a high state of meditation, or experiencing Cosmic Consciousness, but not in the world of action. It draws from all directions at once: above, below, from the past, and the future, converging at a point (the heart). (Could suggest heart trouble for someone who takes on everything at once. Would be tempered by the presence of B's, U's, and H's and made more intense by C's and G's.)

Artistic creativity that comes from such experience. These cross purposes can be expressed and harmonized through art.

C#   THE CAPABILITY OF ACTUALIZING CREATIVITY IN THE PHYSICAL WORLD.

C#   I   (See Strokes: 1) The individual "I Am" creativity. PERSONALITY MANIFESTING IN THE WORLD. A person's unique contribution, idea, goal, or purpose. An individual as a connection between heaven and earth. The potential ability to cut across all horizontal lines between planes. The ability to free oneself from the laws of the Earth plane (time cycles, biorhythms, moon cycles, group karma, thought forms of others, etc.) through the ability to attune vertically (meditation). Mobility of consciousness through uniquely human will and desire. The vertical axis of the cross.

INDIVIDUALLY MOTIVATED ACTUALIZA-
TION OF ARTISTIC CREATIVITY. ABILITY
TO MANIFEST ARTISTIC SENSITIVITY FOR
PERSONAL GROWTH. Personal desire to use ar-
tistic sensitivity for growth in consciousness by
bringing it into physical expression.

C#   O   (see Strokes: O) The ability to complete creative
projects in such a way that they are a replica in the
world of the qualities of God: Wholeness, Universality, Harmony, Unity. The completion of the letter U. Expansion out in all directions from a center.
The ability to draw to a seed idea or project information from all directions, and put it all together
harmoniously. Cosmic Consciousness, the vision to
see that the one can be an expression and manifestation of the One. Integrating the All and its expression as specificity.

ABILITY TO ACTUALIZE ARTISTIC
CREATIVITY IN THE PHYSICAL WHEN
MOTIVATED BY SERVICE OR VALUE TO THE
WHOLE, TO OTHER PEOPLE, TO LIFE. Usual-
ly implies greater co-creation with Higher Forces
to insure universal value.

G#   CREATIVE OR ARTISTIC PATIENCE. The step
or steps we take to manifest creative projects. The
ability to make one particular act further a longer
range artistic or creative plan.

G#   S   The snake (kundalini). The energy that rises. The
individual power called forth by self-motivation,
personal evolution, and renewal. Made up of two
C's or gathering letters: upper half looks forward
in time, and bottom half looks backward, head and
heart forward, heart and root backward. Ability to
integrate past and future.

PATIENCE IN MANIFESTING CONTINUING
ARTISTIC PROJECTS. Ability to sustain the original creative impulse when it serves the development
of self, when it's self motivated; (the project may
also serve others, but this is incidental).

G#	Y	The upper half is gathering from above (to the heart); the lower half is the "I Am" expression, or an event in time. The upper half focuses an awareness of Involution and Evolution in Universal Love, and then can express this through individuality or as an act, or event, in time.

PATIENCE IN COMPLETING THE CREATIVE OR ARTISTIC PROCESS WHEN MOTIVATED BY THE VALUE OF THE PROJECT TO OTHERS, THE GROUP AROUND ONE, OR HUMANITY AS A WHOLE. Selfless dedication and application. More inspired and guided than S.

D#		UNIVERSAL LOVE, UNCONDITIONAL LOVE, CHRIST-LIKE LOVE. Love without thought of return. Higher octave of D (Human Love.)

D#	P	An "I Am" expression projecting into the future: experience from the past in combining the head and the heart. Less grounded than the R and more idealistic—not so much manifestation in action (no root).

UNIVERSAL LOVE EXPERIENCED AND GIVEN IN A PERSONALIZED WAY. THE INDIVIDUAL LOVING THE GROUP, THE COUNTRY, THE WORLD, HUMANITY, ALL LIFE FORMS, THE COSMOS, GOD.

D#	V	Involution and evolution in balance. The sequence suggests the Grand Circle of Creation: out from God into matter and the return. Gathers from above. Is abstract, having no vertical or horizontal lines. This higher understanding leads to a high order of love, based on spiritual principles.

SPIRITUALIZED HUMAN LOVE. The "All" within a person loving the greater "All". This would imply that the Holy Christ Love in the heart had been opened to a large degree.

A#		A HIGHER ASPECT OF THE DIVINE MOTHER PRINICPLE, THE PHYSICAL

PLANE. EXPERIENCE OR KNOWLEDGE OF RELATIONSHIP BETWEEN ONE PLANE AND A HIGHER PLANE.

A#   Z   The line of evolution or ascension connecting a lower plane of existence, or level of understanding, with a higher one. Thus the last letter of our alphabet expresses the final result of the human dance of life in planetary sojourn. To place the small horizontal cross-bar halfway up adds the love of the heart (chakra) to the root and the head of the bottom and top lines. Could also symbolize having run the gamut from the root chakra to the crown.

THE EQUIVALENT OF PHYSICAL FORMS AND ENERGIES ON ANOTHER, USUALLY MORE EVOLVED, PLANET. The ability to bring these into this plane through inspiration or memory. Perception of higher forms of physicality. The higher octave or aspect of the letter A. If E# is present, more ability to manifest and actualize the spiritual essence of that higher dimension.

E#   ATTUNEMENT WITH SPACE AND REALITIES BEYOND THE EARTH, AND POSSIBLY BEYOND THE SOLAR SYSTEM.

E#   W   Gathers from above from two sources (Earth and solar or solar and extra solar). Two V's: Involution-Evolution-Involution-Evolution. SUGGESTS POSSIBLITY THAT A SOUL INCARNATED ON A "HIGHER" PLANET, EVOLVED, THEN TOOK ON INCARNATION ON EARTH (A LOWER PLANET) FOR FURTHER TESTING AND GROWTH, THEN MAY ASCEND ON UP HIGHER STILL. May have dual concepts about the nature of God and higher Realities. This could be confusing or just provide added higher octaves of understanding. May work with descension and ascension. Abstract and needs grounding: no vertical or horizontal lines.

ALL THE PEOPLE I HAVE WORKED WITH WHO HAVE THE LETTER W HAVE A CON-

NECTION WITH OUTER SPACE AND ALSO
A CERTAIN PLANET. They are the "space people" of various kinds among us. The link is through
memory or present-time attunement, or both. This
letter completes the grand circle of this system since
the pitch E# is the equivalent of the pitch F (the
Angelic Order) with which we began. I have found
it true that a person with this letter may channel
the outerspace energies, knowledge and sensitivities, directly into this world; or the aid of the Angelic Order may be enlisted to help translate it into
terms and forms the Earth humans can more readily use. These space people feel somewhat alien, depending on how much experience they've had on
the Earth plane. They need to learn about how
things work here so they can make their special message, or abilities, more understandable to their fellow humans. In this way, they fulfill their destiny,
become accepted and evolve toward ascension.

 Appendix II

AFFIRMATION #1

(For clearing one's being for higher work or even just clearing away negative patterns.)

> Father-Mother God, I ask to be cleared and cleansed, in the Christ Light, the Green Healing Light, and The Violet Transmuting Flame. Within God's Will, and for my highest good, I ask and decree that any and all negativity be completely cut off from me now, encapsulated in its own light, encapsulated in the Ultraviolet Light and returned to its source, such that it cannot re-establish within me, or anyone else, in any form. Now I ask to be surrounded and filled with The White, Protective Light of the Christ, and for this blessing I give humble thanks. I accept this; so be it; manifest on all levels, NOW!

(This is an adapted version of an affirmation channeled by Bonita Brookshire, for which we give thanks. "We" may be substituted for "I" if you wish to think of yourself as a set of Basic Selves plus your conscious mind ego, or if you're saying this with others. This affirmation can be said in the name of another person since it's never wrong to pray for someone. They can accept the effect or reject it, according to their free will.)

AFFIRMATION #2

(To open your channel for intuitive service to others.)

> Father-Mother God, as we once more recognize Thy Presence here, Thy Love, Thy Wisdom, and we bow before these; we ask to be used as channels for (healing and attunement). We understand that The Christ Spirit does the work as He sees fit, we are only channels of love and concern for _____. We ask for the sensitivity to do this kind of work; we're open to Truth only. Father-Mother God, we ask thy protection of Light and Love, surrounding and filling this room, surrounding and filling all those who would come IN THE LIGHT to serve (his/her highest good). We see the channel surrounded, filled, and protected with The Light, the equipment protected (if there is), and all spirits involved.

UNITAS EANOKEE
ONE WORLD ANTHEM

copyright © 1980 Joel Andrews

Brother, sister, take my hands,
Form a ring of nations.
Root us now in Mother Earth,
To Father Sun we rise.

Heart in heart, together stand,
Sing and praise all that is:
Earth, Water, Fire and Air,
Together we can save this world.

Forgive our transgressions, God,
So we may love ourselves.
Forgiving all who ever hurt us,
Resolving not to hurt again.

Now may we create afresh
A New Age based on Love and Light,
Our love and will within God's laws,
Together we can save this world.

Joy in love,
Joy in light,

Work with Love,
Work with Light.

Joel Andrews (August, 1975)

UNITAS EANOKEE
ONE WORLD ANTHEM

LITERAL TRANSLATION FROM EANOKEEAN INTO ENGLISH
copyright © 1980 Joel Andrews

Brother, sister, take my hands,
Form a ring of nations.
Root us, God, now, in Mother Earth,
Spirits rise to Father of the Sun.

Heart in heart, together we stand,
Sing and praise The All that is:
Earth and Water, Fire and Air,
Together we can save this world.

Forgive our transgressions, All-Loving God,
So we may always love ourselves.
We forgive all those who hurt at us (try to),
We resolve never to hurt anything again.

Now may we create a world and time (age) of Love
      and Light,
Our love and will within the Laws of God,
Together we can save this world.

Joy in love, Joy in love
Joy in light, Joy in light

Work with Love, Work with Love
Work with Light, Work with Light

Joel Andrews (August, 1975)

UNITAS EANOKEE
copyright © 1980 Joel Andrews

I
KEPIJOY, HUNTIJOY, ONEETAS IN SANTIAZ
SONT I PHO CU PHOLLEAZ
UNAM ZII, SOHIEZ NI
LO UNITAS UFRAVENTEZ
PANIEZES NIE LEEJ
KENSIRE CU LAÑ SOEN

II
KEYRAM LO KEYRAM JIIROJ III SONAT
SANA DI VAZEY
LANEEAA LEN SOE
UFANTES DI UVRANNES
UFEENNREE DI UVAAEEY
JIIROJ IIIZ EANAH
CAEPUZ LIN UROEZ

III
SOROVEEZ IIIZKO NOXIXC
DAHJEHPAYVEEZ ENN SOHIEZ
JAHNO IIIZ EANAH
HOEEZ JEHPAYVEEZ ZIII
ZIII SOROVEEZ EEAA
III NOXIN LEE ZIII
IIIZ EEIIILLNA EELOY
JEHPAYVEEZ DILOHEE

IV
NI EANAH IIIZ EAN
UROEZ DI LOHEEZ
CU PAEVEEZ DI KAESEE
VEE LORSAY CU SOHIEZ
JIIROJ IIIZ EANAH
CAEPUZ LIN UROEZ

V
ZAHEY LO DAJE, ZAHEY LO JEHPAE
ZAHEY LO NARE, ZAHEY LO REKAE
LISAN VI JEHPAE, LISAN VI PAEVEEZ
LOYAN VI REKAE, LOYAN VI KAESEE

Joel Andrews (1977)

Note: Song sheet, harp (or keyboard) accompaniment and learning cassette are available from Joel Andrews (see address on last page). The cassette includes: Side I, the anthem in English and in Eanokee. Song in Eanokee with harp accompaniment. Side II, Eanokee words with pauses for repeating, and harp accompaniment for practicing singing. Also available arranged for choir: Soprano, Alto, Tenor, and Bass.

Infinite and eternal circulation of Deity Energy, but showing the potential to divide into two aspects, Yang-Yin, Male-Female, to create on lower planes of frequency. The highest-pitched sound humans make (s). Gathering from past experience on higher levels of consciousness; gathering from the "future" on lower levels.

First level of creativity, or manifestation: a universe, a system, condensation around a point (a planet); or expansion, proliferation of an "idea". Wholeness, Unity.

Space-time continuity. Planes of frequency, or consciousness on, or surrounding, a planet. The horizon, an age.

An individualized person, being, thing, place, or event. A human, connecting Sun and Earth, Yang and Yin.

How a human optimally evolves. The "I Am", growing through processing experience with head, heart, and body; or thinking (will), feeling (love), and action.

Ascension from a lower plane of being (frequency) to a higher one. The last letter of the Alphabet symbolizes the end result of the human dance, ascension, and with the crossbar, upliftment through love. The "s" sound of the first letter with the human body vibration now added.

Thus we have the Grand Cycle of Creation: the 8 begins the outbreath of God, the descent into matter; the lowest point is reached with the I (the One becomes the one); then the return, the inbreath of God, through the E and Z. (Please see the Symbolism of the Strokes and the Alphabet for additional symbolism.)

236

Psychic Research, Incorporated

1725 Little Orchard Street, Unit 'C' San Jose, CA 95125 (408)279-2291

Joel Andrews
P.O. Box 335
Ben Lomond, CA 95005

April 30, 1987

Dear Joel,

This is to acknowledge the contribution of your work and sensitivity with the harp in the role of sound in the structuring of water.

In the first set of experiments our laboratory did with you, we found that when you tuned with your mind into the water and played your music we found a change in the water: pH, electro-conductivity and the UV spectrum.

We further did the experments in which you played to a crystal over the water and we noted an even greater degree of change in the water with your music. What we have found is that not only is sound important but the sensitivity of the individual playing these tones as well.

At this time i believe this work of yours indicates that when you play your type of music a change in the electro-physiology of a body listening to this music takes place over and beyond just the beauty of the sound and tonal patterns you create.

I am deeply grateful for your help and participation in the research work we are doing. I wish you the very best on your book.

Very truly yours,

Marcel J. Vogel, Ph.D.

GLOSSARY

AKASHIC RECORDS: "Akasha" is a Hindu word for the basic substance upon which everything that happens is recorded.

ANGELS: Members of the angelic order, generally higher in rank than devas, overlighting individual humans (guardian seraphim), nations, races, languages, the arts, and sciences, etc. There are hundreds of types, supposedly 500 million pairs on Earth at this time, not counting the resident archangel contingent. (See The URANTIA Book, Bibliography.)

ASCENDED MASTER: A teacher from a higher frequency dimension. Some believe they have evolved from humans; others that they have their own particular origin but take embodiment occasionally. The author leans toward the latter. See "midwayers" in the URANTIA Book. "I AM" groups channel from them.

ASCENSION: At the end of life on Earth, the essential aspects of an individual (not the body) passing into higher frequency dimensions of existence, having earned release from the "wheel of karma" and the need to re-embody on Earth. In this book, possible for anyone in any particular life if the major karmic lessons and the basic lessons of Earth life have been mastered (see The URANTIA Book, Bibliography) and also possible for the body consciousness, basic or low selves, to ascend along their own path, even possible (although rare) for the two to happen simultaneously (Jesus and a few others, some in our time).

AURAMETER: A wooden handle with a wire extending from it (first spiralled and then straight) ending in a solid piece of metal (various metals are used) about a foot long. The Cameron Aurameter is longer, all metal and more sensitively suspended. Like all dowsing devices, including the pendulum, it simply makes visible the subtle energies the subconscious or Basic Selves are picking up or what it is trying to tell you. A myriad of uses depending on the developed sensitivities and skill of the Basic Selves .

CAUSAL BODY: Found in the upper mental body.

CHAKRA (with a "ch" as in "chapter"): means in Hindu, "coin". One of twelve vortices of energy, seven of which lie along the spine. Also called psychic centers. They, like transformers, step down the higher frequency energies coming in through the medulla and also focus energies from the root chakra (kundalini) for various uses in the lower bodies: Physical—

Etheric, Emotional—Astral, and Mental. See "Seven Bodies". They gradually open (hopefully in balance and harmony) but drugs and other shocks can open them too fast with extremely challenging results.

CHRIST SPIRIT: Jesus said before the Crucifixion, "I go on so that I can send my spirit, the Comforter". It is reported that on the day of Pentacost, the apostles all felt the descent of this "Spirit of Truth". Their hair stood on end and they spoke in tongues which the many races of people present could all understand. It is this personal presence, acting for The Christ, which has always been with us—The Living Christ. The URANTIA Book explains that the presence on Earth of the Spirit of Truth and Beauty enables us to be assigned High Selves, undiluted fragments of the Highest Deity, the I AM Presence, to lead us ever to God—to be distinguished from The Holy Spirit, the presence of The Divine Mother Spirit, the equal partner of The Christ for this local universe. (See The URANTIA Book.)

COSMIC CONSCIOUSNESS: Expanded awareness and perceptible emanations of Light resulting from an experience of illumination; usually, but not always, around age 33—36. Marked changes in physical appearance, emotional behavior, and especially mental and spiritual upliftment and perception; heightened moral sense and feeling of love for, and connection with, all of life. See Bibliography.

DEVAS: A Hindu word meaning "angel". In the West used to denote members of the angelic order holding essence patterns for, and promoting the growth of, the nature kingdoms: earth, water, fire, and air, minerals, plants, and animals (but not the human evolution). Usually smaller than angels but occasionally quite large if overshadowing a lake, a mountain, or the weather. Much larger than elementals whom they supervise. Visible to clairvoyant sight.

ELEMENTALS: Seen to clairvoyant sight as tiny points of light flitting around and through minerals, plants, animals, and the bodies of humans. Working under the devas they take on prana (life force) and fly into the creation to discharge it. Together with the devas and angels they are called the builders of form.

ESOTERIC CHRISTIANITY: An attempt to extract and reconstruct the true teachings of The Christ from the parables and second- and third-hand stories of the Bible. Draws also on lesser-known gospels such as that of St. Thomas, records of the teachings from Asia, the impressive revelation from higher beings, "The URANTIA Book", and other present-day channelings concerning the days the Master of Masters walked the

Earth, such as the readings of the well-documented Edgar Cayce. Another important source would be the metaphysical dictionary of the Unity Church. Esoteric Christianity is for the serious student who soon develops "eyes to see and ears to hear", who believes that God presents revelations to His/Her children in all ages, and that The Christ, who is very much alive on Earth through his Spirit of Truth and Beauty, can speak to those of true humility and sincere seeking, and will speak not in archaic idioms and symbols which need to be translated, but in language we can understand. An esoteric Christian is liable to believe that the monumental works, "The URANTIA Book" and "The Course In Miracles" are probably a form of "Second Coming", since Jesus said when he came again everyone would be able to see him in a much more true and essential form, and how ready are the people of Earth for that? Some stages of preparation would seem to be in order. Happily, these seem to be more and more frequent!

EXORCISM: To clear the "bodies" of an individual of so-called "negative" patterns, taken on during a period of imbalance. Could be inharmonious physical vibrations, emotional patterns, or mental thought forms. Most effective is to call on the name and power of The Living Christ, and also to have the subject's permission—although the latter is not necessary since they can always reject the action.

FALSETTO: An additional high register voice possible for some men (and the author). There is usually a break between the low voice and the falsetto. Yodelling utilizes this break.

FREE WILL PLAN: The concept that God intends that our type of being (Evolutionary Will Creature with Ascension Potential) shall grow through making choices in a dualistic world (apparent good and evil). Also, that God endowed us with creativity that we might learn to become co-creators with Him/Her (the author calls God "Herm").

FULL TRANCE: A state associated with the giving over of control of the body, the emotions, and the mind to a (hopefully!) higher being, usually to channel information or healing. The subject is usually unconscious of what comes through or takes place during full trance but in experienced channels the mind is taken somewhere and shown images so that on return he/she will have some knowledge of what transpired. Has the advantage of purity of transmission (less tampering by conscious mind of channel) but is usually much more of a strain on the body. Some full trance mediums do it relatively safely for long periods and have brought through impressive material (Jane Roberts, "Seth"; "Ramtha"; and Jach Pursel, "Lazaris"). To be distinguished from conscious channels (such as the author) some of whom have developed high degrees of accuracy through dedication, training of the mind and body, and practice.

HIGH SELF: Pure spark of divinity (God) assigned to a human to point the way toward Godhood. Indwells the mind and adjusts thoughts but always honors the free will of the individual host. Has experience but not individuality, which it achieves eventually, hopefully, through greater and greater fusion with the human person-ality. The God within, the "I AM" Presence, our link with divinity.

HUNA: The wisdom of the Kahunas, priest-healers of Hawaii. An ancient tradition, passed down through language, containing much truth and many effective techniques. Came from the Holy Land through migrations around the time of Christ. The works of Max Freedom Long have preserved much of it, and there are still a few authentic Kahunas in Hawaii.

KARMA, THE LAW OF: Cause and effect operating in our thoughts, emotions, and actions. The universe manifesting and returning to us our creativity, so we can learn from it. Both difficult and a wonderful plan since no one gets away with anything! What you mete out to others (all of life) you will also experience, so that you can know both sides: giving and receiving.

KUNDALINI: The energy that arises from the root chakra and passes along the spine, through the chakras to the crown chakra at the top of the head. Can be thought of as a reflection of the divine energy that comes down through the medulla. In the average person, coiled at the root and not too active. When awakened naturally, can motivate the subject along the path toward the Light and Cosmic Consciousness. If forced by too much desire or drugs can produce experiences which, due to lack of understanding, seem psychotic.

LEMURIA: A huge land mass centered in the Pacific Ocean, supposedly pre-dating Atlantis in the Atlantic. Many historical writings refer to it. Achievements focused more on the intuitive and artistic rather than. the scientific (Atlantis). Some places with records in California.

LIVING CHRIST: See "CHRIST SPIRIT" and "ESOTERIC CHRISTIANITY"

LORDS OF SIRIUS: Advanced beings from the twin-star Sirius. They are supervising the growth in consciousness in a large sector of the universe of which the solar system is a small part. In their channelings through sensitives on Earth they emphasize the yellow-gold, Second Ray, qualities of Love-Wisdom. At this time of great change we are passing into a universe sector under Arcturus and the Violet Ray (Seventh). The author of this book has channeled for the Lords of both Sirius and Arcturus.

LOW SELF: The subconscious, the body consciousness. Called "low self" in Huna, the wisdom of the Kahunas (priest-healers of Hawaii). Low perhaps in positioning in the body, certainly not low in intelligence, since it regulates the 500 functions of the liver—one organ out of many—as well as the five senses and much of their higher octaves of sensing! The author calls the low self the Basic Selves.

MASTER: See "ASCENDED MASTER". Or could also be an exalted teacher or guide from another planet or dimension of space or a human spiritual teacher acting for the above.

OVERTONE SERIES: The natural chord of tones produced by dividing a vibrating string (or any freely vibrating object) successively into segments: 2, 3, 4, 5, 6, 7, etc. The Law of Harmonics. The Chord of Nature. The "Lost Chord".

REINCARNATION: The concept that an aspect, or aspects, of a human being last beyond the transition called death to re-embody in subsequent lives, carrying memory and karmic patterns for further evolution.

SEVEN BODIES: Found in a number of religious disciplines, they are roughly: Physical—Etheric, Emotional—Astral, Mental (lower and higher), Intuitional, Spiritual, Monadic, and Divine. The first three (your own or others) can be felt with your hand, but since each successive body is larger and more rarified, the next four can only be contacted clairvoyantly.

STAR CHILDREN: Souls or perhaps Basic Selves who have come from other planets, probably outside the solar system. Occasionally a "walk in" where a body vehicle that was going to die is completely appropriated.

THE GREAT WHITE BROTHERHOOD: An organization in spirit of ascended masters dedicated to the spiritual upliftment of the human race, as well as the kingdoms of mineral, plant, and animal. Not angels but liaisons between higher spirit personalities and man. Sometimes take bodies for experience and service (such as Joseph, father of Jesus; Iknaton, who brought monotheism to Egypt; St. Francis of Assisi, the Master Kuthumi, etc.). Occasionally, humans are accomplishing such important and dedicated work in co-creation with these masters that they could be called, loosely, members of The White Brotherhood. They always honor your free will.

THE LAW OF SEVEN: Recognised in spiritual disciplines the world over as one of the Great Laws. Actually arises out of the creative combinations of the Triune Aspects of the Godhead, whatever names are used to designate them. Creating alone provides 1, 2, and 3; creating in pairs, 4, 5, and 6; all three creating, the 7th. These fundamental creative possibilities apparently set a pattern which is detectable at many levels throughout the Creation.

TIME OF DIVISION: Edgar Cayce's term for the present transition from the Piscean Age to the Aquarian Age, roughly 1900 to May 5, 2000 (the last date in the Great Pyramid). A time of extreme polarization and challenge described in most religions. In the Bible: Armageddon, the struggle between the forces of Light and and the forces of darkness and possibly the return of The Christ. To an enlightened metaphysician: a healing crisis or "pangs of birth" necessary for the emergence of a Golden Age of peace, understanding, and brother/sisterhood and possible world language and government.

TOUCH-FOR-HEALTH: An all-around system of diagnosis through muscle-testing which includes techniques of achieving balance by acupressure, pressing neurovascular holding points, massaging the two ends of related muscles, and tracing meridians to increase their flow. Touch-For-Health is the name for the system developed by John Thie ("Thee" with a "th" as in "thing") based on 20 years of research by Dr. Richard Goodheart establishing the connection between certain muscles and certain organs. Touch-For-Health also offers therapeutic nutrition and other related modalities.

Bibliography

Andrews, Donald Hatch. *The Symphony of Life.*
Lee's Summit, Missouri: Unity Books, 1966.

David, William. *The Harmonics of Sound, Color and Vibration.*
Marina del Rey, California: De Vorss, 1980.

Diamond, John, M.D. *Behavioral Kinesiology.*
New York: Harper & Row, 1979. (Published in paperback as *Your Body Doesn't Lie.* New York: Warner Books, 1980.)

Diamond, John, M.D. *The Life Energy in Music, Vols I and II.*
New York: Archaeus Press, 1981, 1983.

Hamel, Peter. *Through Music to the Self.* Shambhala, 1979.

Heline, Corrine. *Esoteric Music.*
Marina del Rey, California: De Vorss, 1969.

Heline, Corrine. *Healing and Regeneration through Music.*
Santa Barbara: New Age Press, 1969.

Jenny, Hans. *Cymatics: The Structure and Dynamics of Waves and Vibrations, Vols. I and II.* Basel, Switzerland:
Basiliu Press, 1967.

Keyes, Elizabeth Laurel. *Toning: The Creative Power of the Voice.*
Marina del Rey, California: De Vorss, 1978.

Khan, Hazrat Inayat. *Music.* New York: Samuel Weiser, 1962.

Khan, Hazrat Inayat. *The Mysticism of Sound.*
New York: Weber 1979.

Partch, Harry. *Genesis of a Music.* Da Capo Press, New York, 1974

Retallack, Dorothy. *The Sound of Music and Plants.*
Santa Monica, California: De Vorss, 1973.

Rogo, D. Scott. *A Psychic Study of the Music of the Spheres Vol. 2*
University Books, Secaucus, N.J., 1972.

Rudhyar, Dane. *The Magic of Tone and the Art of Music.*
Boulder, Colorado: Shambhala, 1982.

Schillinger, Joseph. *The Schillinger System of Musical Composition.*
Carl Fischer, 1941, 1946.

Scott, Cyrill. *Music: Its Secret Influence Through the Ages.*
London: Theosophical Publishing House, 1937.

Stebbin, Lionel. *Music: Its Occult Basis and Healing Value.*
London: New Knowledge Books, 1972.

The URANTIA Book. The Urantia Foundation, 533 Diversey Pky., Chicago, Ill. 60614, 1955.

Zuckerkandl, Victor. *Sound and Symbol.*
Princeton University Press, 1969.

244

INDEX

Joel Andrews tours extensively, presenting Concerts, Seminars, and Lectures in many of the subjects covered in this book. He also has produced many cassettes and L.P.s which are distributed worldwide. These highly-inspired recordings have a rich variety of uses: Attunement-Healing, Meditation, Guided Imagery, Dance and Movement, Massage, Romance, Natural Childbirth, and ambient backgroud for masking sound pollution. In production is a series of Therapy Tapes for the Medical Profession: music co-created with Higher Sources conducive to the re-alignment of the most common specific maladies.

For a listing of recordings available by Mail Order, as well as in stores, or for information regarding booking of engagements, or Individual Attunement sessions, please write:

Golden Harp
P.O. Box 335
Ben Lomond, CA 95005

Order Form

Please send me _____ copies of "A Harp Full of Stars."

$14.95 per copy _____

POSTAGE & HANDLING
$2.00 for first book, $1.00 each additional book.   _____
(allow 3 weeks for delivery)

Add to the above $2.00 per book for airmail   _____

Outside U.S.A. add to the above

$5.00 per book surface or   _____

$7.50 per book airmail   _____

California residents add 6% sales tax   _____

TOTAL _____

DISTRIBUTORS AND RETAILERS
May write for account information

Send check or money order to:

GOLDEN HARP PRESS
P.O. Box 335
Ben Lomond, CA 95005

You will receive a catalogue of the available cassettes by Joel Andrews.

Order Form

Please send me _____ copies of "A Harp Full of Stars."

$14.95 per copy _____

POSTAGE & HANDLING
$2.00 for first book, $1.00 each additional book.   _____
(allow 3 weeks for delivery)

Add to the above $2.00 per book for airmail   _____

Outside U.S.A. add to the above

$5.00 per book surface or   _____

$7.50 per book airmail   _____

California residents add 6% sales tax   _____

TOTAL _____

DISTRIBUTORS AND RETAILERS
May write for account information

Send check or money order to:

GOLDEN HARP PRESS
P.O. Box 335
Ben Lomond, CA 95005

You will receive a catalogue of the available cassettes by Joel Andrews.